Server Side
Swift
with
Vapor

By Tim Condon, Tanner Nelson, Jonas Schwartz & Logan Wright

Server Side Swift with Vapor

By Tim Condon, Tanner Nelson, Jonas Schwartz & Logan Wright

ISBN: 978-1-942878-53-7

About the Authors

Tim Condon is a software engineer who has worked in most areas of the industry, including security, back-end, front-end and mobile! He is the founder of Broken Hands, a company specializing in Vapor and also currently works for the BBC on their mobile team. On Twitter he can be found sporadically tweeting @0xTim. You can find more about him at www.brokenhands.io.

Jonas Schwartz had a long career as a backend and server operations developer, before he teamed up with Tanner and Logan in 2017. He came onboard after talks about building a cloud platform. Since then, his focus has been on making hosting easy and more scalable for Vapor applications.

Logan Wright began his career as an iOS Developer working on many categories of applications from navigation, to customized bluetooth communication protocols. Always a major supporter of OSS, Logan met Tanner through the Vapor project. Eventually, that grew into a full-time position and the community as we know it today.

Tanner Wayne Nelson is an American software engineer based in New York City. He started programming in elementary school and went on to study Computer Science at New York University. Tanner created Vapor in 2016 and now works full time maintaining the core framework and the dozens of packages around it.

About the Editors

Richard Critz did double duty as editor and tech editor for this book. He is the iOS Team Lead at raywenderlich.com and has been doing software professionally for nearly 40 years, working on products as diverse as CNC machinery, network infrastructure, and operating systems. He discovered the joys of working with iOS beginning with iOS 6. Yes, he dates back to punch cards and paper tape. He's a dinosaur; just ask his kids. On Twitter, while being mainly read-only, he can be found @rcritz. The rest of his professional life can be found at www.rwcfoto.com.

Darren Ferguson is the final pass editor for this book. He's an experienced software developer and works for M.C. Dean, Inc, a systems integration provider from North Virginia. When he's not coding, you'll find him enjoying EPL Football, traveling as much as possible and spending time with his wife and daughter. Find Darren on Twitter at @darren102.

Dedications

"To the Vapor team, thank you for creating the framework —
none of this would exist without you! To the Vapor community,
thank you for being the best open source community anywhere
in the world! To my editors, Richard and Darren, thank you for
putting up with the constant cycles of change as we followed the
early betas and RCs and turning my early attempts at writing
into something almost resembling that of an author. To my
friends and family, sorry I've been locked away for so long!
Finally, thank you to Amy, who has put up with endless hours of
me writing and being absent but supported me throughout."

— *Tim Condon*

"To the entire Vapor community, thank you very much for your
hard work, without all of you, Vapor wouldn't exist, and an
extended thanks to Tim Condon for all the hard work on the
book. To the editors Richard and Darren thanks for all your
feedback and help getting the book. To my friends and family
thank you for all your support, and last but not least, thanks to
Heidi for always having faith and support, even when I am glued
to the computer day in and day out."

— *Jonas Schwartz*

"To everybody in the open source community that saw value and
supported Vapor as we grew. This project wouldn't exist without
their continued support. Also, the Ray Wenderlich team for
making videos early on and helping us create this book. Tim
Condon for being one of our biggest contributors and writing so
much great content here. Finally, Jonas and Tanner for being
great people to work with and giving so much to Vapor."

— *Logan Wright*

"Thank you to the amazing community that supports Vapor. We're incredibly grateful for the opportunity you give us to work on something that we love and believe in. These past few years have been a wonderful experience and I can't wait to see where the future takes us."

— *Tanner Wayne Nelson*

Table of Contents

Book License 15

Book Source Code & Forums 17

What You Need.. 19
    About this book 20

About the Cover 21

Section I: Creating a Simple Web API........ 23

Chapter 1: Introduction................................... 25
    About Vapor... 25
    How to read this book 26

Chapter 2: Hello Vapor 27
    Vapor Toolbox 27
    Building your first app 29
    Swift Package Manager... 31
    Creating your own routes 32
    Accepting data 34
    Returning JSON 36
    Troubleshooting Vapor 38
    Where to go from here? 39

Chapter 3: HTTP Basics 41
    Powering the web 41
    HTTP in web browsers... 43
    HTTP in iOS apps 44
    HTTP 2.0 44
    REST 44
    Why use Vapor? 45

Chapter 4: Async 47

Async...47
Working with futures 49
SwiftNIO 56

Chapter 5: Fluent & Persisting Models........................... 59

Fluent 59
Acronyms 60
Saving models 64
Deploying to Vapor Cloud 66
Where to go from here? 79

Chapter 6: Configuring a Database 81

Why use a database? 81
Choosing a database 82
Configuring Vapor 83
Deploying to Vapor Cloud 92
Where to go from here? 98

Chapter 7: CRUD Database Operations........................ 99

CRUD and REST 99
Fluent queries..109
Deploy to Vapor Cloud 114
Where to go from here? 116

Chapter 8: Controllers 117

Controllers..117
Getting started with controllers 118
Deploy to Vapor Cloud..125
Where to go from here?...127

Chapter 9: Parent Child Relationships......................... 129

Parent-child relationships..129
Creating a user 130
User model 130
Setting up the relationship..134
Querying the relationship..137

Foreign key constraints 140

Deploy to Vapor Cloud 143

Running migrations 145

Where to go from here? 148

Chapter 10: Sibling Relationships 149

Sibling relationships.. 149

Creating a category 150

Creating a pivot 153

Querying the relationship 157

Removing the relationship 160

Foreign key constraints 162

Deploy to Vapor Cloud 165

Where to go from here? 168

Chapter 11: Testing 169

Why should you write tests? 169

Writing tests with SPM 170

Testing users.. 170

Testing the User API 180

Testing acronyms and categories 183

Testing on Linux 184

Where to go from here? 188

Chapter 12: Creating a Simple iPhone App, Part 1 191

Getting started 192

Viewing the acronyms 192

Viewing the users 196

Viewing the categories.. 197

Creating users 199

Creating acronyms 202

Where to go from here? 208

Chapter 13: Creating a Simple iPhone App, Part 2 209

Getting started.. 209

Editing acronyms 213
Deleting acronyms 217
Creating categories 219
Adding acronyms to categories 221
Where to go from here? 225

Section II: Making a Simple Web App 227

Chapter 14: Templating with Leaf 229

Leaf.. 229
Configuring Leaf 230
Rendering a page 231
Injecting variables 233
Using tags 235
Acronym detail page 237
Deploying to Vapor Cloud 240
Where to go from here? 242

Chapter 15: Beautifying Pages 243

Embedding templates 243
Bootstrap... 246
Navigation 247
Tables.. 249
Serving files 250
Users 251
Deploying to Vapor Cloud 257
Where to go from here? 259

Chapter 16: Making a Simple Web App, Part 1 261

Categories 261
Create acronyms 266
Editing acronyms.. 270
Deleting acronyms 274
Where to go from here?... 276

Chapter 17: Making a Simple Web App, Part 2 277
Adding categories to acronyms 277
Deploy to Vapor Cloud 288
Where to go from here? 290

Section III: Validation, Users & Authentication 291

Chapter 18: API Authentication, Part 1 293
Passwords 293
Basic authentication 300
Token authentication 305
Database seeding 313
Where to go from here? 315

Chapter 19: API Authentication, Part 2 317
Updating the tests 317
Deploying to Vapor Cloud 325
Updating the iOS application 327
Where to go from here? 334

Chapter 20: Web Authentication, Cookies & Sessions .. 335
Web authentication 335
Cookies 347
Sessions 350
Deploying to Vapor Cloud 352
Where to go from here? 354

Chapter 21: Validation 355
The registration page 355
Basic validation 360
Custom validation 361
Displaying an error 362
Deploy to Vapor Cloud 363

Where to go from here? 365

Section IV: Advanced Server Side Swift ... 367

Chapter 22: Google Authentication 369
OAuth 2.0 369
Imperial 370
Integrating with web authentication 377
Deploying to Vapor Cloud 381
Where to go from here? 383

Chapter 23: Database/API Versioning & Migration 385
Modifying tables 385
Adding users' Twitter handles 387
Making categories unique 393
Seeding based on environment 395
Deploy to Vapor Cloud 395
Where to go from here? 396

Chapter 24: Caching 397
Cache storage 397
Example: Pokédex 399
Where to go from here? 405

Chapter 25: Middleware 407
Vapor's middleware 408
Example: Todo API 409
Where to go from here? 415

Chapter 26: Deploying with Heroku 417
Setting up Heroku 417
Where to go from here? 425

Chapter 27: WebSockets 427
Tools 427
A basic server 427

iOS project 429

Server word API 430

Session Manager 430

Endpoints... 434

Observer endpoint 436

iOS follow location 437

Where to go from here? 441

Conclusion 443

More Books You Might Enjoy 445

New to iOS or Swift? 445

Experienced iOS developer?... 447

Want to make games? 458

Want to learn Android or Kotlin?....................................... 461

Book License

By purchasing *Server Side Swift with Vapor*, you have the following license:

- You are allowed to use and/or modify the source code in *Server Side Swift with Vapor* in as many apps as you want, with no attribution required.

- You are allowed to use and/or modify all art, images and designs that are included in *Server Side Swift with Vapor* in as many apps as you want, but must include this attribution line somewhere inside your app: "Artwork/images/designs: from *Server Side Swift with Vapor*, available at www.raywenderlich.com".

- The source code included in *Server Side Swift with Vapor* is for your personal use only. You are NOT allowed to distribute or sell the source code in *Server Side Swift with Vapor* without prior authorization.

- This book is for your personal use only. You are NOT allowed to sell this book without prior authorization, or distribute it to friends, coworkers or students; they would need to purchase their own copies.

Book Source Code & Forums

You can get the source code for the book here:

https://store.raywenderlich.com/products/server-side-swift-with-vapor-source-code

There, you'll find all the code from the chapters for your use.

We've also set up an official forum for the book at forums.raywenderlich.com. This is a great place to ask questions about the book or to submit any errors you may find.

What You Need

To follow along with this book, you'll need the following:

- **Swift 4.1** Vapor 3 requires Swift 4.1 minimum in both Xcode and from the command line.

- **Xcode 9 or later.** Xcode is the main development tool for writing code in Swift. You need Xcode 9.4 at a minimum, since that version includes Swift 4.1. You can download the latest version of Xcode for free from the Mac App Store.

If you haven't installed the latest version of Xcode, be sure to do that before continuing with the book. The code covered in this book depends on Swift 4.1 and Xcode 9 — you may get lost if you try to work with an older version.

This book provides the building blocks for developers who wish to use Vapor to create server-side Swift applications. It shows you how to take the familiar type-safe, compiler-driven world of Swift you know from iOS and use it on the server.

The only prerequisites for this book are an intermediate understanding of Swift and iOS development. If you've worked through our classic beginner books — *Swift Apprentice* https://store.raywenderlich.com/products/swift-apprentice and *iOS Apprentice* https://store.raywenderlich.com/products/ios-apprentice — or have similar development experience, you're ready to read this book.

As you work through the book, you'll develop a server-side app called TIL — Today I Learned — for recording and categorizing acronyms. You'll first build a REST API to support iOS and other client apps. Then, you'll build a web site with direct access to the data and protect it all with authentication.

About this book

This book provides the building blocks for developers who wish to use Vapor to create server-side Swift applications. It shows you how to take the familiar type-safe, compiler-driven world of Swift you know from iOS and use it on the server.

The only prerequisites for this book are an intermediate understanding of Swift and iOS development. If you've worked through our classic beginner books — *Swift Apprentice* https://store.raywenderlich.com/products/swift-apprentice and *iOS Apprentice* https://store.raywenderlich.com/products/ios-apprentice — or have similar development experience, you're ready to read this book.

As you work through the book, you'll develop a server-side app called TIL — Today I Learned — for recording and categorizing acronyms. You'll first build a REST API to support iOS and other client apps. Then, you'll build a web site with direct access to the data and protect it all with authentication.

About the Cover

The Mexican salamander, or axolotl, is an especially unique amphibian in that it remains a fully aquatic creature in adulthood and retains its gills instead of growing lungs like most amphibians.

Axolotls are exceptionally easy to breed in captivity, and for this reason are studied extensively in such wide-ranging fields as heart defects and neural tube development. But perhaps the most fascinating feature is their ability to completely regenerate entire limbs, other appendages, and even brain sections when damaged.

Unfortunately, the wild axolotl's habitat is limited to a few lakes in central Mexico, which are under stress due to rapid urban development along with the introduction of non-native predators to their natural habitat. Consequently, the axolotl has earned a categorization of "Critically Endangered" on global conservation lists.

For more information, check out the following great resources:

- http://www.iucnredlist.org/details/1095/0
- http://www.pbs.org/wgbh/nova/next/nature/saving-axolotls/

Section I: Creating a Simple Web API

This section teaches you the beginnings of building Vapor applications, including how to use Swift Package Manager. You'll learn how routing works and how Vapor leverages the power of Swift to make routing type-safe. You'll learn how to create models, set up relationships between them and save them in a database. You'll see how to provide an API to access this data from a REST client. You'll also build an iOS app which leverages this API to allow users to display and interact with the data. Finally, you'll learn how to use Vapor Cloud and deploy your application to the internet for real users.

Some things you'll learn in this section are below:

- **Chapter 2: Hello, Vapor!:** In this chapter, you'll start by installing the Vapor Toolbox, then use it to build and run your first project. You'll finish by learning about routing, accepting data and returning JSON.

- **Chapter 4: Async:** In this chapter, you'll learn about asynchronous and non-blocking architectures. You'll discover Vapor's approach to these architectures and how to use them. Finally, the chapter provides a small overview of SwiftNIO, a core technology used by Vapor.

- **Chapter 5: Fluent & Persisting Models:** This chapter explains how to use Fluent to save data in Vapor applications. Fluent is Vapor's ORM or **object relational mapping** tool. It's an abstraction layer between the Vapor application and the database, and it's designed to make working with databases easier.

- **Chapter 6: Configuring a Database:** Databases allow you to persist data in your applications. In this chapter you'll learn how to configure your Vapor application to integrate with the database of your choice. Currently Vapor only has support for releational (SQL) databases but this will change in the future.

- **Chapter 7: CRUD Database Operations:** This chapter concentrates on how to interact with models in the database. You'll learn about CRUD (Create, Retrieve, Update, Delete) operations and how they relate to REST APIs. You'll also see how to leverage Fluent to perform complex queries on your models.

- **Chapter 9: Parent Child Relationships:** In this chapter, you'll learn how to set up a parent-child relationship between two models. You'll learn the purpose of these relationships, how to model them in Vapor and how to use them with routes.

- **Chapter 10: Sibling Relationships:** In this chapter, you'll learn how to implement the other type of relationship: sibling relationships. You'll learn how to model them in Vapor and how to use them in routes.

Chapter 1: Introduction

Vapor is an open-source web framework written in Swift. It's built on top of Apple's SwiftNIO library to provide a powerful, asynchronous framework. Vapor allows you to build back-end applications for iOS apps, front-end web sites and stand-alone server applications.

About Vapor

Apple open-sourced Swift in December 2015, thereby enabling developers to create applications for macOS and Linux written in Swift. Almost immediately, a number of web frameworks written in Swift appeared. Tanner Nelson started Vapor in January 2016, and Logan Wright joined him shortly thereafter. Over time, a large and engaged user community has embraced the framework. Vapor has a Swift-like API and makes heavy use of many powerful language features. As a result, it has become the most popular server-side Swift framework on GitHub.

Vapor consists of a number of packages including Leaf — a templating engine for front-end development — and Fluent, a Swift Object Relational Mapping (ORM) framework with native, asynchronous database drivers. One of its biggest strengths is its community. There's a very dedicated following on GitHub and an extremely active chat server on Discord.

How to read this book

The chapters in the first three sections build on each other. If you're new to Vapor, you should read them in sequence. If you're experienced with Vapor, you can skip from chapter to chapter to learn how to use the latest features and treat this book as a reference.

Each chapter provides starter and final projects. The book is *very* code heavy and you should follow along with the code to truly understand it all.

The chapters in Section 4 stand alone and you can read them in any order. Written by the core Vapor team, they provide deeper insight into how best to use Vapor.

The best way to learn about Vapor is to roll up your sleeves and start coding. Enjoy the book!

Chapter 2: Hello Vapor

By Tim Condon

Beginning a project using a new technology can be daunting. Vapor makes it easy to get started. It even provides handy scripts to make sure your computer is configured correctly.

In this chapter, you'll start by installing the Vapor Toolbox, then use it to build and run your first project. You'll finish by learning about routing, accepting data and returning JSON.

Vapor Toolbox

The Vapor Toolbox is a command line interface (CLI) tool that you use when developing Vapor apps. It provides several features, including:

- Creating new apps from templates.
- Building and running projects using the Swift toolchain.
- Generating Xcode projects.
- Deploying projects with Vapor Cloud.

Before you can install the toolbox, you need to ensure your system is compatible. To do this, you run the Vapor Check script, which verifies you have the necessary version of Swift installed.

Open **Terminal**, and execute the following command:

```
eval "$(curl -sL check.vapor.sh)"
```

This command also works on Linux.

```
● ● ●                    ⌂ timc — -bash — 64×7
Tims-MBP:~ timc$ eval "$(curl -sL check.vapor.sh)"
 ☑  Xcode 9 is compatible with Vapor 2.
 ☑  Xcode 9 is compatible with Vapor 3.
 ☑  Swift 4.1 is compatible with Vapor 2.
 ☑  Swift 4.1 is compatible with Vapor 3.
Tims-MBP:~ timc$ ▊
```

If you receive errors when running this script, you'll need to install Swift. On macOS, simply install Xcode from the Mac App Store. On Linux, use APT to install it as described below.

> Vapor 3 requires Swift 4.1, both in Xcode and from the command line.

Installing on macOS

Vapor uses Homebrew to install the Toolbox.

> If you don't have Homebrew installed, visit https://brew.sh and run the installation command.

In **Terminal** run the following command:

```
brew install vapor/tap/vapor
```

Installing on Linux

This book focuses primarily on using Xcode and macOS for developing your apps. However, everything you build with Vapor will work on versions of Linux that Swift supports. At the time of writing, these are Ubuntu 14.04, Ubuntu 16.04 and Ubuntu 16.10. The Vapor Toolbox works in exactly the same way, with the exception that you can't use Xcode projects on Linux.

You install Vapor on Linux using the Vapor APT repository. Vapor maintains an open source APT repo at https://github.com/vapor/apt. which serves the same purpose as Vapor's Brew tap. It allows for easy installation of packages and manages all the dependencies for you. When you install Vapor, it also installs Swift for you.

This book uses Ubuntu 16.04 throughout when referring to Linux, but the other supported versions of Ubuntu should work in exactly the same way.

To use the Vapor APT repo, add it to your repository list. Enter the following at a shell prompt:

```
eval "$(curl -sL https://apt.vapor.sh)"
```

> **Note**: You may need to install curl first before you can run this command if you are starting with a fresh Ubuntu image. Run **sudo apt-get install curl -y** to do so.

Once this has completed, you can then install the Toolbox (and Swift):

```
sudo apt-get install vapor -y
```

When this completes, you should be able to run the check script from above and get a successful result:

```
demo@demo-VirtualBox: ~
demo@demo-VirtualBox:~$ eval "$(curl -sL check.vapor.sh)"
  Compatible with Vapor 3
demo@demo-VirtualBox:~$
```

Building your first app

Setting up a Vapor project can seem complicated at first as there are a number of required files and directories. To help with this, the Toolbox can create a new project from a template. The default template is a simple API template, but it also has templates for web sites and authentication. You can even create your own templates.

First, create a new directory in your home directory or somewhere sensible to work on your Vapor projects. For example, enter the following commands in Terminal:

```
mkdir ~/vapor
cd ~/vapor
```

This creates a new directory in your home folder called **vapor** and navigates you there. Next, create your project with:

```
vapor new HelloVapor
```

You should see the following:

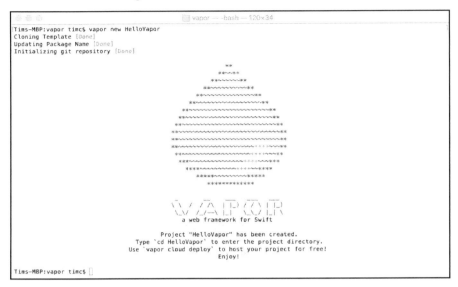

To build and start your app, run:

```
# 1
cd HelloVapor
# 2
vapor build
# 3
vapor run
```

Here's what this does:

1. `cd` is the "Change Directory" command and takes you into the project directory.

2. This builds the app. This can take some time the first time since it must fetch all the dependencies.

3. This runs the app. If the macOS Application Firewall pops up asking you to allow network connections, click **Allow**.

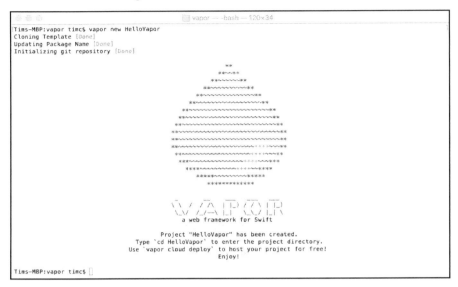

The template has a predefined route, so open your browser and visit **http://localhost:8080/hello** and see the response!

Swift Package Manager

Vapor Toolbox uses Swift Package Manager, or SPM, — a dependency management system similar to Cocoapods on iOS — to configure and build Vapor apps. Open your project directory and look at the structure. On macOS in **Terminal**, enter:

```
open .
```

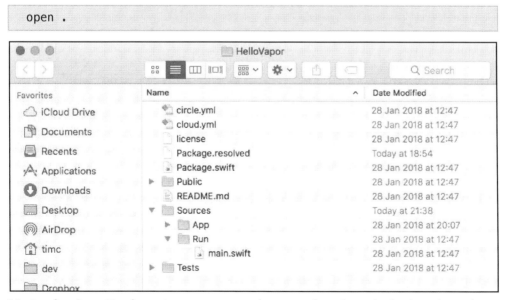

Notice there's no Xcode project in your template even though you've built and run the app. This is deliberate. In fact, the project file is explicitly excluded from source control using the **.gitignore** file. When using SPM, Xcode projects are discardable and regenerated whenever you make project changes.

An SPM project is defined in the **Package.swift** manifest file. It declares targets, dependencies and how they link together. The project layout is also different from a traditional Xcode project. There is a **Tests** directory for tests. There is a **Sources** directory for source files. Each module defined in your manifest has its own directory inside **Sources**. Your sample app has an App module and a Run module, so **Sources** contains an **App** directory and a **Run** directory.

Inside the **Run** directory, there's a single **main.swift** file. This is the entry point required by all Swift apps.

> On iOS this is usually synthesized with an `@UIApplicationMain` attribute on the `AppDelegate`.

The template contains everything you need to set up your app and you shouldn't need to change **main.swift** or the Run module. Your code lives in App or any other modules you define.

Creating your own routes

> This section, as does most of the book, uses Xcode. If you're developing on Linux, use your favorite editor, then use the commands **vapor build** and **vapor run** to build and run your app.

Now that you've made your first app, it's time to see how easy it is to add new routes with Vapor. If the Vapor app is still running, stop it by pressing **Control-C** in Terminal. Next enter:

```
vapor xcode -y
```

This generates an Xcode project and open it. Open **routes.swift** in **Sources/App**. You'll see the route you visited above. To create another route, add the following after the `router.get("hello")` closure:

```
router.get("hello", "vapor") { req -> String in
  return "Hello Vapor!"
}
```

Here's what this does:

- Add a new route to handle a GET request. Each parameter to `router.get` is a path component in the URL. This route is invoked when a user enters **http://localhost:8080/hello/vapor** as the URL.

- Supply a closure to run when this route is invoked. The closure receives a `Request` object; you'll learn more about these later.

- Return a string as the result for this route.

In the Xcode toolbar, select the **Run** scheme and choose **My Mac** as the device.

Build and run. In your browser, visit **http://localhost:8080/hello/vapor**.

What if you want to say hello to anyone who visits your app? Adding every name in the world would be quite impractical! There must be a better way. There is and Vapor makes it easy.

Add a new route that says hello to whomever visits. For example, if your name is Tim, you'll visit the app using the URL **http://localhost:8080/hello/Tim** and it says "Hello, Tim!". Add the following after the code you just entered:

```
// 1
router.get("hello", String.parameter) { req -> String in
  //2
  let name = try req.parameters.next(String.self)
  // 3
  return "Hello, \(name)!"
}
```

Here's the play-by-play:

1. Use `String.parameter` to specify that the second parameter can be any `String`.

2. Extract the user's name which is passed in the `Request` object.

3. Use the name to return your greeting.

Build and run. In your browser, visit **http://localhost:8080/hello/Tim**. Try replacing **Tim** with some other values.

Accepting data

Most web apps must accept data. A common example is user login. To do this, a client sends a POST request with a JSON body which the app must decode and process. To learn more about POST requests and how they work, see Chapter 3, "HTTP Basics."

Vapor 3 makes decoding data easy thanks to its strong integration with Swift 4's `Codable`. You give Vapor a `Codable` struct that matches your expected data and Vapor does the rest. Create a POST request to see how this works.

> This book uses the RESTed app, available as a free download from the Mac App Store. If you like, you may use another REST client to test your APIs.

Set up the request as follows:

- **URL**: **http://localhost:8080/info**

- **Method**: **POST**

- Add a single parameter called **name**. Use your name as the value.

- Select **JSON-encoded** as the request type. This ensures that the data is sent as JSON and that the Content-Type header is set to application/json. If you are using a different client you may need to set this manually.

Your request should look similar to the following:

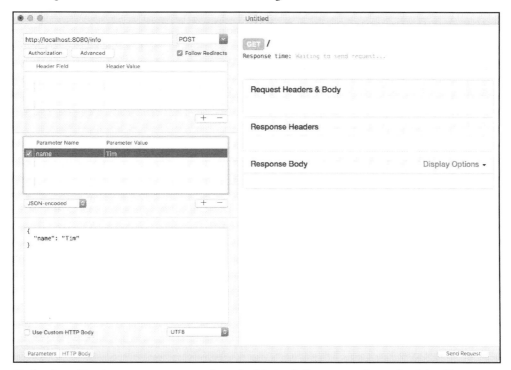

Go back to Xcode, open **routes.swift** and add the following to the end of the file to create a struct called InfoData to represent this request:

```
struct InfoData: Content {
  let name: String
}
```

This struct conforms to Content which is Vapor's wrapper around Codable. Vapor uses Content to extract the request data, whether it's the default JSON-encoded or form URL-encoded. InfoData contains the single parameter name.

Next add a new route after the router.get("hello", "vapor") closure:

```
router.post(InfoData.self, at: "info") { req, data -> String in
  return "Hello \(data.name)!"
}
```

Here's what this does:

- Add a new route handler to handle a POST request for the URL **http://localhost: 8080/info**. This route handler returns a `String`. The route handler accepts a `Content` type as the first parameter and any path parameters after the `at:` parameter name. The route handler decodes the data and passes it to the closure as the second parameter.

- Return the string by pulling the name out of the `data` variable.

Build and run the app. Send the request from RESTed and you'll see the response come back:

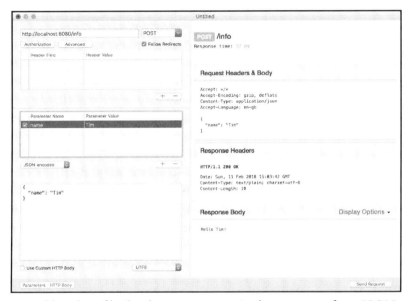

This may seem like a lot of boilerplate to extract a single parameter from JSON. However, `Codable` scales up and allows you to decode complex, nested JSON objects with multiple types in a single line.

Returning JSON

Vapor also makes it easy to return JSON in your route handlers. This is a common need when your app provides an API service. For example, a Vapor app that processes requests from an iOS app needs to send JSON responses. Vapor again uses `Content` to encode the response as JSON.

Open **routes.swift** and add the following struct to the end of the file called
InfoResponse to return the incoming request:

```
struct InfoResponse: Content {
  let request: InfoData
}
```

This struct conforms to Content and contains a property for the request. Next, replace
router.post(InfoData.self, at: "info") with the following:

```
// 1
router.post(InfoData.self, at: "info") {
  req, data -> InfoResponse in
  // 2
  return InfoResponse(request: data)
}
```

Here's what changed:

1. The route handler now returns the new InfoResponse type.

2. Construct a new InfoResponse type using the decoded request.

Build and run the app. Send the same request from RESTed. You'll see a JSON response
containing your original request data:

Troubleshooting Vapor

Throughout the course of this book, and in any future Vapor apps, you may encounter errors in your projects. There are a number of steps to take to troubleshoot any issues.

Regenerate your project

First and foremost, you should regenerate your Xcode project. In Terminal, type:

```
vapor xcode -y
```

This regenerates your project like the first time you created the Xcode project. This can fix issues such as missing files or project configuration errors.

Update your dependencies

Another scenario you may encounter is hitting a bug in Vapor or another dependency you use. Make sure you are on the latest package version of any dependencies to see if the update fixes the issue. In Terminal, type:

```
vapor update
```

This uses the underlying `swift package update` command to pull down any updates to your dependencies and use the latest releases you support in **Package.swift**. Note that while packages are in the beta or release candidate stages, there may be breaking changes between updates.

Clean and rebuild

Finally, if you are still having issues, you can use the software equivalent of "turn it off and on again". In Xcode use **Command-Option-Shift-K** to clean the build folder. You may also need to remove the build products created by the Vapor Toolbox. To do this, enter the following in Terminal:

```
rm -rf .build
```

This removes all build artifacts and your dependencies. You may also need to clear your derived data for the Xcode project as well. The "nuclear" option involves:

• Remove the **.build** directory to remove any build artifacts.

• Remove your **.xcodeproj** to delete the Xcode project and any misconfigurations.

- Remove **Package.resolved** to ensure you get the latest dependencies next time you build.

- Remove derived data to clear extra Xcode build artifacts.

Vapor Discord

The above steps usually fix most issues encountered that aren't caused by your code. If all else fails, head to Vapor's Discord server. There are thousands of developers discussing Vapor, it's changes, and helping people with issues. Click the **Join Chat** button on Vapor's web site: https://vapor.codes.

Where to go from here?

This chapter provides an overview of how to get started with Vapor and how to create basic routes. The first two sections of this book show you how to build a complex app, including an API, a website, and authentication in both parts. As you progress through them, you'll learn how to use core Vapor concepts, such as futures, Fluent and Leaf. By the end of section 2, you'll have a solid foundation on which to build any server-side Swift app in Vapor.

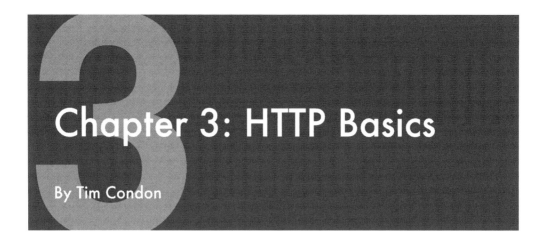

Chapter 3: HTTP Basics

By Tim Condon

Before you begin your journey with Vapor, you'll first review the fundamentals of how the web and HTTP operate.

This chapter explains what you need to know about HTTP, its methods, and its most common response codes. You'll also learn how Vapor can augment your web development experience, its benefits, and what differentiates it from other Swift frameworks.

Powering the web

HyperText Transfer Protocol, or HTTP, is the foundation of the web. Each time you visit a website, your browser sends HTTP requests to and receives responses from the server. Many dedicated apps — ordering coffee from your smartphone, streaming video to your TV, or playing an online game — use HTTP behind the scenes.

At its core, HTTP is simple. There's a client — an iOS application, a web browser or even a simple cURL session — and a server. The client sends an HTTP request to the server which returns an HTTP response.

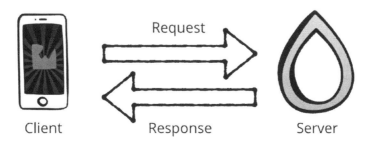

HTTP requests

An HTTP request consists of several parts:

- **The request line**: This specifies the HTTP method to use, the resource requested and the HTTP version. `GET /about.html HTTP/1.1` is one example. You'll learn about HTTP versions later in this chapter.
- **The host**: The name of server to handle the request. This is needed when multiple servers are hosted at the same address.
- **Other request headers** such as Authorization, Accept, Cache-Control, Content-Length, Content-Type etc.
- **Optional request data**, if required by the HTTP method.

The HTTP method specifies the type of operation requested by the client. The HTTP specifications define the following methods:

- GET
- HEAD
- POST
- PUT
- DELETE
- CONNECT
- OPTIONS
- TRACE
- PATCH

The most common HTTP method is `GET`. It allows a client to retrieve a resource from a server. Clicking a link in a browser or tapping a story in a News app both trigger a `GET` request to the server.

Another common HTTP method is `POST`. It allows a client to send data to a server. Clicking the login button after entering your username and password can trigger a `POST` request to the server. You'll learn about other HTTP methods as you work through the book.

Frequently, the server needs more than the resource's name to properly service a request. This additional information is sent in **request headers**. Request headers are nothing more than key-value pairs.

Some common request headers are: `Authorization`, `Cookie`, `Content-Type` and `Accept`. You'll learn in later chapters how Vapor can use some of these to make your server-side apps more robust.

HTTP responses

The server returns an HTTP response when it has processed a request. An HTTP response consists of:

- **The status line**: contains the version, status code and message

- **Response headers**

- **An optional response body**

The **status code** and its associated message indicate the outcome of the request. There are many status codes but you won't use or encounter most of them. They're broken into 5 groups, based on the first digit:

- **1**: informational response. These don't occur frequently.

- **2**: success response. The most common, `200 OK`, means the request was completed successfully.

- **3**: redirection response. These are used frequently.

- **4**: client error. One of the most common is `404 Not Found`. You've probably seen some different and entertaining 404 pages!

- **5**: server error. This frequently indicates an improperly configured server, resource exhaustion or a bug in the server-side app.

There is even an April Fools' joke status code: `418 I'm a teapot`!

The response may include a **response body** such as the HTML content of a page, an image file, or a JSON description of a resource. The response body is optional, however, and some response codes — `204 No Content` for example — won't have one.

Finally, the response may include some **response headers**. These are analogous to the **request headers** described earlier. Some common response headers are: `Set-cookie`, `WWW-Authenticate`, `Cache-Control` and `Content-Length`.

HTTP in web browsers

When you ask your browser to load a page, it sends an HTTP `GET` request for that page. The server returns the HTML in the response's body. As the browser parses the HTML, it generates additional HTTP GET requests for any assets — images, JavaScript, CSS — the page references.

A properly formatted HTML page contains both a <head> and a <body> section. When processing a page, the browser waits until it receives all external resources referenced in the <head> section to render the page. The client renders assets referenced in the <body> section as it receives them.

Web browsers use only the GET and POST HTTP methods. The majority of browser requests are GET requests. The browser may use POST to submit form data or upload a file. This will become important in later chapters; you'll learn techniques to address this then. It's also impossible to customize the request headers sent by a browser.

HTTP in iOS apps

Your iOS apps — this also applies to other HTTP clients, such as Rested, JavaScript, Postman — are far less constrained. These apps are able to use all HTTP methods, add custom request headers and implement custom response handling. This is more work but the flexibility allows you the freedom to develop exactly what you need.

HTTP 2.0

Most web services today use HTTP version 1.1 — released in January 1997 as RFC 2068. Everything you've learned so far is part of HTTP/1.1 and, unless otherwise noted, is the version used throughout this book.

HTTP/2 expands the communications between client and server to improve efficiency and reduce latency. Individual requests are identical to those in HTTP/1.1, but they may proceed in parallel. The server can anticipate the client's requests and push data, such as stylesheets and images, to the client before it requests them. Vapor supports HTTP/1.1 and HTTP/2 in both its client and server functions.

REST

REST, or representational state transfer, is an architectural standard closely related to HTTP. Many APIs used by apps are REST APIs and you'll hear the term often. You'll learn more about REST and how it relates to HTTP and CRUD in Chapter 7: "CRUD Database Operations". REST provides a way of defining a common standard for accessing resources from an API. For example, for an acronyms API, you might define the following endpoints:

- **GET /api/acronyms/**: get all acronyms.

- **POST /api/acronyms**: create a new acronym.

- **GET /api/acronyms/1**: get the acronym with ID 1.

- **PUT /api/acronyms/1**: update the acronym with ID 1.

- **DELETE /api/acronyms/1**: delete the acronym with ID 1.

Having a common pattern to access resources from a REST API simplifies the process of building clients.

Why use Vapor?

Server-side app development with Swift and Vapor is a unique experience. In contrast to many traditional server-side languages — for example PHP, JavaScript, Ruby — Swift is strongly- and statically-typed. This characteristic has greatly reduced the number of runtime crashes in iOS apps and your server-side apps will also enjoy this benefit.

Another potential benefit of server-side Swift is improved performance. Because Swift is a compiled language, apps written using Swift are likely to perform better than those written in an interpreted language.

However, the biggest reason to write server-side Swift apps is you get to use Swift! Swift is one of the fastest-growing and most-loved languages, its modern syntax and features combining the best of many languages. If you currently develop for iOS, you probably already know the language well. This means you can start sharing core business logic code between your server-side apps and your iOS apps.

Choosing Swift also means you get to use Xcode to develop your server applications! Though Foundation on Linux is a subset of what you'll find on iOS and macOS, you can do the majority of your development in Xcode. This gives you access to powerful debugging capabilities in the IDE, a feature most server-side languages don't have.

How Vapor compares

Vapor isn't the only server-side Swift framework available so why choose Vapor? There are a number of good reasons to choose Vapor; here are a few.

At the time of writing, Vapor is the only server-side framework that uses `Codable` throughout its API. This allows you to write very little code to save models in the database and return them as JSON. It also allows you to accept data and convert it into a type-safe `struct` in a single line of code. Compared with previous versions of the framework, Vapor 3's use of `Codable` has dramatically reduced the amount of code you need to write.

Vapor also employs a fully non-blocking architecture. As you've learned, when a server application receives an HTTP request, it must return an HTTP response. In a blocking architecture, if your application takes a long time to process a request — for example, waiting for a database query to return — then the application can't respond to further requests on that thread. As you'll learn in the next chapter, spawning multiple threads and switching between them brings additional overhead. In a non-blocking architecture, the request is handed off and other requests are handled until the results of original request are ready. As a result, non-blocking frameworks perform significantly better than those that block. Vapor is non-blocking at every level, including the database drivers.

Finally, the best feature about Vapor is its community. Vapor has the most active and vibrant community, a major factor in its ever-increasing popularity!

Chapter 4: Async

By Tim Condon

In this chapter, you'll learn about asynchronous and non-blocking architectures. You'll discover Vapor's approach to these architectures and how to use them. Finally, the chapter provides a small overview of SwiftNIO, a core technology used by Vapor.

Async

One of Vapor 3's most important new features is `Async`. It can also be one of the most confusing. Why is it important?

Consider a scenario where your server has only a single thread and four client requests, in order:

1. A request for a stock quote. This results in a call to an API on another server.

2. A request for a static CSS style sheet. The CSS is available immediately without a lookup.

3. A request for a user's profile. The profile must be fetched from a database.

4. A request for some static HTML. The HTML is available immediately without a lookup.

In a synchronous server, the server's sole thread blocks until the stock quote is returned. It then returns the stock quote and the CSS style sheet. It blocks again while the database fetch completes. Only then, after the user's profile is sent, will the server return the static HTML to the client.

On the other hand, in an asynchronous server, the thread initiates the call to fetch the stock quote and puts the request aside until it completes. It then returns the CSS style sheet, starts the database fetch and returns the static HTML. As the requests that were put aside complete, the thread resumes work on them and returns their results to the client.

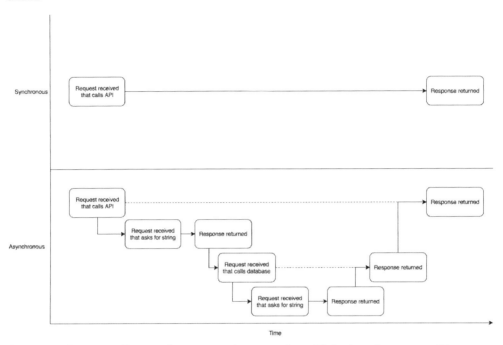

"But, wait!" you say, "Servers have more than one thread." And you're correct. However, there are limits to how many threads a server can have. Switching context between threads is expensive, and ensuring all your data accesses are thread-safe is time-consuming and error-prone. As a result, trying to solve the problem solely by adding threads is a poor, inefficient solution.

Futures and promises

In order to "put aside" a request while it waits for a response, you must wrap it in a **promise** to resume work on it when you receive the response. In practice, this means you must change the return type of functions that can be put aside. In a synchronous environment, you might have a function:

```
func getAllUsers() -> [User] {
  // do some database queries
}
```

In an asynchronous environment, that won't work because your database call may not have completed by the time `getAllUsers()` must return. You know you'll be able to return [User] in the future but can't do so now. In Vapor, your promise to deliver the results is called a **Future**. You'd write your function as shown below:

```
func getAllUsers() -> Future<[User]> {
  // do some database queries
}
```

Working with futures

Working with `Futures` can be confusing at first but, since Vapor uses them extensively, they'll quickly become second nature.

Unwrapping futures

Vapor has a number of convenience functions to work with futures to avoid having to deal with them directly. However, there are lots of scenarios where you need to use a future and wait for the promise to be executed. To demonstrate, imagine you have a route that returns the HTTP status code `204 No Content`. This route fetches a list of users from a database using a function like the one described above and modifies the first user in the list before returning. In order to use the result of that call, you must unwrap the result and provide a closure to execute when the `Future` has resolved. There are two main functions you'll use to do this:

- **flatMap(to:)**: Use when the promise closure returns a `Future`.

- **map(to:)**: Use when the promise closure returns a type other than `Future`.

Both choices produce another `Future`. For example:

```
// 1
return database
      .getAllUsers()
      .flatMap(to: HTTPStatus.self) { users in
  // 2
  let user = users[0]
  user.name = "Bob"
  // 3
  return user.save().map(to: HTTPStatus.self) { user in
    //4
    return HTTPStatus.noContent
  }
}
```

Here's what this does:

1. Fetch all users from the database. As you saw above, `getAllUsers()` returns `Future<[User]>`. Since the result of completing this `Future` is yet another `Future` (see step 3), use `flatMap(to:)` to unwrap the result. The closure for `flatMap(to:)` receives the completed future - `[User]` as its parameter. This `.flatMap(to:)` returns `Future<HTTPStatus>`.

2. Update the first user's name.

3. Save the updated user to the database. This returns `Future<User>` but the HTTPStatus value you need to return isn't yet a `Future` so use `map(to:)`.

4. Return the appropriate `HTTPStatus` value.

As you can see, for the top-level promise you use `flatMap(to:)` since the closure you provide it returns a `Future`. The inner promise, which returns a non-future HTTPStatus, uses `map(to:)`.

Transform

Sometimes you don't care about the result of a future, only that it completed successfully. In the above example, you don't use the unwrapped result of `save()` and are returning a different type back. For this scenario, you can simplify step 3 by using `transform(to:)`:

```
return database
        .getAllUsers()
        .flatMap(to: HTTPStatus.self) { users in
    let user = users[0]
    user.name = "Bob"
    return user.save().transform(to: HTTPStatus.noContent)
}
```

This helps reduce the amount of nesting and can make your code easier to read and maintain. You'll see this used throughout the book.

Flatten

There are times when you must wait for a number of futures to complete. One example occurs when you're saving multiple models in a database. In this case, you use `flatten(on:)`. For instance:

```
static func save(_ users: [User], request: Request)
    -> Future<HTTPStatus> {
    // 1
    var userSaveResults: [Future<User>] = []
    // 2
```

```
    for user in users {
      userSaveResults.append(user.save())
    }
    // 3
    return userSaveResults.flatten(on: request)
      //4
      .transform(to: HTTPStatus.created)
  }
```

Here's what this does:

1. Define an array of `Future<User>`s, the return type of `save()` in step 2.

2. Loop through each user in the `users` array and append the return value of `user.save()` to the array.

3. Use `flatten(on:)` to wait for all the futures to complete. This takes a `Worker`, the thread that actually performs the work. This is normally a `Request` in Vapor, but you'll learn about this later. The closure for `flatten(on:)`, if needed, takes the returned collection as a parameter.

4. Return a **201 Created** status.

`flatten(on:)` waits for all the futures to return as they're executed asynchronously by the same `Worker`.

Multiple futures

Occasionally, you need to wait for a number of futures of different types that don't rely on one another. For example, you encounter this situation when decoding request data and getting a user from the database. Vapor provides a number of global convenience functions that allow waiting for up to five different futures. This helps avoid deeply nested code or confusing chains.

If you have two futures — get all the users from the database and decode some data from a request — you can do:

```
// 1
flatMap(
  to: HTTPStatus.self,
  database.getAllUsers(),
  // 2
  request.content.decode(UserData.self)) { allUsers, userData in
    // 3
    return allUsers[0]
      .addData(userData)
      .transform(to: HTTPStatus.noContent)
}
```

Here's what this does:

1. Use the global `flatMap(to:_:_:)` to wait for the two futures to complete.

2. The closure takes the completed futures as parameters.

3. Call `addData(_:)`, which returns some future result and transform the return type to `.noContent`.

If the closure returns a non-future result, you can use the global `map(to:_:_:)` instead:

```
// 1
map(
  to: HTTPStatus.self,
  database.getAllUsers(),
  // 2
  request.content.decode(UserData.self)) { allUsers, userData in
    // 3
    allUsers[0].syncAddData(userData)
    // 4
    return HTTPStatus.noContent
}
```

Here's what this does:

1. Use the global `map(to:_:_:)` to wait for the two futures to complete.

2. The closure takes the completed futures as parameters.

3. Call the synchronous `syncAddData(_:)`

4. Return `.noContent`.

Creating futures

Sometimes you need to create your own futures. If an `if` statement returns a non-future and the `else` block returns a `Future`, the compiler will complain that these must be the same type. To fix this, you must convert the non-future into a `Future` using `request.future(_:)`. For example:

```
// 1
func createTrackingSession(for request: Request)
  -> Future<TrackingSession> {
  return request.makeNewSession()
}

// 2
func getTrackingSession(for request: Request)
  -> Future<TrackingSession> {
  // 3
  let session: TrackingSession? =
```

```
    TrackingSession(id: request.getKey())
  // 4
  guard let createdSession = session else {
    return createTrackingSession(for: request)
  }
  // 5
  return request.future(createdSession)
}
```

Here's what this does:

1. Define a function that creates a `TrackingSession` from the request. This returns `Future<TrackingSession>`.

2. Define a function that gets a tracking session from the request.

3. Attempt to create a tracking session using the request's `key`. This returns `nil` if the tracking session could not be created.

4. Ensure the session was created successfully, otherwise create a new tracking session.

5. Create a `Future<TrackingSession>` from `createdSession` using `request.future(_:)`. This returns the future on the same `Worker` the request runs on.

Since `createTrackingSession(for:)` returns `Future<TrackingSession>` you have to use `request.future(_:)` to turn the `createdSession` into a `Future<TrackingSession>` to make the compiler happy.

Dealing with errors

Vapor makes heavy use of Swift's error handling throughout the framework. Many functions `throw`, allowing you to handle errors at different levels. You may choose to handle errors inside your route handlers or by using middleware to catch the errors at a higher level, or both.

However, dealing with errors is a little different in an asynchronous world. You can't use Swift's `do`/`catch` as you don't know when the promise will execute. Vapor provides a number of functions to help handle these cases. At a basic level, Vapor has its own `do`/`catch` callbacks that work with Futures:

```
let futureResult = user.save()
futureResult.do { user in
  print("User was saved")
}.catch { error in
  print("There was an error saving the user: \(error)")
}
```

If save() succeeds, the do block is executed, with the unwrapped value of the future as the first parameter. If the future fails, it'll execute the .catch block, passing in the Error.

In Vapor, you must return something when handling requests, even if it's a future. Using the above do/catch method won't stop the error happening, but it'll allow you to see what the error is. If the save() call fails and you return futureResult, the failure still propagates up the chain. In most circumstances, however, you want to try and rectify the issue.

Vapor provides catchMap(_:) and catchFlatMap(_:) to handle this type of failure. This allows you to handle the error and, either fix it or throw a different error. For example:

```
// 1
return user.save(on: req).catchMap { error -> User in
  // 2
  print("Error saving the user: \(error)")
  // 3
  return User(name: "Default User")
}
```

Here's what this does:

1. Attempt to save the user. Provide a catchMap(_:) to handle the error if it occurs. The closure takes the error as the parameter and must return the type of the resolved future — in this case User.

2. Log the error received.

3. Create a default user to return.

Vapor also provides the related catchFlatMap(_:) for when the associated closure returns a future:

```
return user.save().catchFlatMap { error -> Future<User> in
  print("Error saving the user: \(error)")
  return User(name: "Default User").save()
}
```

Since save() returns a future, you must call catchFlatMap(_:) instead.

catchMap and catchFlatMap only execute their closures on a failure. But what if you want both to handle errors and handle the success case? Simple! Just chain to the appropriate method!

Chaining futures

Dealing with futures can sometimes seem overwhelming. It's easy to end up with code that's nested multiple levels deeps.

Vapor allows you to chain futures together instead of nesting them. For example, consider a snippet that looks like the following:

```
return database
    .getAllUsers()
    .flatMap(to: HTTPStatus.self) { users in
  let user = users[0]
  user.name = "Bob"
  return user.save().map(to: HTTPStatus.self) { user in
    return HTTPStatus.noContent
  }
}
```

map(to:) and flatMap(to:) can be chained together to avoid nesting like below:

```
return database
    .getAllUsers()
    // 1
    .flatMap(to: User.self) { users in
            let user = users[0]
            user.name = "Bob"
            return user.save()
    // 2
    }.map(to: HTTPStatus.self) { user in
        return HTTPStatus.noContent
    }
```

Changing the return type of flatMap(to:) allows you to chain the map(to:), which receives the Future<User>. The final map(to:) then returns the type you returned originally.

Chaining futures allows you to reduce the nesting in your code and may make it easier to reason about, which is especially helpful in an asynchronous world. However whether you nest or chain is completely personal preference.

Always

Sometimes you want to execute something no matter the outcome of a future. You may need to close connections, trigger a notification or just log that the future has been executed. For this use the always callback. For example:

```
// 1
let userResult: Future<User> = user.save()
```

```
// 2
userResult.always {
  // 3
  print("User save has been attempted")
}
```

Here's what this does:

1. Save a user and set the result to `userResult`. This is of type `Future<User`.

2. Chain an `always` to the result.

3. Print a string when the app executes the future.

The `always` closure gets executed no matter the result of the future, whether it fails or succeeds. It also has no effect on the future. You can combine this with other chains as well.

Waiting

In certain circumstances you may want to actually wait for the result to return. To do this, use `wait()`.

> **Note**: There's a large caveat around this: you can't use `wait()` on the main event loop, which means all request handlers and most other circumstances.

However, as you'll see in Chapter 11, "Testing", this can be especially useful in tests, where writing asynchronous tests is difficult. For example:

```
let savedUser = try user.save(on: connection).wait()
```

Instead of `savedUser` being a `Future<User>`, because you use `wait()`, in this instance `savedUser` is a `User` object. Be aware `wait()` throws an error if executing the promise fails.

It's worth saying again: this can only be used off the main event loop!

SwiftNIO

Vapor 3 is built on top of Apple's SwiftNIO library. SwiftNIO is a cross-platform, asynchronous networking library, like Java's Netty. It's open-source, just like Swift itself!

SwiftNIO handles all HTTP communications for Vapor. It's the plumbing that allows

Vapor to receive requests and send responses. SwiftNIO manages the connections and the transfer of data. It also manages all the **EventLoops** for your futures that perform work and execute your promises. Each `EventLoop` has its own thread.

Vapor manages all the interactions with NIO and provides a clean, Swifty API to use. Vapor is responsible for the higher-level aspects of a server, such as routing requests. It provides the features to build great server-side Swift applications. SwiftNIO provides a solid foundation to build on.

Chapter 5: Fluent & Persisting Models

By Tim Condon

In Chapter 2, "Hello, Vapor!" you learned the basics of creating a Vapor app, including how to create routes. This chapter explains how to use Fluent to save data in Vapor applications. You'll also learn how to deploy the application using Vapor Cloud.

Fluent

Fluent is Vapor's ORM or **object relational mapping** tool. It's an abstraction layer between the Vapor application and the database, and it's designed to make working with databases easier. Using an ORM such as Fluent has a number of benefits.

The biggest benefit is you don't have to use the database directly! When you interact directly with a database, you write database queries as strings. These aren't type-safe and can be painful to use from Swift.

Fluent benefits you by allowing you to use any of a number of database engines, even in the same app. Finally, you don't need to know how to write queries since you can interact with your **models** in a "Swifty" way.

Models are the Swift representation of your data and are used throughout Fluent. **Models** are the objects, such as user profiles, you save and access in your database. Fluent returns and uses type-safe models when interacting with the database, giving you compile-time safety.

Acronyms

Over the next several chapters you'll build a complex "Today I Learned" application that can save different acronyms and their meanings. Start by creating a new project, using the Vapor Toolbox. In Terminal, enter the following commands:

```
cd ~/vapor
vapor new TILApp
```

The first command takes you into a directory called **vapor** inside your home directory and assumes that you completed the steps in Chapter 2, "Hello Vapor!". The second command creates a new Vapor 3 project called **TILApp** using the default template.

The template provides examples files for models and controllers. You'll build your own so delete the examples. In Terminal, enter:

```
cd TILApp
rm -rf Sources/App/Models/*
rm -rf Sources/App/Controllers/*
```

Since Xcode projects are discardable when using Vapor — they're entirely optional — it's best practice to create your project files outside of Xcode. This lets the Swift Package

Manager, which is used by the Vapor Toolbox, ensure that they link to the correct targets. Create a file to hold the `Acronym` model:

```
touch Sources/App/Models/Acronym.swift
```

This command creates a Swift file inside the **App** module's **Models** directory called **Acronym.swift**. Now generate your Xcode project:

```
vapor xcode -y
```

Open **configure.swift**, find the **Configure migrations** group and delete the following line:

```
migrations.add(model: Todo.self, database: .sqlite)
```

Next, open **routes.swift** and delete the following lines:

```
// Example of configuring a controller
let todoController = TodoController()
router.get("todos", use: todoController.index)
router.post("todos", use: todoController.create)
router.delete("todos", Todo.parameter,
              use: todoController.delete)
```

This removes the remaining references to the template's example model and controller.

Open **Acronym.swift** and replace its contents with the following to create the basic model for the acronym:

```
import Vapor
import FluentSQLite

final class Acronym: Codable {
  var id: Int?
  var short: String
  var long: String

  init(short: String, long: String) {
    self.short = short
    self.long = long
  }
}
```

The model contains two `String` properties to hold the acronym and its definition. It also contains an optional `id` property that stores the ID of the model, if one has been set.

All Fluent models must conform to `Codable`. It's also good practice to mark classes `final`, where possible, as it provides a performance benefit. The ID is set by the database when the acronym is saved.

Next make `Acronym` conform to Fluent's `Model`. Add the following at the end of the file:

```
extension Acronym: Model {
  // 1
  typealias Database = SQLiteDatabase
  // 2
  typealias ID = Int
  // 3
  public static var idKey: IDKey = \Acronym.id
}
```

Here's what this does:

1. Tell Fluent what database to use for this model. The template is already configured to use SQLite.

2. Tell Fluent what type the ID is.

3. Tell Fluent the key path of the model's ID property.

This code can be improved further with `SQLiteModel`. Replace:

```
extension Acronym: Model {
  typealias Database = SQLiteDatabase
  typealias ID = Int
  public static var idKey: IDKey = \Acronym.id
}
```

with the following:

```
extension Acronym: SQLiteModel {}
```

The Fluent packages provide `Model` helper protocols for each database provider so you don't have to specify the database or ID types, or the key. The `SQLiteModel` protocol must have an ID of type `Int?` called `id`, but there are `SQLiteUUIDModel` and `SQLiteStringModel` protocols for models with IDs of type `UUID` or `String`. If you want to customize the ID property name, you must conform to the standard `Model` protocol.

To save the model in the database, you must create a table for it. Fluent does this with a **migration**. Migrations allow you to make reliable, testable, reproducible changes to your database. They are commonly used to create a **database schema**, or table description, for your models. They are also used to seed data into your database or make changes to your models after they've been saved.

Add the following at the end of **Acronym.swift** to make the model conform to `Migration`:

```
extension Acronym: Migration {}
```

That is all you need to do! Fluent infers the schema for your model thanks to `Codable`. For basic models you can use the default implementations for `Migration`. If you need to change your model later or do more complex things, such as marking a property as unique, you may need to implement your own migrations. This is covered in a later chapter.

Now that `Acronym` conforms to `Migration`, you can tell Fluent to create the table when the application starts. Open **configure.swift** and find the section labeled `// Configure migrations`. Add the following before `services.register(migrations)`:

```
migrations.add(model: Acronym.self, database: .sqlite)
```

Fluent supports mixing multiple databases in a single application so you specify which database holds each model. Migrations only run *once*; once they have run in a database, they are never executed again. Fluent won't attempt to create a table that already exists, but it's important to remember if you change your model.

Set the active scheme to **Run** with **My Mac** as the destination. Build and run. Check the console and see that the migrations have run. You should see something similar to the console output below:

Saving models

When your app's user enters a new acronym, you need a way to save it. In Swift 4 and Vapor 3, `Codable` makes this trivial. Vapor provides `Content`, a wrapper around `Codable`, which allows you to convert models and other data between various formats. This is used extensively in Vapor and you'll see it throughout the book.

Open **Acronym.swift** and add the following to the end of the file to make `Acronym` conform to `Content`:

```
extension Acronym: Content {}
```

Since `Acronym` already conforms to `Codable`, you don't have to add anything else. To create an acronym, the user's browser sends a POST request containing a JSON payload that looks similar to the following:

```
{
  "short": "OMG",
  "long": "Oh My God"
}
```

You'll need a route to handle this POST request and save the new acronym. Open **routes.swift** and add the following to the end of `routes(_:)`:

```
// 1
router.post("api", "acronyms") { req -> Future<Acronym> in
  // 2
  return try req.content.decode(Acronym.self)
    .flatMap(to: Acronym.self) { acronym in
      // 3
      return acronym.save(on: req)
  }
}
```

Here's what this does:

1. Register a new route at **/api/acronyms** that accepts a POST request and returns `Future<Acronym>`. It returns the acronym once it's saved.

2. Decode the request's JSON into an `Acronym` model using `Codable`. This returns a `Future<Acronym>` so it uses a `flatMap(to:)` to extract the acronym when the decoding is complete. Note this is different from how data is decoded in Chapter 2, "Hello Vapor!". In this route handler, you are calling `decode(_:)` on `Request` yourself. You are then unwrapping the result as `decode(_:)` returns a `Future<Acronym>`.

3. Save the model using Fluent. This returns `Future<Acronym>` as it returns the model once it's saved.

Fluent and Vapor's integrated use of `Codable` makes this simple. Since `Acronym` conforms to `Content`, it's easily converted between JSON and `Model`. This allows Vapor to return the model as JSON in the response without any effort on your part. Build and run the application to try it out. A good tool to test this is **RESTed**, available as a free download from the Mac App Store. Other tools such as Paw and Postman are suitable as well.

In RESTed, configure the request as follows:

- **URL**: http://localhost:8080/api/acronyms

- **method**: POST

- **Parameter encoding**: JSON-encoded

Add two parameters with names and values:

- **short**: OMG

- **long**: Oh My God

Setting the parameter encoding to **JSON-encoded** ensures the data is sent as JSON. It is important to note this also sets the `Content-Type` header to `application/json`, which tells Vapor the request contains JSON. If you are using a different client to send the request you may need to set this manually. Click **Send Request** and you'll see the acronym provided in the response. The `id` field will have a value as it has now been saved in the database:

Deploying to Vapor Cloud

Vapor Cloud is a Platform as a Service (PaaS) built by the Vapor team specifically for hosting Vapor applications. It's designed to simplify configuring servers and managing deployments so you can concentrate on writing code.

At the end of each chapter in this section of the book, you'll deploy your application to Vapor Cloud. First, sign up for an account, if you don't have one. Visit https://dashboard.vapor.cloud and follow the signup process:

Before you use Vapor Cloud, you must configure your application. Vapor Cloud applications are configured in **cloud.yml**, provided in the template. The template is already configured for Vapor 3. It looks similar to the following:

```
# 1
type: "vapor"
# 2
swift_version: "4.1.0"
# 3
run_parameters: "serve --port 8080 --hostname 0.0.0.0"
```

Here's what this does:

1. Specify this is a Vapor application.

2. Specify the Swift version to build the project.

3. Specify the parameters required to run the application.

You use the Vapor Toolbox to interact with Vapor Cloud commands. First, login to Vapor Cloud with the Toolbox. In Terminal, type:

```
vapor cloud login
```

This asks for your username and password, use the credentials you provided when registering. When successful, the Toolbox logs you in to Vapor Cloud:

Now deploy the application. In Terminal, type:

```
vapor cloud deploy
```

This takes you through all steps necessary to deploy your project to Vapor Cloud.

Adding a repository

> **Note**: Vapor Cloud works with both SSH and HTTPS for the GitHub URL below. If you have set up two factor authentication on GitHub you **must** use the SSH URL, otherwise you'll be unable to push. This also applies if you are using a private repository.

Vapor Cloud first reads your local repository. Because the application is set up from the template, no remote repository has been configured. Vapor Cloud guides you through the process for doing so. Vapor Cloud asks if you want to set up a remote, so type **y** followed by **Enter**:

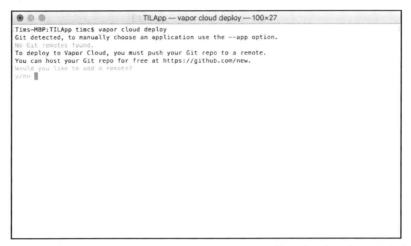

This opens GitHub so you can create a new repository. Fill in the details and click **Create repository**:

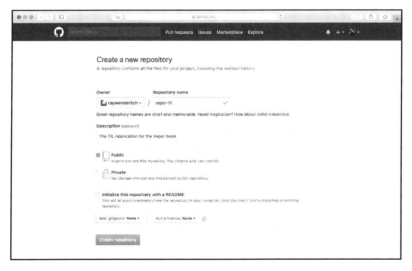

Once you have the repository, copy the SSH or HTTPS URL provided on the empty repository screen:

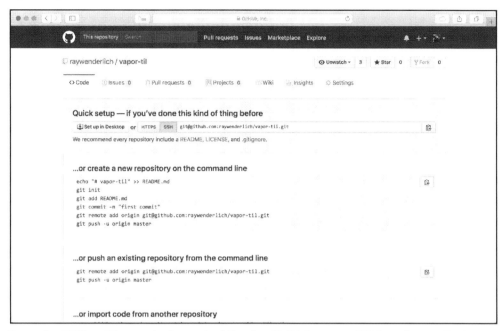

Paste the URL in Terminal when asked for the **GitHub origin URL** and press **Enter**:

This commits your code and pushes it up to the new GitHub remote repository.

Creating a project and application

Next Vapor Cloud asks you to create an application. Type **y** and press **Enter**:

Before you create an application, you must create a project for the application to live in. For example, the TIL project could contain a TIL API application and a TIL website application. When asked to create a project, enter **y** and press **Enter**:

Vapor Cloud asks you to select the **organization** to own the project. This is the organization you specified when you registered. Organizations can also include any that you have been joined after registration.

Select the organization, in this case **1**, and press **Enter**:

```
●  ●  ●                    TILApp — vapor cloud deploy — 100×28
 * [new branch]      master -> master
Branch 'master' set up to track remote branch 'master' from 'origin'.
Added Git origin: git@github.com:raywenderlich/vapor-til.git
No applications matching Git remotes found.
    - git@github.com:raywenderlich/vapor-til.git
Create application: vapor cloud create app
Would you like to create an application now?
y/n> y
Creating an application
You will normally create one application for each Vapor project.
You can then add services to this application such as hosting.
Choosing a project
If paid services are added to this application,
they will be billed to the project's organization.
No projects found.
Create project: vapor cloud create proj
Would you like to create a project now?
y/n> y
Creating a project
Projects are a way to group applications together.
If you are an app developer, you might create a new project
for each client to keep things organized.
Choosing an organization
If paid services are added to applications in this project,
they will be billed to the project's organization.
Which organization?
1: Ray Wenderlich
> 1█
```

Once selected, Vapor Cloud asks you to name the project. This section of the book builds a TIL application, so the name is **TIL**. Vapor Cloud then asks you to confirm this. Enter **y** and press **Enter**:

```
●  ●  ●                    TILApp — vapor cloud deploy — 100×28                    ?
Branch 'master' set up to track remote branch 'master' from 'origin'.
Added Git origin: git@github.com:raywenderlich/vapor-til.git
No applications matching Git remotes found.
    - git@github.com:raywenderlich/vapor-til.git
Create application: vapor cloud create app
Would you like to create an application now?
y/n> y
Creating an application
You will normally create one application for each Vapor project.
You can then add services to this application such as hosting.
Choosing a project
If paid services are added to this application,
they will be billed to the project's organization.
No projects found.
Create project: vapor cloud create proj
Would you like to create a project now?
y/n> y
project: TIL
Is the above information correct?
y/n> y█
```

Finally, Vapor Cloud asks you to name the application. Again, enter **TIL**.

Next, Vapor Cloud asks you to provide a **slug**. A slug is a unique identifier for your application that forms part of the URL. For this book, the slug is **rw-til**. You must choose a unique slug. Vapor Cloud then asks you to confirm the information provided. Enter **y** and press **Enter**:

Setting up hosting

Next Vapor asks you if you would like to add a **hosting service**. A hosting service allows you to deploy code to Vapor Cloud, for example GitHub. Vapor Cloud already knows this Git URL as it helped create the repository, so select **1** and press **Enter**. Vapor Cloud then asks for confirmation that all the information is correct. Enter **y** and press **Enter** to continue:

> **Note**: If you are using a private Git repository, you must provide Vapor Cloud with an SSH key so that it can read the repository to build your code. See the Vapor Cloud documentation at https://docs.vapor.cloud/advanced/general/using-private-git/ for details on how to do this.

Setting up environments

Once you have configured the hosting, Vapor Cloud asks you to set up **environments**. An application can have multiple environments. These can be used for testing your application at different stages before releasing. For instance, you can have a testing environment to test your application without using real data. You can have a staging environment to check everything works with production configuration. Finally you can have a production environment, which is what your users will use. In Vapor Cloud **production** is the default environment.

Vapor Cloud asks if you want to create an environment, so enter **y** followed by **Enter**.

Provide **production** for the name when prompted and press **Enter**:

Each environment can use a different Git branch by default. This book uses the **master** branch for production. Enter **master** when asked for the Git branch and press **Enter**:

Final configuration

Once you have configured an environment, you must choose a **replica size** for that environment. Replicas are the hardware that host your application: the bigger the replica, the more processing power and memory it has.

To start with, select the **Free** option:

```
●  ●  ●                    TILApp — vapor cloud deploy — 100×26
Tims-MBP:TILApp timc$ vapor cloud deploy
app: TIL
git: git@github.com:raywenderlich/vapor-til.git
No environments found.
Create environment: vapor cloud create env
Would you like to create an environment now?
y/n> y
app: TIL
git: git@github.com:raywenderlich/vapor-til.git
environment: production
default branch: master
What size replica(s)?
1: Free ($0/month)
2: Hobby ($6/month)
3: Small ($30/month)
4: Medium ($65/month)
5: Large ($225/month)
6: X-Large ($375/month)
> 1
```

Vapor Cloud asks you to confirm your choice. Type **y** followed by **Enter**:

```
●  ●  ●                    TILApp — vapor cloud deploy — 100×26
Tims-MBP:TILApp timc$ vapor cloud deploy
app: TIL
git: git@github.com:raywenderlich/vapor-til.git
No environments found.
Create environment: vapor cloud create env
Would you like to create an environment now?
y/n> y
app: TIL
git: git@github.com:raywenderlich/vapor-til.git
environment: production
default branch: master
replica size: Free
Is the above information correct?
y/n> y
```

Next, Vapor Cloud asks if you would like to configure a database. The application is currently using the in-memory SQLite database so a database isn't required for now. Enter **n** followed by **Enter** to skip configuring a database.

The final option to choose is the **build type**. Vapor Cloud offers three build types:

• **Incremental**: this compiles the code using any existing build artifacts to speed up build times.

• **Update**: this updates any dependencies as allowed by your manifest.

• **Clean**: this cleans any dependencies and existing build artifacts.

As this is the initial build, type **3** for Clean and press **Enter**:

Build, deploy and test

Finally, Vapor Cloud asks you to confirm that all the options are correct before proceeding. Ensure everything is as expected and press **y** followed by **Enter**:

```
Tims-MBP:TILApp timc$ vapor cloud deploy
app: TIL
git: git@github.com:raywenderlich/vapor-til.git
env: production
db: none
replicas: 1
replica size: free
branch: master
build: clean
Is the above information correct?
y/n> y
```

This kicks off a build in Vapor Cloud. Vapor Cloud clones the project, compiles the application, creates a Docker image and pushes the image to the Vapor Cloud container repository. When the build finishes, Vapor Cloud prints a **Successfully deployed** message with a URL to the app:

```
app: TIL
git: git@github.com:raywenderlich/vapor-til.git
env: production
db: none
replicas: 1
replica size: free
branch: master
build: clean
Creating deployment [Done]
Connecting to build logs ...
Waiting in Queue [Done]
Starting deployment: 'rw-til' [Done]
Getting project from Git 'git@github.com:raywenderlich/vapor-til.git' [Done]
Checkout branch 'master' [Done]
Verifying base folder [Done]
Selected swift version: 4.1.0-beta [Done]
Building vapor (release) [Done]
Trying to find executable [Done]
Found executable: Run [Done]
Creating container registry [Done]
Building container [Done]
Pushing container to registry [Done]
Updating replicas [Done]
Deployment succeeded: https://rw-til.vapor.cloud [Done]
Successfully deployed.
Tims-MBP:TILApp timc$
```

As this book uses the **rw-til** slug, the URL for the application is **https://rw-til.vapor.cloud**. The URL for your deployed application will print in Terminal.

Open RESTed and configure a new request as follows:

- **URL**: http://**<your URL>**/hello

- **method**: GET

Send the request and you get a "Hello, world!" response back:

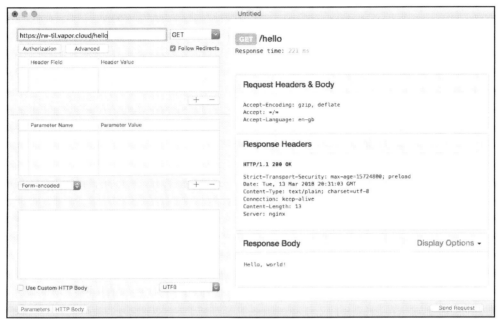

Finally, reconfigure the request as follows:

- **URL**: http://**<your URL>**/api/acronyms/

- **method**: POST

- **Parameter encoding**: JSON-encoded

Add two parameters with names and values:

- **short**: OMG

- **long**: Oh My God

Send the request, and you'll receive the acronym you have created in Vapor Cloud in the response:

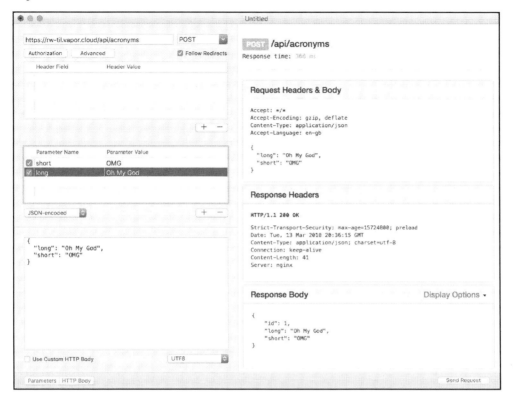

Where to go from here?

This chapter has introduced you to Fluent and how to create models in Vapor. You have also learned how to deploy your application to Vapor Cloud. The next chapters build on this application to create a full featured TIL application.

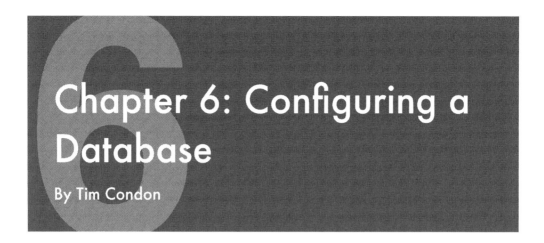

Chapter 6: Configuring a Database

By Tim Condon

Databases allow you to persist data in your applications. In this chapter you'll learn how to configure your Vapor application to integrate with the database of your choice. Finally you'll deploy your application to **Vapor Cloud** and learn how to set up the database there.

> This chapter, and most of the book, uses **Docker** to host the database. Docker is a containerization technology that allows you to run independent images on your machine without the overhead of virtual machines. You can spin up different databases and not worry about installing dependencies or databases interfering with each other.

Why use a database?

Databases provide a reliable, performant means of storing and retrieving data. If your application stores information in memory, it is lost when you stop the application. It's good practice to decouple storage from your application as this allows you to scale your application across multiple instances, all backed by the same database. Indeed, most hosting solutions, such as Vapor Cloud and Heroku, don't have persistent file storage.

Choosing a database

Vapor has official, Swift-native drivers for:

- **SQLite**

- **MySQL**

- **PostgreSQL**

There are two types of databases: **relational**, or **SQL** databases, and **non-relational**, or **NoSQL** databases. Relational databases store their data in structured tables with defined columns. They are efficient at storing and querying data whose structure is known up front. You create and query tables with a **structured query language** (SQL) that allows you to retrieve data from multiple, related tables. For example, if you have a list of pets in one table and list of owners in another, you can retrieve a list of pets with their owners' names with a single query. Currently Vapor only has support for relational (SQL) databases but this will change in the future.

While relational databases are good for rigid structures, this can be an issue if you must change that structure. Recently, NoSQL databases have become popular as a way of storing large amounts of unstructured data. Social networks, for example, can store settings, images, locations, statuses and metrics all in a single document. This allows for much greater flexibility than traditional databases.

SQLite

SQLite is a simple, file-based relational database system. It is designed to be embedded into an application and is useful for single-process applications such as iOS applications. It relies on file locks to maintain database integrity, so it's not suitable for write-intensive applications. This also means it can't be used across servers. It is, however, a good database for both testing and prototyping applications.

MySQL

MySQL is another open-source, relational database made popular by the LAMP web application stack (Linux, Apache, MySQL, PHP). It's become the most popular database due to its ease of use and support from most cloud providers and website builders.

PostgreSQL

PostgreSQL — frequently shortened to Postgres — is an open-source, relational database system focused on extensibility and standards and is designed for enterprise use. Postgres also has native support for geometric primitives, such as coordinates. Fluent supports these primitives as well as saving nested types, such as dictionaries, directly into Postgres.

Configuring Vapor

Configuring your Vapor application to use a database follows the same steps for all supported databases as shown below.

• Add the **Fluent Provider** for that database to the application's services.

• Configure the **database**.

• Configure **migrations**.

> **Services** are a way of creating and accessing things from a container. The most common containers you'll interact with in Vapor are the application itself, requests and responses. You should use the application to create services required for booting your app. You'll use the request and response containers to create services such as instances of the `BCryptHasher` if you wanted to hash a password while dealing with that request.

Each database recipe in this chapter starts with **TILApp** as you left it in Chapter 5, "Fluent and Persisting Models". You'll also need to have Docker installed and running. Visit https://www.docker.com/get-docker and follow the instructions to install it.

SQLite

The default template provided by the Vapor Toolbox uses SQLite as its database. The `Acronym` model in Chapter 5 uses SQLite. However to understand how it works, open **Package.swift** in your project directory. It will look similar to the following:

```
// swift-tools-version:4.0
import PackageDescription

let package = Package(
  name: "TILApp",
  dependencies: [
```

```
    // 💧 A server-side Swift web framework.
    .package(url: "https://github.com/vapor/vapor.git",
             from: "3.0.0"),

    // 🖊 Swift ORM framework (queries, models, and relations)
    // for building NoSQL and SQL database integrations.
    .package(url: "https://github.com/vapor/fluent-sqlite.git",
             from: "3.0.0"),
  ],
  targets: [
    .target(name: "App", dependencies: ["FluentSQLite",
                                         "Vapor"]),
    .target(name: "Run", dependencies: ["App"]),
    .testTarget(name: "AppTests", dependencies: ["App"]),
  ]
)
```

You can see your app depends upon FluentSQLite. You might be wondering where the database configuration happens. Database configuration happens in **Sources/App/ configure.swift**:

```
// 1
try services.register(FluentSQLiteProvider())

// 2
var databases = DatabasesConfig()
try databases.add(database: SQLiteDatabase(storage: .memory),
                  as: .sqlite)
services.register(databases)

// 3
var migrations = MigrationConfig()
migrations.add(model: Acronym.self, database: .sqlite)
services.register(migrations)
```

Here's what this does:

1. Register the `FluentSQLiteProvider` as a service to allow the application to interact with SQLite via Fluent.

2. Create a `DatabasesConfig` type which registers an instance of `SQLiteDatabase`, identified as `.sqlite` throughout the application. Note this uses `.memory` storage. This means the database resides in memory, is not persisted to disk and is lost when the application terminates.

3. Create a `MigrationConfig` type which tells the application which database to use for each model as discussed in Chapter 5, "Fluent and Persisting Models".

If you want persistent storage with SQLite, provide `SQLiteDatabase` with a path:

```
let database = SQLiteDatabase(storage: .file(path: "db.sqlite"))
try databases.add(database: database), as: .sqlite)
```

This creates a database file at the specified path, if the file doesn't exist. If the file exists, `SQLiteDatabase` uses it.

MySQL

To test with MySQL, run the MySQL server in a Docker container. Enter the following command in Terminal:

```
docker run --name mysql -e MYSQL_USER=vapor \
  -e MYSQL_PASSWORD=password -e MYSQL_DATABASE=vapor \
  -p 3306:3306 -d mysql/mysql-server:5.7
```

Here's what this does:

- Run a new container named **mysql**.

- Specify the database name, username and password through environment variables.

- Allow applications to connect to the MySQL server on its default port: 3306.

- Run the server in the background as a daemon.

- Use the Docker image named **mysql/mysql-server** for this container. If the image is not present on your machine, Docker automatically downloads it. This also specifies the image tagged with version 5.7, the version compatible with Fluent.

To check that your database is running, enter the following in Terminal to list all active containers:

```
docker ps
```

Now that MySQL is running, set up your Vapor application. Open **Package.swift**; replace its contents with the following:

```
// swift-tools-version:4.0
import PackageDescription
```

```
let package = Package(
  name: "TILApp",
  dependencies: [
    .package(url: "https://github.com/vapor/vapor.git",
             from: "3.0.0"),

    // 1
    .package(url: "https://github.com/vapor/fluent-mysql.git",
             from: "3.0.0-rc"),
  ],
  targets: [
    // 2
    .target(name: "App", dependencies: ["FluentMySQL",
                                        "Vapor"]),
    .target(name: "Run", dependencies: ["App"]),
    .testTarget(name: "AppTests", dependencies: ["App"]),
  ]
)
```

Here's what this does:

1. Specify `FluentMySQL` as a package dependency.

2. Specify that the `App` target depends on `FluentMySQL` to ensure it links correctly.

In Terminal, type the following, to regenerate your Xcode project (close the project first if you have it open) to bring in the new dependencies:

```
vapor xcode -y
```

When Xcode opens, open **configure.swift**. To switch to MySQL, replace the contents with the following:

```
// 1
import FluentMySQL
import Vapor

public func configure(
  _ config: inout Config,
  _ env: inout Environment,
  _ services: inout Services
) throws {
  // 2
  try services.register(FluentMySQLProvider())

  let router = EngineRouter.default()
  try routes(router)
  services.register(router, as: Router.self)

  var middlewares = MiddlewareConfig()
  middlewares.use(ErrorMiddleware.self)
```

```
    services.register(middlewares)

    var databases = DatabasesConfig()
    // 3
    let databaseConfig = MySQLDatabaseConfig(
      hostname: "localhost",
      username: "vapor",
      password: "password",
      database: "vapor")
    let database = MySQLDatabase(config: databaseConfig)
    databases.add(database: database, as: .mysql)
    services.register(databases)
    var migrations = MigrationConfig()
    // 4
    migrations.add(model: Acronym.self, database: .mysql)
    services.register(migrations)
  }
```

The changes are:

1. Import `FluentMySQL`.

2. Register the `FluentMySQLProvider`.

3. Set up a MySql database configuration using the same values supplied to Docker.

4. Change the `Acronym` migration to use the `.mysql` database.

Finally, change the `Acronym` model to conform to `MySQLModel`. Open **Acronym.swift** and replace the contents with the following:

```
import Vapor
import FluentMySQL

final class Acronym: Codable {
  var id: Int?
  var short: String
  var long: String

  init(short: String, long: String) {
    self.short = short
    self.long = long
  }
}

extension Acronym: MySQLModel {}
extension Acronym: Migration {}
extension Acronym: Content {}
```

Make sure you have the **Run** scheme selected with the deployment target **My Mac**, then build and run your application.

Look for the migration messages in the console.

PostgreSQL

To test with PostgreSQL, you'll run the Postgres server in a Docker container. Open `Terminal` and enter the following command:

```
docker run --name postgres -e POSTGRES_DB=vapor \
  -e POSTGRES_USER=vapor -e POSTGRES_PASSWORD=password \
  -p 5432:5432 -d postgres
```

Here's what this does:

- Run a new container named **postgres**.

- Specify the database name, username and password through environment variables.

- Allow applications to connect to the Postgres server on its default port: 5432.

- Run the server in the background as a daemon.

- Use the Docker image named **postgres** for this container. If the image is not present on your machine, Docker automatically downloads it.

To check that your database is running, enter the following in Terminal to list all active containers:

```
docker ps
```

```
Tims-MBP:vapor timc$ docker run --name postgres -e POSTGRES_DB=vapor -e POSTGRES_USER=vapor -e POSTGRES_PASSWORD=password -p 5432:5432 -d postgres
Unable to find image 'postgres:latest' locally
latest: Pulling from library/postgres
723254a2c089: Pull complete
39ec0e6c372c: Pull complete
ba1542fb91f3: Pull complete
c7195e642388: Pull complete
95424deca6a2: Pull complete
2d7d4b3a4ce2: Pull complete
fbde41d4a8cc: Pull complete
43a0cfa9789d: Pull complete
371d656a7cd4: Pull complete
6b98f92bd478: Pull complete
1899e8510879: Pull complete
5d421aa09a81: Pull complete
8423a5b1da74: Pull complete
Digest: sha256:92f5c1043096c56119f5d4a71a5ca382f652a4d02b814f6970c0021031422a2d
Status: Downloaded newer image for postgres:latest
882203d316180f81026d3309960a73dd778b1ec59c8042978ff58d353cdd109d
Tims-MBP:vapor timc$ docker ps
CONTAINER ID    IMAGE       COMMAND            CREATED                STATUS        PORTS                   NAMES
862203d31618    postgres    "docker-entrypoint.s…"  Less than a second ago  Up 4 seconds  0.0.0.0:5432->5432/tcp  postgres
Tims-MBP:vapor timc$
```

Now that Postgres is running, set up your Vapor application. Open **Package.swift**; replace its contents with the following:

```swift
// swift-tools-version:4.0
import PackageDescription

let package = Package(
  name: "TILApp",
  dependencies: [
    .package(url: "https://github.com/vapor/vapor.git",
             from: "3.0.0"),

    // 1
    .package(
      url: "https://github.com/vapor/fluent-postgresql.git",
      from: "1.0.0-rc"),
  ],
  targets: [
    // 2
    .target(name: "App", dependencies: ["FluentPostgreSQL",
                                        "Vapor"]),
    .target(name: "Run", dependencies: ["App"]),
    .testTarget(name: "AppTests", dependencies: ["App"]),
  ]
)
```

Here's what this does:

1. Specify FluentPostgreSQL as a package dependency.

2. Specify that the App target depends on FluentPostgreSQL to ensure it links correctly.

In Terminal, type the following, to regenerate your Xcode project (close the project first if you have it open) to bring in the new dependencies:

```
vapor xcode -y
```

When Xcode opens, open **configure.swift**. To switch to PostgreSQL, replace the contents with the following:

```
// 1
import FluentPostgreSQL
import Vapor

public func configure(
    _ config: inout Config,
    _ env: inout Environment,
    _ services: inout Services
) throws {
    // 2
    try services.register(FluentPostgreSQLProvider())

    let router = EngineRouter.default()
    try routes(router)
    services.register(router, as: Router.self)

    var middlewares = MiddlewareConfig()
    middlewares.use(ErrorMiddleware.self)
    services.register(middlewares)

    // Configure a database
    var databases = DatabasesConfig()
    // 3
    let databaseConfig = PostgreSQLDatabaseConfig(
      hostname: "localhost",
      username: "vapor",
      database: "vapor",
      password: "password")
    let database = PostgreSQLDatabase(config: databaseConfig)
    databases.add(database: database, as: .psql)
    services.register(databases)

    var migrations = MigrationConfig()
    // 4
    migrations.add(model: Acronym.self, database: .psql)
    services.register(migrations)
}
```

The changes are:

1. Import `FluentPostgreSQL`.

2. Register `FluentPostgreSQLProvider`.

3. Set up a PostgreSQL database configuration using the same values supplied to Docker.

4. Change the `Acronym` migration to use the `.psql` database.

Finally, change the `Acronym` model to conform to `PostgreSQLModel`. Open
Acronym.swift and replace the contents with the following:

```swift
import Vapor
import FluentPostgreSQL

final class Acronym: Codable {
  var id: Int?
  var short: String
  var long: String

  init(short: String, long: String) {
    self.short = short
    self.long = long
  }
}

extension Acronym: PostgreSQLModel {}
extension Acronym: Migration {}
extension Acronym: Content {}
```

Make sure you have the **Run** scheme selected with the deployment target **My Mac**, then
build and run your application. Look for the migration messages in the console.

Deploying to Vapor Cloud

Note: This section assumes that you have completed the Vapor Cloud deployment steps in Chapter 5, "Fluent and Persisting Models".

This book uses PostgreSQL as the database when deploying the application to Vapor Cloud. Ensure that you have followed the PostgreSQL section above to set up your application.

Database setup

Earlier in the chapter you configured the `PostgreSQLDatabaseConfig` type in **configure.swift** with hard-coded values. You must change these to use a database in Vapor Cloud. Vapor Cloud sets environment variables for the database information at runtime.

In `configure.swift`, remove the following lines in the section labeled `// Configure a database`:

```
var databases = DatabasesConfig()
let databaseConfig = PostgreSQLDatabaseConfig(
  hostname: "localhost",
  port: 5432,
  username: "vapor",
  database: "vapor",
  password: "password")
let database = PostgreSQLDatabase(config: databaseConfig)
databases.add(database: database, as: .psql)
services.register(databases)
```

Replace these lines with the following:

```
// 1
var databases = DatabasesConfig()
// 2
let hostname = Environment.get("DATABASE_HOSTNAME")
  ?? "localhost"
let username = Environment.get("DATABASE_USER") ?? "vapor"
let databaseName = Environment.get("DATABASE_DB") ?? "vapor"
let password = Environment.get("DATABASE_PASSWORD")
  ?? "password"
// 3
let databaseConfig = PostgreSQLDatabaseConfig(
  hostname: hostname,
  username: username,
```

```
   database: databaseName,
   password: password)
// 4
let database = PostgreSQLDatabase(config: databaseConfig)
// 5
databases.add(database: database, as: .psql)
// 6
services.register(databases)
```

Here's what this does:

1. Create a `DatabasesConfig` to configure the database.

2. Use `Environment.get(_:)` to fetch environment variables set by Vapor Cloud. If the function call returns `nil` (i.e. the application is running locally), default to the values required for the Docker container.

3. Use the properties to create a new `PostgreSQLDatabaseConfig`.

4. Create a `PostgreSQLDatabase` using the configuration.

5. Add the database object to the `DatabasesConfig` using the default `.psql` identifier.

6. Register `DatabasesConfig` with the services.

Build and run the application and ensure that it still connects to the database running in the Docker container:

Deploying

Now that you've configured the application to work with either Docker locally or Vapor Cloud, you're ready to deploy it. In Terminal, commit your code to Git:

```
# 1
git commit -am "Use PostgreSQL as the database"
# 2
git push
```

Here's what these commands do:

1. Commit all the local change to the local repository. The commit message is "Use PostgreSQL as the database".

2. Push the commits in the local repository to the remote repository on GitHub.

Finally, deploy your application to Vapor Cloud. In Terminal, type:

```
vapor cloud deploy
```

This loads the application and then asks you the environment to deploy to. Select **1** for production and press **Enter**:

```
● ● ●                  TILApp — vapor cloud deploy — 100×26
Tims-MBP:TILApp timc$ git commit -am "Use PostgreSQL as the database"
[master d42a4c1] Use PostgreSQL as the database
 4 files changed, 39 insertions(+), 21 deletions(-)
Tims-MBP:TILApp timc$ git push
Counting objects: 9, done.
Delta compression using up to 4 threads.
Compressing objects: 100% (9/9), done.
Writing objects: 100% (9/9), 1.35 KiB | 1.35 MiB/s, done.
Total 9 (delta 6), reused 0 (delta 0)
remote: Resolving deltas: 100% (6/6), completed with 6 local objects.
To github.com:raywenderlich/vapor-til.git
   4e70832..d42a4c1  master -> master
Tims-MBP:TILApp timc$ vapor cloud deploy
app: TIL
git: git@github.com:raywenderlich/vapor-til.git
Which environment?
1: production
> 1
```

Next, Vapor Cloud asks if you'd like to add a database. This time, enter **y** followed by **Enter**:

```
● ● ●                    TILApp — vapor cloud deploy — 100×26
Tims-MBP:TILApp timc$ git commit -am "Use PostgreSQL as the database"
[master d42a4c1] Use PostgreSQL as the database
 4 files changed, 39 insertions(+), 21 deletions(-)
Tims-MBP:TILApp timc$ git push
Counting objects: 9, done.
Delta compression using up to 4 threads.
Compressing objects: 100% (9/9), done.
Writing objects: 100% (9/9), 1.35 KiB | 1.35 MiB/s, done.
Total 9 (delta 6), reused 0 (delta 0)
remote: Resolving deltas: 100% (6/6), completed with 6 local objects.
To github.com:raywenderlich/vapor-til.git
   4e70832..d42a4c1  master -> master
Tims-MBP:TILApp timc$ vapor cloud deploy
app: TIL
git: git@github.com:raywenderlich/vapor-til.git
env: production
No database service found.
Would you like to add a database?
y/n> y
```

In this section, you've configured the application to use PostgreSQL so select **2** followed by **Enter**:

```
● ● ●                    TILApp — vapor cloud deploy — 100×26
[master d42a4c1] Use PostgreSQL as the database
 4 files changed, 39 insertions(+), 21 deletions(-)
Tims-MBP:TILApp timc$ git push
Counting objects: 9, done.
Delta compression using up to 4 threads.
Compressing objects: 100% (9/9), done.
Writing objects: 100% (9/9), 1.35 KiB | 1.35 MiB/s, done.
Total 9 (delta 6), reused 0 (delta 0)
remote: Resolving deltas: 100% (6/6), completed with 6 local objects.
To github.com:raywenderlich/vapor-til.git
   4e70832..d42a4c1  master -> master
Tims-MBP:TILApp timc$ vapor cloud deploy
app: TIL
git: git@github.com:raywenderlich/vapor-til.git
env: production
No database service found.
Would you like to add a database?
y/n> y
app: TIL
env: production
Tip: Vapor and Vapor Cloud work best with MySQL databases.
Which database server?
1: Shared MySQL ($7/month)
2: Shared PostgreSQL ($7/month)
3: Shared MongoDB ($7/month)
> 2
```

> **Note**: The PostgreSQL database costs $7/month to use. However, you can try it
> out before you must configure a payment option in Vapor Cloud.

Vapor Cloud then asks for you to configure the build type. Since the application has a new package — FluentPostgreSQL — select **2** for update:

```
●　●　●                    TILApp — vapor cloud deploy — 100×26
  4 files changed, 39 insertions(+), 21 deletions(-)
[Tims-MBP:TILApp timc$ git push
Counting objects: 9, done.
Delta compression using up to 4 threads.
Compressing objects: 100% (9/9), done.
Writing objects: 100% (9/9), 1.35 KiB | 1.35 MiB/s, done.
Total 9 (delta 6), reused 0 (delta 0)
remote: Resolving deltas: 100% (6/6), completed with 6 local objects.
To github.com:raywenderlich/vapor-til.git
   4e70832..d42a4c1  master -> master
[Tims-MBP:TILApp timc$ vapor cloud deploy
app: TIL
git: git@github.com:raywenderlich/vapor-til.git
env: production
db: yes
replicas: 1
replica size: free
branch: master
Which build type?
1: incremental (fastest: just compile the code)
2: update (normal: update dependencies before compiling)
3: clean (slowest: clear cached dependencies and build data before compiling)
> 2
```

Finally, Vapor Cloud asks you to confirm all the information. Ensure that everything is correct and type **y** followed by **Enter**:

```
●　●　●                    TILApp — vapor cloud deploy — 100×26
  4 files changed, 39 insertions(+), 21 deletions(-)
[Tims-MBP:TILApp timc$ git push
Counting objects: 9, done.
Delta compression using up to 4 threads.
Compressing objects: 100% (9/9), done.
Writing objects: 100% (9/9), 1.35 KiB | 1.35 MiB/s, done.
Total 9 (delta 6), reused 0 (delta 0)
remote: Resolving deltas: 100% (6/6), completed with 6 local objects.
To github.com:raywenderlich/vapor-til.git
   4e70832..d42a4c1  master -> master
[Tims-MBP:TILApp timc$ vapor cloud deploy
app: TIL
git: git@github.com:raywenderlich/vapor-til.git
env: production
db: yes
replicas: 1
replica size: free
branch: master
build: update
Is the above information correct?
y/n> y
```

This builds your application and deploys it to Vapor Cloud. Terminal shows "Successfully deployed" when Vapor Cloud has finished:

```
● ● ●                         TILApp — -bash — 100×26
git: git@github.com:raywenderlich/vapor-til.git
env: production
db: yes
replicas: 1
replica size: free
branch: master
build: update
Creating deployment [Done]
Connecting to build logs ...
Waiting in Queue [Done]
Starting deployment: 'rw-til' [Done]
Getting project from Git 'git@github.com:raywenderlich/vapor-til.git' [Done]
Checkout branch 'master' [Done]
Verifying base folder [Done]
Selected swift version: 4.1.0-beta [Done]
Running swift package update [Done]
Building vapor (release) [Done]
Trying to find executable [Done]
Found executable: Run [Done]
Creating container registry [Done]
Building container [Done]
Pushing container to registry [Done]
Updating replicas [Done]
Deployment succeeded: https://rw-til.vapor.cloud [Done]
Successfully deployed.
Tims-MBP:TILApp timc$ ▌
```

Test your application out by saving an acronym in Vapor Cloud. Open RESTed and configure a new request as follows:

- **URL**: https://<YOUR_URL>/api/acronyms

- **method**: POST

- **Parameter encoding**: JSON-encoded

Add two parameters with names and values:

- **short**: OMG

- **long**: Oh My God

Click **Send Request** and you'll receive the saved acronym in the response.

You should see the following:

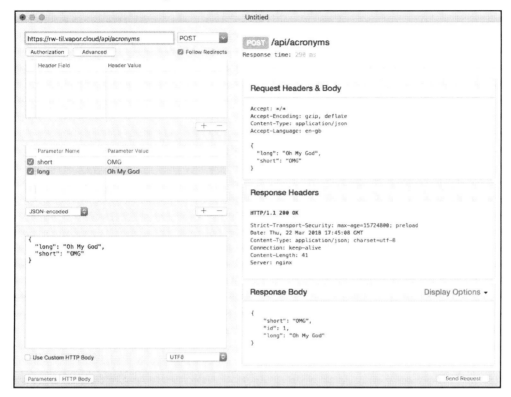

Where to go from here?

In this chapter, you've learned how to configure a database for your application. The next chapter introduces CRUD operations so you can create, retrieve, update and delete your acronyms.

Chapter 7: CRUD Database Operations

By Tim Condon

Chapter 5, "Fluent and Persisting Models," explained the concept of models and how to store them in a database using Fluent. This chapter concentrates on how to interact with models in the database. You'll learn about CRUD operations and how they relate to REST APIs. You'll also see how to leverage Fluent to perform complex queries on your models. Finally, like all chapters in this section, you'll deploy your code to Vapor Cloud.

> **Note**: This chapter requires you to use PostgreSQL. Follow the steps in Chapter 6, "Configuring a Database", to set up PostgreSQL in Docker and configure your Vapor application.

CRUD and REST

CRUD operations — Create, Retrieve, Update, Delete — form the four basic functions of persistent storage. With these, you can perform most actions required for your application. You actually implemented the first function, create, in a previous chapter.

RESTful APIs provide a way for clients to call the CRUD functions in your application. Typically you have a resource URL for your models. For the TIL application, this is the acronym resource: **https://localhost:8080/api/acronyms**. You then define routes on this resource, paired with appropriate HTTP request methods, to perform the CRUD operations. For example:

- **GET https://localhost:8080/api/acronyms/**: get all the acronyms.

- **POST https://localhost:8080/api/acronyms**: create a new acronym.

- **GET https://localhost:8080/api/acronyms/1**: get the acronym with ID 1.

- **PUT https://localhost:8080/api/acronyms/1**: update the acronym with ID 1.

- **DELETE https://localhost:8080/api/acronyms/1**: delete the acronym with ID 1.

Create

In Chapter 5, "Fluent and Persisting Models", you implemented the create route for an Acronym. You can either continue with your project or open the TILApp in the starter folder for this chapter. To recap, you created a new route handler in **routes.swift**:

```
// 1
router.post("api", "acronyms") { req -> Future<Acronym> in
  // 2
  return try req.content.decode(Acronym.self)
                   .flatMap(to: Acronym.self) { acronym in
    // 3
    return acronym.save(on: req)
  }
}
```

Here's what this does:

1. Register a new route at **/api/acronyms/** that accepts a POST request and returns `Future<Acronym>`.

2. Decode the request's JSON into an `Acronym`. This is made simple because `Acronym` conforms to `Content`. `decode(_:)` returns a `Future`; use `flatMap(to:)` to extract the acronym when decoding completes.

3. Save the model using Fluent. When the save completes, it returns the model as a `Future` — in this case, `Future<Acronym>`.

Build and run the application, then open RESTed. Configure the request as follows:

- **URL**: http://localhost:8080/api/acronyms/

- **method**: POST

- **Parameter encoding**: JSON-encoded

Add two parameters with names and values:

- **short**: OMG

- **long**: Oh My God

Send the request and you'll see the response containing the created acronym:

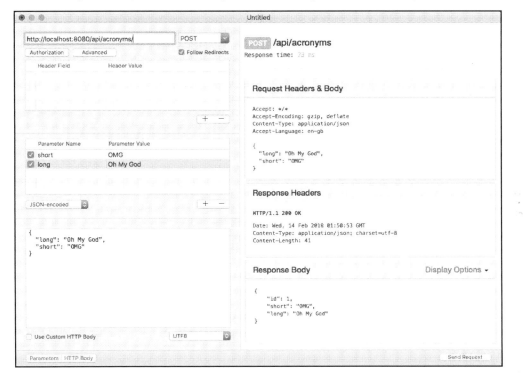

Retrieve

For TILApp, retrieve consists of two separate operations: retrieve all the acronyms and retrieve a single, specific acronym. Fluent makes both of these tasks easy.

Retrieve all acronyms

To retrieve all acronyms, you'll create a route handler for GET requests to **/api/acronyms/**. Open **routes.swift** and add the following at the end of routes(_:):

```
// 1
router.get("api", "acronyms") { req -> Future<[Acronym]> in
  // 2
  return Acronym.query(on: req).all()
}
```

Here's what this does:

1. Register a new route handler for the request which returns Future<[Acronym]>, a future array of Acronyms.

2. Perform a query to get all the acronyms.

Fluent adds functions to models to be able to perform queries on them. You must give the query a `DatabaseConnectable`. This is almost always the request and provides a thread to perform the work. `all()` returns all the models of that type in the database. This is equivalent to the SQL query `SELECT * FROM Acronyms;`.

Build and run your application, then create a new request in RESTed. Configure the request as follows:

*   **URL**: http://localhost:8080/api/acronyms/

*   **method**: GET

Send the request to see the acronyms already in the database:

Retrieve a single acronym

Vapor's powerful type safety for parameters extends to models that conform to `Parameter`. To make this work for `Acronym`, open **Acronym.swift** and add the following at the end of the file:

```
extension Acronym: Parameter {}
```

To get a single acronym, you need a new route handler. Open **routes.swift** and add the following at the end of routes(_:):

```
// 1
router.get("api", "acronyms", Acronym.parameter) {
  req -> Future<Acronym> in
  // 2
  return try req.parameters.next(Acronym.self)
}
```

Here's what this does:

1. Register a route at **/api/acronyms/<ID>** to handle a GET request. The route takes the acronym's id property as the final path segment. This returns Future<Acronym>.

2. Extract the acronym from the request using the parameter function. This function performs all the work necessary to get the acronym from the database. It also handles the error cases when the acronym does not exist, or the ID type is wrong, for example, when you pass it an integer when the ID is a UUID.

Build and run your application, then create a new request in RESTed. Configure the request as follows:

• **URL**: http://localhost:8080/api/acronyms/1 (1 is the ID of the first acronym created)

• **method**: GET

Send the request and you'll receive the first acronym as the response:

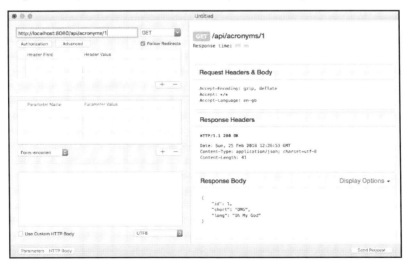

Update

In RESTful APIs, updates to single resources use a PUT request, with the request data containing the new information. Add the following at the end of routes(_:) to register a new route handler:

```
// 1
router.put("api", "acronyms", Acronym.parameter) {
  req -> Future<Acronym> in
  // 2
  return try flatMap(to: Acronym.self,
                     req.parameters.next(Acronym.self),
                     req.content.decode(Acronym.self)) {
    acronym, updatedAcronym in
    // 3
    acronym.short = updatedAcronym.short
    acronym.long = updatedAcronym.long

    // 4
    return acronym.save(on: req)
  }
}
```

Here's the play-by-play:

1. Register a route for a PUT request to **/api/acronyms/<ID>** that returns Future<Acronym>.

2. Use flatMap(to:_:_:), the dual future form of flatMap, to wait for both the parameter extraction and content decoding to complete. This provides both the acronym from the database and acronym from the request body to the closure.

3. Update the acronym's properties with the new values.

4. Save the acronym and return the result.

Build and run the application, then create a new acronym using RESTed. Configure the request as follows:

• **URL**: http://localhost:8080/api/acronyms/

• **method**: POST

• **Parameter encoding**: JSON-encoded

Add two parameters with names and values:

• **short**: WTF

• **long**: What The Flip

Send the request and you'll see the response containing the created acronym:

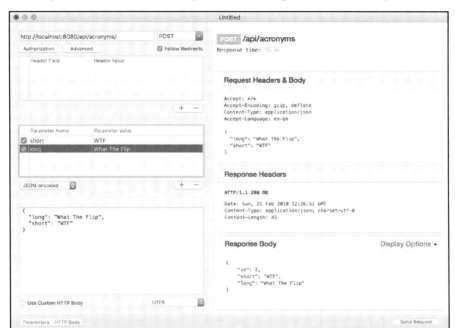

It turns out the meaning of WTF is not in fact "What The Flip" so it needs updating. Change the request in RESTed as follows:

- **URL**: http://localhost:8080/api/acronyms/<ID>

> Use the ID from the returned create request.

- **method**: PUT
- **long**: What The Fudge

Send the request. You'll receive the updated acronym in the response:

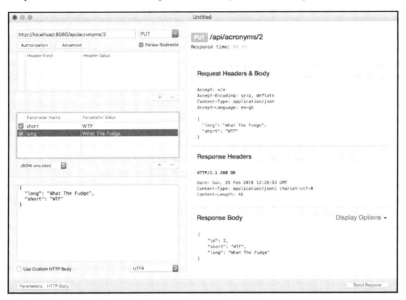

To ensure this has worked, send a request in RESTed to get all the acronyms. You'll see the updated acronym returned:

Delete

To delete a model in a RESTful API, you send a DELETE request to the resource. Add the following to the end of routes(_:) to create a new route handler:

```
// 1
router.delete("api", "acronyms", Acronym.parameter) {
  req -> Future<HTTPStatus> in
  // 2
  return try req.parameters.next(Acronym.self)
                // 3
                .delete(on: req)
                // 4
                .transform(to: HTTPStatus.noContent)
}
```

Here's what this does:

1. Register a route for a DELETE request to **/api/acronyms/<ID>** that returns Future<HTTPStatus>.

2. Extract the acronym to delete from the request's parameters.

3. Delete the acronym using delete(on:). Instead of requiring you to unwrap the returned Future, Fluent allows you to call delete(on:) directly on that Future. This helps tidy up code and reduce nesting. Fluent provides convenience functions for delete, update, create and save.

4. Transform the result into a **204 No Content** response. This tells the client the request has successfully completed but there's no content to return.

Build and run the application. The "WTF" acronym is a little risqué so delete it. Configure a new request in RESTed as follows:

• **URL**: http://localhost:8080/api/acronyms/<ID>

Use ID of the WTF acronym from the previous request

• **method**: DELETE

Send the request; you'll receive a 204 No Content response.

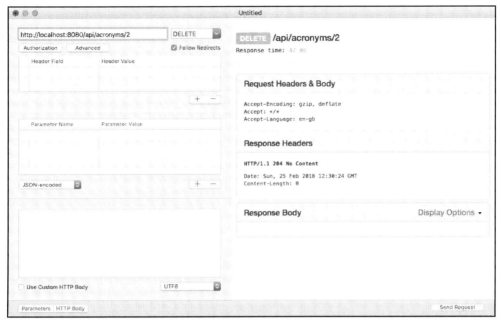

Send a request to get all the acronyms and you'll see the WTF acronym is no longer in the database.

Fluent queries

You've seen how easy Fluent makes basic CRUD operations. It can perform more powerful queries just as easily.

Filter

Search functionality is a common feature in applications. If you want to search all the acronyms in the database, Fluent makes this easy. Add the following below the `import Vapor` statement at the top of **routes.swift**:

```
import Fluent
```

Next, add a new route handler for searching at the end of `routes(_:)`:

```
// 1
router.get("api", "acronyms", "search") {
  req -> Future<[Acronym]> in
  // 2
  guard
    let searchTerm = req.query[String.self, at: "term"] else {
      throw Abort(.badRequest)
  }
  // 3
  return Acronym.query(on: req)
                  .filter(\.short == searchTerm)
                  .all()
}
```

Here's what's going on to search the acronyms:

1. Register a new route handler for **/api/acronyms/search** that returns `Future<[Acronym]>`.

2. Retrieve the search term from the **URL query string**. You can do this with any `Codable` object by calling `req.query.decode(_:)`. If this fails, throw a `400 Bad Request` error.

> **Query strings** in URLs allow clients to pass information to the server that doesn't fit sensibly in the path. For example, they are commonly used for defining the page number of a search result.

3. Use `filter(_:)` to find all acronyms whose `short` property matches the `searchTerm`. Because this uses key paths, the compiler can enforce type-safety on

the properties and filter terms. This prevents run-time issues caused by specifying an invalid column name or invalid type to filter on.

Build and run your application, then create a new request in RESTed. Configure the request as follows:

• **URL**: http://localhost:8080/api/acronyms/search?term=OMG

• **method**: GET

Send the request and you'll see the OMG acronym returned with its meaning:

If you want to search multiple fields — for example both the short and long fields — you need to change your query. You can't chain `filter(_:)` functions as that would only match acronyms whose `short` and `long` properties were identical. Instead, you must use a **filter group**. Replace `return Acronym.query(on: req).filter(\.short == searchTerm).all()` with the following:

```
// 1
return Acronym.query(on: req).group(.or) { or in
  // 2
  or.filter(\.short == searchTerm)
  // 3
  or.filter(\.long == searchTerm)
// 4
}.all()
```

Here's what this extra code does:

1. Create a filter group using the `.or` relation.

2. Add a filter to the group to filter for acronyms whose `short` property matches the search term.

3. Add a filter to the group to filter for acronyms whose `long` property matches the search term.

4. Return all the results.

This returns all acronyms that match the first filter *or* the second filter. Build and run the application and go back to RESTed. Resend the request from above and you'll still see the same result.

Change the URL to **http://localhost:8080/api/acronyms/search?term=Oh+My+God** and send the request. You'll get the OMG acronym back as a response:

> **Note**: Spaces in URLs must be URL-encoded as either **%20** or **+** to be valid.

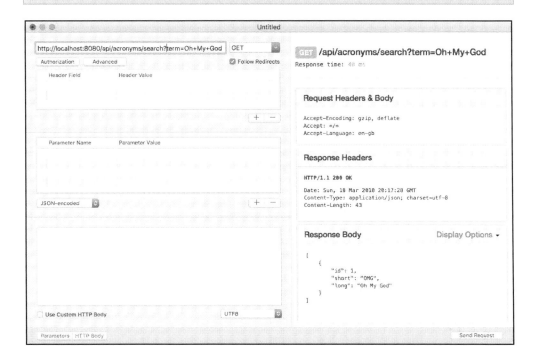

First result

Sometimes an application needs only the first result of a query. Creating a specific handler for this ensures the database only returns one result rather than loading all results into memory. Create a new route handler to return the first acronym at the end of `routes(_:)`:

```
// 1
router.get("api", "acronyms", "first") {
  req -> Future<Acronym> in
  // 2
  return Acronym.query(on: req)
                .first()
                .map(to: Acronym.self) { acronym in
    // 3
    guard let acronym = acronym else {
      throw Abort(.notFound)
    }
    // 4
    return acronym
  }
}
```

Here's what this function does:

1. Register a new HTTP GET route for **/api/acronyms/first** that returns `Future<Acronym>`.

2. Perform a query to get the first acronym. Use the `map(to:)` function to unwrap the result of the query.

3. Ensure an acronym exists. `first()` returns an optional as there may be no acronyms in the database. Throw a `404 Not Found` error if no acronym is returned.

4. Return the first acronym.

You can also apply `.first()` to any query, such as the result of a filter.

Build and run the application, then open RESTed. Create new acronym with:

• **short**: IKR

• **long**: I Know Right

Now create a new RESTed request configured as:

• **URL**: http://localhost:8080/api/acronyms/first

• **method**: GET

Send the request and you'll see the first acronym you created returned:

Sorting results

Apps commonly need to sort the results of queries before returning them. For this reason, Fluent provides a sort function. Write a new route handler at the end of the `routes(_:)` function to return all the acronyms, sorted in ascending order by their `short` property:

```
// 1
router.get("api", "acronyms", "sorted") {
  req -> Future<[Acronym]> in
  // 2
  return Acronym.query(on: req)
                .sort(\.short, .ascending)
                .all()
}
```

Here's how this works:

1. Register a new HTTP GET route for **/api/acronyms/sorted** that returns `Future<[Acronym]>`.

2. Create a query for `Acronym` and use `sort(_:_:)` to perform the sort. This function takes the field to sort on and the direction to sort in. Finally use `all()` to return all the results of the query.

Build and run the application, then create a new request in RESTed:

- **URL**: http://localhost:8080/api/acronyms/sorted

- **method**: GET

Send the request and you'll see the acronyms sorted alphabetically by their `short` property:

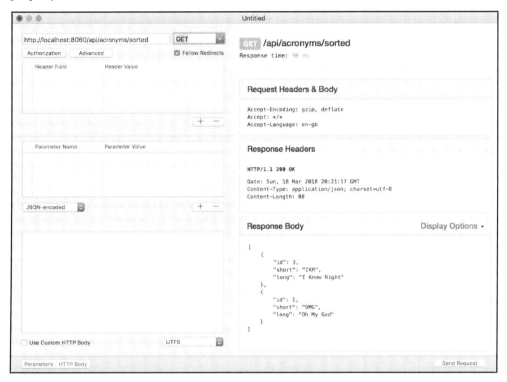

Deploy to Vapor Cloud

Note: This section requires that you have followed through Chapter 5, "Fluent and Persisting Models" to set up Vapor Cloud. It also requires that you have configured a database as shown in Chapter 6, "Configuring a Database."

In previous chapters, you performed some configuration to be able to get your updated application running on Vapor Cloud. This chapter has only added new routes.

To deploy your updated application to Vapor Cloud, you simply need to commit your code and deploy.

In Terminal, type the following, to commit and push your code:

```
# 1
git commit -am "Add CRUD operations"
# 2
git push
```

Here's what these commands do:

1. Commit your changes with the message "Add CRUD operations".

2. Push your local commits to the remote repository on GitHub.

Now that you have committed and pushed, deploy your updated application. In Terminal, run the following:

```
vapor cloud deploy --env=production --build=incremental -y
```

This command is the same as previous **vapor cloud deploy** commands, but with extra parameters:

- Deploy the application to the **production** environment.

- Use the **incremental** build type since you have included no new packages.

- Automatically deploy without waiting at the confirmation screen.

```
● ● ●                    TILApp — -bash — 100×27
Tims-MBP:TILApp timc$ vapor cloud deploy --env=production --build=incremental -y
app: TIL
git: git@github.com:raywenderlich/vapor-til.git
env: production
db: yes
replicas: 1
replica size: free
branch: master
build: incremental
Creating deployment [Done]
Connecting to build logs ...
Waiting in Queue [Done]
Starting deployment: 'rw-til' [Done]
Getting project from Git 'git@github.com:raywenderlich/vapor-til.git' [Done]
Checkout branch 'master' [Done]
Verifying base folder [Done]
Selected swift version: 4.1.0-beta [Done]
Building vapor (release) [Done]
Trying to find executable [Done]
Found executable: Run [Done]
Creating container registry [Done]
Building container [Done]
Pushing container to registry [Done]
Updating replicas [Done]
Deployment succeeded: https://rw-til.vapor.cloud [Done]
Successfully deployed.
Tims-MBP:TILApp timc$ ▓
```

When this has finished, open RESTed and configure the request as follows:

- **URL**: https://<YOUR_URL>/api/acronyms/1

- **method**: GET

Click **Send Request** and you'll get the first acronym created in a previous chapter:

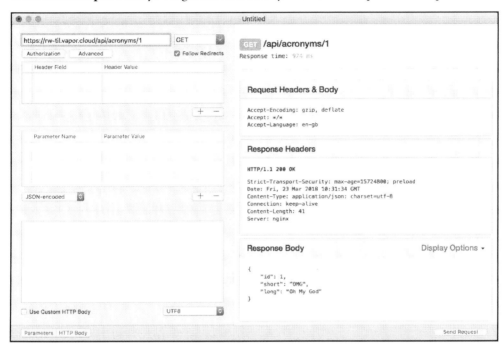

Where to go from here?

You now know how to use Fluent to perform the different CRUD operations and advanced queries. At this stage, **routes.swift** is getting cluttered with all the code from this chapter. The next chapter looks at how to better organize your code using controllers.

Chapter 8: Controllers

By Tim Condon

In previous chapters, you've written all the route handlers in **routes.swift**. This isn't sustainable for large projects as the file quickly becomes too big and cluttered. This chapter introduces the concept of controllers to help manage your routes and models, using both basic controllers and RESTful controllers. Finally, as in the other chapters in this section, you'll deploy your code to Vapor Cloud.

> **Note**: this chapter requires PostgreSQL to be set up and configured. Follow the steps in Chapter 6, "Configuring a Database", to set up PostgreSQL in Docker and configure the Vapor application.

Controllers

Controllers in Vapor serve a similar purpose to controllers in iOS. They handle interactions from a client, such as requests, process them and return the response. Controllers provide a way of better organizing your code. It's good practice to have all interactions with a model in a dedicated controller. For example in the TIL application, an acronym controller can handle all CRUD operations on an acronym.

Controllers are also used to organize your application. For instance, you may use one controller to manage an older version of your API and another to manage the current version. This allows a clear separation of responsibilities in your code and keeps code maintainable.

Getting started with controllers

Create a new file to hold the acronyms controller. In Terminal, enter:

```
# 1
cd ~/vapor/TILApp/
# 2
touch Sources/App/Controllers/AcronymsController.swift
# 3
vapor xcode -y
```

Here's what this does:

1. Navigate to the directory where the TIL application lives.

2. Create a new file, **AcronymsController.swift**, in the **Controllers** directory of the **App** module.

3. Regenerates the Xcode project to add the new file to the **App** target.

Route collections

Inside a controller, you define different route handlers. To access these routes, you must register these handlers with the router. A simple way to do this is to call the functions inside your controller from **routes.swift**. For example:

```
router.get(
    "api",
    "acronyms",
    use: acronymsController.getAllHandler)
```

This example calls `getAlllHandler(_:)` on the `acronymsController`. This call is like the route handlers you wrote in Chapter 7. However, instead of passing a closure as the final parameter, you pass the function to use.

This works well for small applications. But if you've a large number of routes to register, **routes.swift** again becomes unmanageable. It's good practice for controllers to be responsible for registering the routes they control. Vapor provides the protocol `RouteCollection` to enable this.

Open **AcronymsController.swift** in Xcode and add the following to create an `AcronymsController` controller that conforms to `RouteCollection`:

```
import Vapor
import Fluent

struct AcronymsController: RouteCollection {
```

```
    func boot(router: Router) throws {

    }
}
```

RouteCollection requires you to implement boot(router:) to register routes. Add a new route handler after boot(router:):

```
func getAllHandler(_ req: Request) throws -> Future<[Acronym]> {
    return Acronym.query(on: req).all()
}
```

The body of the handler is identical to the one you wrote earlier and the signature matches the signature of the closure used before. Register the route in boot(router:):

```
router.get("api", "acronyms", use: getAllHandler)
```

This makes a GET request to **/api/acronyms** call getAllHandler(_:). You wrote this same route earlier in **routes.swift**. Now, it's time to remove that one. Open **routes.swift** and delete the following handler:

```
router.get("api", "acronyms") { req -> Future<Acronym> in
    return try req.content.decode(Acronym.self)
      .flatMap(to: Acronym.self) { acronym in
        return acronym.save(on: req)
      }
}
```

Next, add the following to the end of routes(_:):

```
// 1
let acronymsController = AcronymsController()
// 2
try router.register(collection: acronymsController)
```

Here's what this does:

1. Create a new AcronymsController.

2. Register the new type with the router to ensure the controller's routes get registered.

Build and run the application, then create a new request in RESTed. Configure the request as follows:

• **URL**: http://localhost:8080/api/acronyms/

• **method**: GET

Send the request and you'll get the existing acronyms in your database:

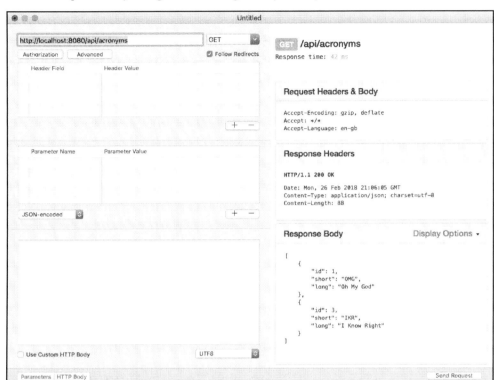

Route groups

All of the REST routes created for acronyms in the previous chapters use the same initial path, e.g.:

```
router.get(
  "api",
  "acronyms",
  Acronym.parameter
) { req -> Future<Acronym> in
  return try req.parameters.next(Acronym.self)
}
```

If you need to change the **/api/acronyms/** path, you have to change the path in multiple locations. If you add a new route, you have to remember to add both parts of the path. Vapor provides **route groups** to simplify this. Open **AcronymsController.swift** and create a route group at the beginning of boot(router:):

```
let acronymsRoutes = router.grouped("api", "acronyms")
```

This creates a new route group for the path **/api/acronyms**. Next, replace:

```
router.get("api", "acronyms", use: getAllHandler)
```

with the following:

```
acronymsRoutes.get(use: getAllHandler)
```

This works as it did before but greatly simplifies the code, making it easier to maintain.

Next, open **routes.swift** and remove the remaining acronym routes:

- router.post("api", "acronyms") route handler.
- router.get("api", "acronyms", Acronym.parameter)
- router.put("api", "acronyms", Acronym.parameter)
- router.delete("api", "acronyms", Acronym.parameter)
- router.get("api", "acronyms", "search")
- router.get("api", "acronyms", "first")
- router.get("api", "acronyms", "sorted")

Next, open **AcronymsController.swift** and recreate the handlers by adding each of the following at the end of boot(router:)

```
func createHandler(_ req: Request) throws -> Future<Acronym> {
  return try req
    .content
    .decode(Acronym.self)
    .flatMap(to: Acronym.self) { acronym in
    return acronym.save(on: req)
  }
}

func getHandler(_ req: Request) throws -> Future<Acronym> {
  return try req.parameters.next(Acronym.self)
}

func updateHandler(_ req: Request) throws -> Future<Acronym> {

  return try flatMap(
    to: Acronym.self,
    req.parameters.next(Acronym.self),
    req.content.decode(Acronym.self)
  ) { acronym, updatedAcronym in
    acronym.short = updatedAcronym.short
    acronym.long = updatedAcronym.long
    return acronym.save(on: req)
  }
```

```
  }

  func deleteHandler(_ req: Request)
    throws -> Future<HTTPStatus> {

    return try req
      .parameters
      .next(Acronym.self)
      .delete(on: req)
      .transform(to: HTTPStatus.noContent)
  }

  func searchHandler(_ req: Request) throws -> Future<[Acronym]> {
    guard let searchTerm = req
      .query[String.self, at: "term"] else {
      throw Abort(.badRequest)
    }
    return Acronym.query(on: req).group(.or) { or in
      or.filter(\.short == searchTerm)
      or.filter(\.long == searchTerm)
    }.all()
  }

  func getFirstHandler(_ req: Request) throws -> Future<Acronym> {
    return Acronym.query(on: req)
      .first()
      .map(to: Acronym.self) { acronym in
      guard let acronym = acronym else {
        throw Abort(.notFound)
      }
      return acronym
    }
  }

  func sortedHandler(_ req: Request) throws -> Future<[Acronym]> {
    return Acronym.query(on: req).sort(\.short, .ascending).all()
  }
```

Each of these handlers is identical the ones you created in Chapter 7. If you need a reminder of what they do, that's the place to look!

Finally, register these route handlers using the route group. Add the following to the bottom of `boot(router:)`:

```
// 1
acronymsRoutes.post(use: createHandler)
// 2
acronymsRoutes.get(Acronym.parameter, use: getHandler)
// 3
acronymsRoutes.put(Acronym.parameter, use: updateHandler)
// 4
acronymsRoutes.delete(Acronym.parameter, use: deleteHandler)
```

```
// 5
acronymsRoutes.get("search", use: searchHandler)
// 6
acronymsRoutes.get("first", use: getFirstHandler)
// 7
acronymsRoutes.get("sorted", use: sortedHandler)
```

Here's what this does:

1. Register createHandler(_:) to process POST requests to **/api/acronyms**.

2. Register getHandler(_:) to process GET requests to **/api/acronyms/<ACRONYM ID>**.

3. Register updateHandler(:_) to process PUT requests to **/api/acronyms/ <ACRONYM ID>**.

4. Register deleteHandler(:_) to process DELETE requests to **/api/acronyms/ <ACRONYM ID>**.

5. Register searchHandler(:_) to process GET requests to **/api/acronyms/search**.

6. Register getFirstHandler(:_) to process GET requests to **/api/acronyms/first**.

7. Register sortedHandler(:_) to process GET requests to **/api/acronyms/sorted**.

Build and run the application, then create a new request in RESTed. Configure the request as follows:

- **URL**: http://localhost:8080/api/acronyms/1

- **method**: GET

Send the request and you'll see a previously created acronym using the new controller:

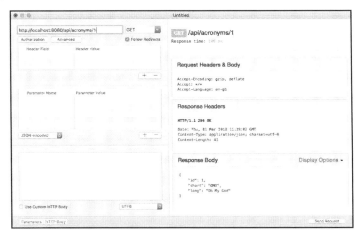

Accepting POST data

As mentioned in Chapter 2, "Hello Vapor!", Vapor provides helper functions for PUT, POST and PATCH routes for decoding incoming data. This helps remove a layer of nesting. To use this helper function, open **AcronymsController.swift** and replace `createHandler(_:)` with the following:

```
func createHandler(
  _ req: Request,
  acronym: Acronym
) throws -> Future<Acronym> {
  return acronym.save(on: req)
}
```

The function signature now has an `Acronym` as a parameter. This is the decoded acronym from the request, so you don't have to decode the data yourself. In `boot(router:)` replace:

```
acronymsRoutes.post(use: createHandler)
```

with the following:

```
acronymsRoutes.post(Acronym.self, use: createHandler)
```

This helper function takes the type to decode as the first parameter. You can provide any path components before the `use:` parameter, if required.

Build and run the application, then create a new request in RESTed. Configure the request as follows:

• **URL**: http://localhost:8080/api/acronyms/

• **method**: POST

• **Parameter encoding**: JSON-encoded

Add two parameters with names and values:

• **short**: IRL

• **long**: In Real Life

Send the request and you'll see the response containing the created acronym:

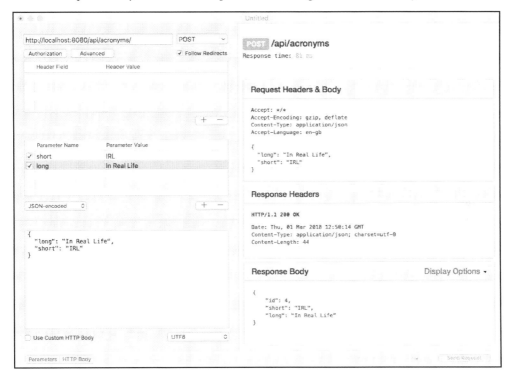

Fluent provides convenience functions for save(on:), create(on:), update(on:) and delete(on:) for Future<Model> types. This is useful if you don't need to manipulate the model before saving it, for example.

Deploy to Vapor Cloud

Note: This section requires that you have followed through Chapter 5, "Fluent and Persisting Models" to set up Vapor Cloud. It also requires that you have configured a database as shown in Chapter 6, "Configuring a Database."

Like the previous chapter, deploying the changes from this chapter to Vapor Cloud are simple.

In Terminal, type the following:

```
# 1
git commit -am "Split routes out into a separate controller"
# 2
git push
```

Here's what these commands do:

1. Commit your changes with the message "Split routes out into a separate controller".

2. Push your local commits up to the remote repository on GitHub.

Now you've committed and pushed, you can deploy your updated application to Vapor Cloud. In Terminal, type the following:

```
vapor cloud deploy --env=production --build=incremental -y
```

This command is the same as previous **vapor cloud deploy** commands, but with extra parameters:

*   Deploy the application to the **production** environment.

*   Use the **incremental** build type since you have included no new packages.

*   Automatically deploy without waiting at the confirmation screen.

When this has finished, open RESTed to ensure the routes still work. Configure your request as follows:

*   **URL**: https://<YOUR_URL>/api/acronyms/

*   **method**: GET

Click **Send Request** and you'll get all the acronyms created in previous chapters:

Where to go from here?

This chapter has introduced controllers as a way of better organizing code. They help split out route handlers into separate areas on responsibility. This allows applications to grow in a maintainable way. The next chapters looks at how to bring together different models with relationships in Fluent.

Chapter 9: Parent Child Relationships

By Tim Condon

Chapter 5, "Fluent and Persisting Models," introduced the concept of models. In this chapter, you'll learn how to set up a parent-child relationship between two models. You'll learn the purpose of these relationships, how to model them in Vapor and how to use them with routes. Finally, like every chapter in this section, you'll deploy your code to Vapor Cloud.

> **Note**: This chapter requires PostgreSQL to be set up and configured. Follow the steps in Chapter 6, "Configuring a Database", to set up PostgreSQL in Docker and configure the Vapor application.

Parent-child relationships

Parent-child relationships describe a relationship where one model has "ownership" of one or more models. They are also known as **one-to-one** and **one-to-many** relationships.

For instance, if you model the relationship between people and pets, one person can have one or more pets. A pet can only ever have one owner. In the TIL application, users will create acronyms. Users (the parent) can have many acronyms, and an acronym (the child) can only be created by one user.

Creating a user

Create a new file for the User class and a new file for the UsersController. In Terminal, type:

```
# 1
cd ~/vapor/TILApp
# 2
touch Sources/App/Models/User.swift
# 3
touch Sources/App/Controllers/UsersController.swift
# 4
vapor xcode -y
```

Here's what this does:

1. Change to the directory where the TIL application is.

2. Create a new file **User.swift**.

3. Create a new file **UsersController.swift**.

4. Regenerate the Xcode project and open it.

User model

In Xcode, open **User.swift** and create a basic model for the user:

```
import Foundation
import Vapor
import FluentPostgreSQL

final class User: Codable {
  var id: UUID?
  var name: String
  var username: String

  init(name: String, username: String) {
    self.name = name
    self.username = username
  }
}
```

The model contains two String properties to hold the user's name and username. It also contains an optional id property that stores the ID of the model assigned by the database when it's saved. Note that unlike the Acronym model, this time the ID is a UUID. Since the ID is a UUID type, you must import Foundation.

Next, make the `User` model conform to Fluent's `Model` by adding the following at the end of the file:

```
extension User: PostgreSQLUUIDModel {}
```

Use the `FluentPostgreSQL` model helpers to make conforming to `Model` simple. Because the model's `id` property is a `UUID`, you must use `PostgreSQLUUIDModel` instead of `PostgreSQLModel`. Next, at the bottom of the file make `User` conform to `Content`, `Migration` and `Parameter`:

```
extension User: Content {}
extension User: Migration {}
extension User: Parameter {}
```

Finally, open **configure.swift** and add the `User` model to the migration list, after `migrations.add(model: Acronym.self, database: .psql)`:

```
migrations.add(model: User.self, database: .psql)
```

This adds the new model to the migrations so Fluent prepares the table in the database at the next application start.

User controller

Open **UsersController.swift** and create a new controller that can create users:

```
import Vapor

// 1
struct UsersController: RouteCollection {
  // 2
  func boot(router: Router) throws {
    // 3
    let usersRoute = router.grouped("api", "users")
    // 4
    usersRoute.post(User.self, use: createHandler)
  }

  // 5
  func createHandler(
    _ req: Request,
    user: User
  ) throws -> Future<User> {
    // 6
    return user.save(on: req)
  }
}
```

This should look familiar by now. Let's go over this step-by-step.

1. Define a new type `UsersController` that conforms to `RouteCollection`.

2. Implement `boot(router:)` as required by `RouteCollection`.

3. Create a new route group for the path **/api/users**.

4. Register `createHandler(_:user:)` to handle a POST request to **/api/users**. This uses the POST helper method to decode the request body into a `User` object.

5. Define the route handler function.

6. Save the decoded user from the request.

Finally, open **routes.swift** and add the following to the end of `routes(_:)`:

```
// 1
let usersController = UsersController()
// 2
try router.register(collection: usersController)
```

Here's what this does:

1. Create a `UsersController` instance.

2. Register the new controller instance with the router to hook up the routes.

Open **UsersController.swift** again and add the following to the end of `UsersController`. These functions return a list of all users and a single user:

```
// 1
func getAllHandler(_ req: Request) throws -> Future<[User]> {
  // 2
  return User.query(on: req).all()
}

// 3
func getHandler(_ req: Request) throws -> Future<User> {
  // 4
  return try req.parameters.next(User.self)
}
```

Here's what this does:

1. Define a new route handler, `getAllHandler(_:)`, that returns `Future<[User]>`.

2. Return all the users using a Fluent query.

3. Define a new route handler, `getHandler(_:)`, that returns `Future<User>`.

4. Return the user specified by the request's parameter.

Register these two route handlers at the end of boot(router:):

```
// 1
usersRoute.get(use: getAllHandler)
// 2
usersRoute.get(User.parameter, use: getHandler)
```

Here's what this does:

1. Register getAllHandler(_:) to process GET requests to **/api/users/**.

2. Register getHandler(_:) to process GET requests to **/api/users/<USER ID>**.

Build and run the application, then create a new request in RESTed. Configure the request as follows:

- **URL**: http://localhost:8080/api/users

- **method**: POST

- **Parameter encoding**: JSON-encoded

Add two parameters with names and values:

- **name**: your name

- **username**: a username of your choice

Send the request and you'll see the saved user in the response:

Setting up the relationship

Modeling a parent-child relationship in Vapor matches how a database models the relationship. Because a user owns each acronym, you add a reference to the user in the acronym. This allows Fluent to search the database efficiently.

To get all the acronyms for a user, you retrieve all acronyms that contain that user reference. To get the user of an acronym. you use the user reference from that acronym.

Open **Acronym.swift** and add a new property after `var long: String`:

```
var userID: User.ID
```

This adds a property of type `User.ID` to the model. This is a `typealias` defined by `PostgreSQLUUIDModel`, which resolves to `UUID`. Note this type is not optional, so an acronym must have a user.

Replace the initializer with the following to reflect this:

```
init(short: String, long: String, userID: User.ID) {
  self.short = short
  self.long = long
  self.userID = userID
}
```

That's all you need to do to set up the relationship! Before you run the application, you need to reset the database. Fluent has already run the `Acronym` migration but the table has a new column now. To add the new column to the table, you must delete the database so Fluent will run the migration again. Stop the application in Xcode and then in Terminal, enter:

```
# 1
docker stop postgres
# 2
docker rm postgres
# 3
docker run --name postgres -e POSTGRES_DB=vapor \
  -e POSTGRES_USER=vapor -e POSTGRES_PASSWORD=password \
  -p 5432:5432 -d postgres
```

Here's what this does:

1. Stop the running Docker container **postgres**. This is the container currently running the database.

2. Remove the Docker container **postgres** to delete any existing data.

3. Start a new Docker container running PostgreSQL. For more information, see Chapter 6, "Configuring a Database".

```
● ● ●                          ⌂ timc — -bash — 100×8
Tims-MBP:~ timc$ docker stop postgres
postgres
Tims-MBP:~ timc$ docker rm postgres
postgres
Tims-MBP:~ timc$ docker run --name postgres -e POSTGRES_DB=vapor -e POSTGRES_USER=vapor -e POSTGRES_
PASSWORD=password -p 5432:5432 -d postgres
8ef2bd564fc117b6c774ef1c1596221f209e6544d7466a8aa8bb19396097519f
Tims-MBP:~ timc$
```

> **Note**: New migrations can also alter tables so you don't lose production data when changing your models. Chapter 23, "Database/API Versioning and Migration" covers this.

Build and run the application in Xcode and the migrations run. Open RESTed and create a user following the steps from earlier in the chapter. Make sure you copy the returned ID.

Create a new request in RESTed and configure it as follows:

- **URL**: http://localhost:8080/api/acronyms/
- **method**: POST
- **Parameter encoding**: JSON-encoded

Add three parameters with names and values:

- **short**: OMG
- **long**: Oh My God
- **userID**: the ID you copied earlier

Click **Send Request**. Your application creates the acronym with the user specified:

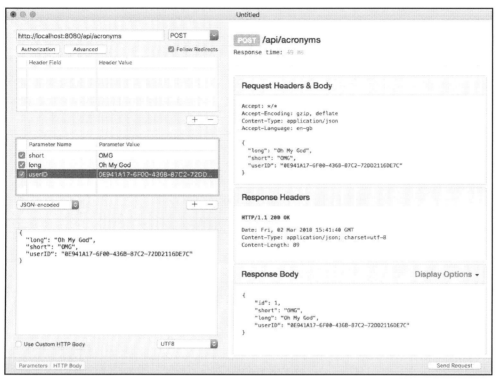

Finally, open **AcronymsController.swift** and replace updateHandler(_:) with the following to account for the new property on Acronym:

```
func updateHandler(_ req: Request) throws -> Future<Acronym> {
  return try flatMap(
    to: Acronym.self,
    req.parameters.next(Acronym.self),
    req.content.decode(Acronym.self)
  ) { acronym, updatedAcronym in

    acronym.short = updatedAcronym.short
    acronym.long = updatedAcronym.long
    acronym.userID = updatedAcronym.userID
    return acronym.save(on: req)
  }
}
```

This updates the acronym's properties with the new values provided in the request.

Querying the relationship

Users and acronyms are now linked with a parent-child relationship. However, this isn't very useful until you can query these relationships. Once again, Fluent makes that easy.

Getting the parent

Open **Acronym.swift** and add an extension at the bottom of the file to get the acronym's parent:

```
extension Acronym {
  // 1
  var user: Parent<Acronym, User> {
    // 2
    return parent(\.userID)
  }
}
```

Here's what this does:

1. Add a computed property to `Acronym` to get the `User` object of the acronym's owner. This returns Fluent's generic `Parent` type.

2. Use Fluent's `parent(_:)` function to retrieve the parent. This takes the key path of the user reference on the acronym.

Open **AcronymsController.swift** and add a new route handler after `sortedHandler(_:)`:

```
// 1
func getUserHandler(_ req: Request) throws -> Future<User> {
  // 2
  return try req
    .parameters.next(Acronym.self)
    .flatMap(to: User.self) { acronym in
      // 3
      acronym.user.get(on: req)
  }
}
```

Here's what this route handler does:

1. Define a new route handler, `getUserHandler(_:)`, that returns `Future<User>`.

2. Fetch the acronym specified in the request's parameters and unwrap the returned future.

3. Use the new computed property created above to get the acronym's owner.

Register the route handler at the end of boot(router:):

```
acronymsRoutes.get(
  Acronym.parameter, "user",
  use: getUserHandler)
```

This connects an HTTP GET request to **/api/acronyms/<ACRONYM ID>/user** to getUserHandler(_:).

Build and run the application, then create a new request in RESTed. Configure the request as follows:

- **URL**: http://localhost:8080/api/acronyms/1/user

- **method**: GET

Send the request and you'll see the response returns the acronym's user:

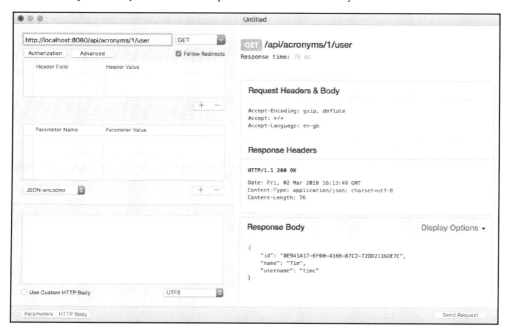

Getting the children

Getting the children of a model follows a similar pattern. Open **User.swift** and add an extension at the bottom of the file to get the user's acronyms:

```
extension User {
  // 1
  var acronyms: Children<User, Acronym> {
    // 2
```

```
    return children(\.userID)
  }
}
```

Here's what this does:

1. Add a computed property to `User` to get a user's acronyms. This returns Fluent's generic `Children` type.

2. Use Fluent's `children(_:)` function to retrieve the children. This takes the key path of the user reference on the acronym.

Open **UsersController.swift** and add a new route handler after `getHandler(_:)`:

```
// 1
func getAcronymsHandler(_ req: Request)
  throws -> Future<[Acronym]> {
  // 2
  return try req
    .parameters.next(User.self)
    .flatMap(to: [Acronym].self) { user in
      // 3
      try user.acronyms.query(on: req).all()
  }
}
```

Here's what this route handler does:

1. Define a new route handler, `getAcronymsHandler(_:)`, that returns `Future<[Acronym]>`.

2. Fetch the user specified in the request's parameters and unwrap the returned future.

3. Use the new computed property created above to get the acronyms using a Fluent query to return all the acronyms.

Register the route handler at the end of `boot(router:)`:

```
usersRoute.get(
  User.parameter, "acronyms",
  use: getAcronymsHandler)
```

This connects an HTTP GET request to **/api/users/<USER ID>/acronyms** to `getAcronymsHandler(_:)`.

Build and run the application, then create a new request in RESTed. Configure the request as follows:

*   **URL**: http://localhost:8080/api/users/<ID of your user>/acronyms

*   **method**: GET

Send the request and you'll see the response returns the user's acronyms:

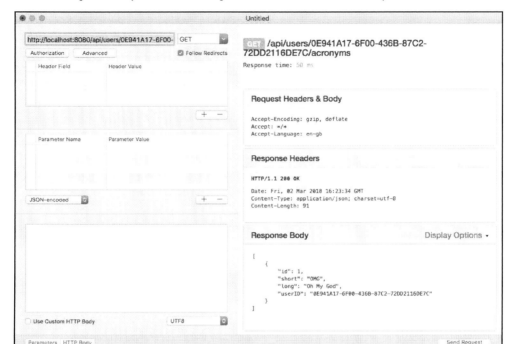

Foreign key constraints

Foreign key constraints describe a link between two tables. They are frequently used for validation. Currently there's no link between the user table and the acronym table in the database. Fluent is the only thing that has knowledge of the link.

Using foreign key constraints has a number of benefits:

- It ensures you can't create acronyms with users that don't exist.

- You can't delete users until you've deleted all their acronyms.

- You can't delete the user table until you've deleted the acronym table.

Foreign key constraints are set up in the migration. Open **Acronym.swift**, and remove the following `Migration` extension:

```
extension Acronym: Migration {}
```

Next, add the following extension at the bottom of the file:

```
// 1
extension Acronym: Migration {
  // 2
  static func prepare(
    on connection: PostgreSQLConnection
  ) -> Future<Void> {
    // 3
    return Database.create(self, on: connection) { builder in
      // 4
      try addProperties(to: builder)
      // 5
      builder.reference(from: \.userID, to: \User.id)
    }
  }
}
```

Here's what this does:

1. Conform `Acronym` to `Migration` again.

2. Implement `prepare(on:)` as required by `Migration`. This overrides the default implementation.

3. Create the table for `Acronym` in the database.

4. Use `addProperties(to:)` to add all the fields to the database. This means you don't need to add each column manually.

5. Add a reference between the `userID` property on `Acronym` and the `id` property on `User`. This sets up the foreign key constraint between the two tables.

Finally, because you're linking the acronym's `userID` property to the `User` table, you must create the `User` table first. In **configure.swift** move the `User` migration to before the `Acronym` migration:

```
migrations.add(model: User.self, database: .psql)
migrations.add(model: Acronym.self, database: .psql)
```

This ensures Fluent creates the tables in the correct order.

Stop the application in Xcode and follow the steps from earlier to **delete the database**.

Build and run the application, then create a new request in RESTed. Configure the request as follows:

- **URL**: http://localhost:8080/api/acronyms/

- **method**: POST

- **Parameter encoding**: JSON-encoded

Add three parameters with names and values:

- **short**: OMG

- **long**: Oh My God

- **userID**: E92B49F2-F239-41B4-B26D-85817F0363AB

This is a valid UUID string, but does not refer to any user since the database is empty. Send the request; you'll get an error saying there's a foreign key constraint violation:

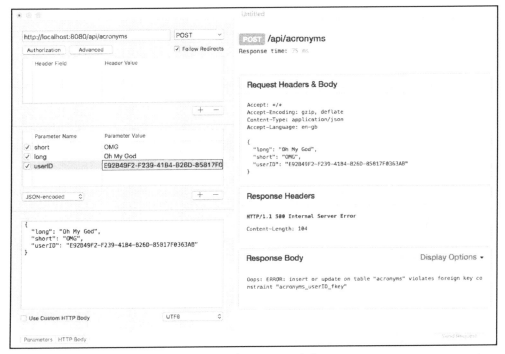

Create a user as you did earlier and copy the ID. Send the create acronym request again, this time using the valid ID. The application creates the acronym without any errors.

Deploy to Vapor Cloud

Note: This section requires that you have followed through Chapter 5, "Fluent and Persisting Models" to set up Vapor Cloud. It also requires that you have configured a PostgreSQL database as shown in Chapter 6, "Configuring a Database".

Reset database

Earlier in the chapter you wiped the database running in Docker due to the model changes. You must do the same thing on Vapor Cloud so the `Acronym` table gets the `userID` column. Vapor provides a **revert** command that reverts all migrations, in effect wiping the database. Vapor also provides a **migrate** command to run all new migrations. As mentioned earlier, in a real application you should use another migration to alter the table but this is covered in a later chapter. Open **configure.swift** and add the following at the end of `configure(_:_:_:)`:

```
// 1
var commandConfig = CommandConfig.default()
// 2
commandConfig.useFluentCommands()
// 3
services.register(commandConfig)
```

Here's what this does:

1. Create a `CommandConfig` with the default configuration.

2. Add the Fluent commands to your `CommandConfig`. This adds both the revert command with the identifier **revert** and the migrate command with the identifier **migrate**. You use these strings to invoke the commands.

3. Register the `commandConfig` as a service.

Build the application to ensure the code is correct. Next, in Terminal, type the following:

```
# 1
git add .
# 2
git commit -m "Add parent-child relationship"
# 3
git push
# 4
vapor cloud deploy --env=production --build=incremental -y
```

Here's what this does:

1. Adds all files so that Git picks up the new user files.

2. Commit your changes with the message "Add parent-child relationship".

3. Push your local commits to the remote repository on GitHub.

4. Deploy the application containing the revert command to Vapor Cloud. It's important you deploy first as Vapor Cloud runs any commands — such as revert — on an existing application. If you try and run the revert command before deploying, it will fail.

> **Note**: If you try and interact with your application at this point you may receive errors since the application is expecting a `userID` column in the Acronyms table.

When the new application has been successfully deployed, type the following in Terminal:

```
vapor cloud run "revert --all --yes"
```

When asked, specify the production environment by typing **1** followed by **Enter**. This executes the revert command on Vapor Cloud, which wipes your database, with the following options:

- **--all**: revert all migrations

- **--yes**: don't ask for confirmation

```
● ● ●                        TILApp — -bash — 101×25
Tims-MBP:TILApp timc$ vapor cloud run "revert --all --yes"
app: TIL
env: production
Running '.build/release/Run --env=production revert --all --yes'
[Deprecated] --option=value syntax is deprecated. Please use --option value (with no =) instead.
[ INFO ] Migrating 'psql' database (FluentProvider.swift:28)
[ INFO ] Migrations complete (FluentProvider.swift:32)
[ INFO ] Revert all migrations requested (RevertCommand.swift:42)
[ WARNING ] This will revert all migrations for all configured databases (RevertCommand.swift:43)
Are you sure you want to revert all migrations?
y/n> yes
[ INFO ] Reverting all migrations on 'psql' database (RevertCommand.swift:50)
[ INFO ] Reverting migration 'Acronym' (MigrationContainer.swift:94)
Tims-MBP:TILApp timc$ ▊
```

Running migrations

At this stage the database has no tables, having executed the revert. So in Terminal type:

```
vapor cloud run "migrate"
```

When asked, specify the production environment by typing **1** followed by **Enter**. This runs the **migrate** command on your application. **migrate** runs all your migrations to create the tables with the new information:

```
● ● ●                              TILApp — -bash — 107×18
Tims-MBP:TILApp timc$ vapor cloud run "migrate"
app: TIL
env: production
Running '.build/release/Run --env=production migrate'
[Deprecated] --option=value syntax is deprecated. Please use --option value (with no =) instead.
[ INFO ] Migrating 'psql' database (/vapor/rw-til-production/code/.build/checkouts/fluent.git--104656239611
2595480/Sources/Fluent/Migration/MigrationConfig.swift:69)
[ INFO ] Preparing migration 'User' (/vapor/rw-til-production/code/.build/checkouts/fluent.git--10465623961
12595480/Sources/Fluent/Migration/Migrations.swift:109)
[ INFO ] Preparing migration 'Acronym' (/vapor/rw-til-production/code/.build/checkouts/fluent.git--10465623
96112595480/Sources/Fluent/Migration/Migrations.swift:109)
[ INFO ] Migrations complete (/vapor/rw-til-production/code/.build/checkouts/fluent.git--104656239611259548
0/Sources/Fluent/Migration/MigrationConfig.swift:73)
[ INFO ] Migrating 'psql' database (/vapor/rw-til-production/code/.build/checkouts/fluent.git--104656239611
2595480/Sources/Fluent/Migration/MigrationConfig.swift:69)
[ INFO ] Migrations complete (/vapor/rw-til-production/code/.build/checkouts/fluent.git--104656239611259548
0/Sources/Fluent/Migration/MigrationConfig.swift:73)
Tims-MBP:TILApp timc$
```

When this has finished, open RESTed and create a new request:

- **URL**: https://<YOUR_URL>/api/users
- **method**: POST
- **Parameter encoding**: JSON-encoded

Add parameters to create a user:

- **name**: your name
- **username**: a username of your choice

Send the request and you'll receive the created user in the response:

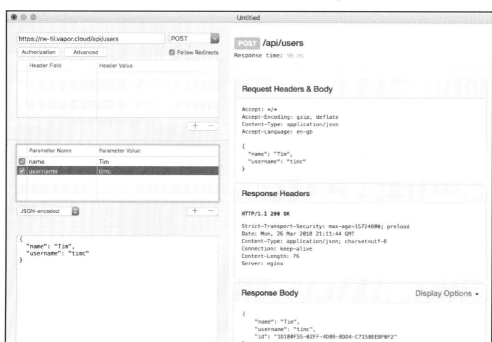

Copy the returned user ID. Create a new request in RESTed and configure it as follows:

- **URL**: https://<YOUR_URL>/api/acronyms
- **method**: POST
- **Parameter encoding**: JSON-encoded

Add three parameters with names and values:

- **short**: OMG
- **long**: Oh My God
- **userID**: the ID you copied above

Send the request and you'll see the created acronym in the response:

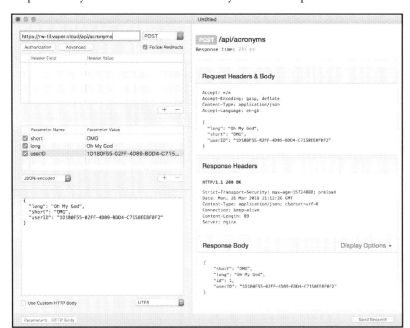

In RESTed, remove the parameters and create a final request:

- **URL**: https://<YOUR_URL>/api/users/<ID>/acronyms, where ID is the ID of the user you copied above

- **method**: GET

Send the request and you'll see the acronym created above under that user's acronyms:

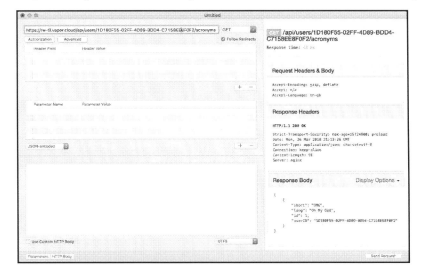

Where to go from here?

In this chapter, you learned how to implement parent-child relationships in Vapor using Fluent. This allows you to start creating complex relationships between models in the database. The next chapter covers the other type of relationship in databases: sibling relationships.

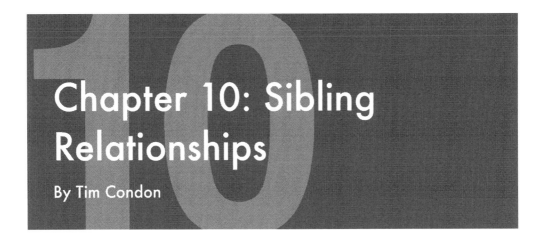

Chapter 10: Sibling Relationships

By Tim Condon

In Chapter 9, "Parent Child Relationships," you learned how to use Fluent to build parent-child relationships between models. This chapter shows you how to implement the other type of relationship: sibling relationships. You'll learn how to model them in Vapor and how to use them in routes. Finally, like every chapter in this section, you'll deploy your code to Vapor Cloud.

> **Note**: This chapter requires PostgreSQL to be set up and configured. Follow the steps in Chapter 6, "Configuring a Database," to set up PostgreSQL in Docker and configure the Vapor application.

Sibling relationships

Sibling relationships describe a relationship that links two models to each other. They are also known as **many-to-many** relationships. Unlike parent-child relationships, there are no constraints between models in a sibling relationship.

For instance, if you model the relationship between pets and toys, a pet can have one or more toys and a toy can be used by one or more pets. In the TIL application, you'll be able to categorize acronyms. An acronym can be part of one or more categories and a category can contain one or more acronyms.

Creating a category

Create new files for `Category` and `CategoriesController`. In Terminal, type:

```
# 1
cd ~/vapor/TILApp
# 2
touch Sources/App/Models/Category.swift
# 3
touch Sources/App/Controllers/CategoriesController.swift
# 4
vapor xcode -y
```

Here's what that does:

1. Change to TILApp's project directory.

2. Create a new file **Category.swift**.

3. Create a new file **CategoriesController.swift**.

4. Regenerate the Xcode project and open it.

Category model

In Xcode, open **Category.swift** and create a basic model for a category:

```
import Vapor
import FluentPostgreSQL

final class Category: Codable {
  var id: Int?
  var name: String

  init(name: String) {
    self.name = name
  }
}
```

The model contains a `String` property to hold the category's name. The model also contains an optional `id` property that stores the ID of the model when it's set. Make the `Category` model conform to Fluent's `PostgreSQLModel`, `Content`, `Migration`, and `Parameter`, by adding the following extensions below the class:

```
extension Category: PostgreSQLModel {}
extension Category: Content {}
extension Category: Migration {}
extension Category: Parameter {}
```

Finally, open **configure.swift** and add the `Category` model to the migration list, after `migrations.add(model: Acronym.self, database: .psql)`:

```
migrations.add(model: Category.self, database: .psql)
```

This adds the new model to the `MigrationConfig` so that Fluent creates the table in the database at the next application start.

Category controller

Open **CategoriesController.swift** and create a new controller to create and retrieve categories:

```swift
import Vapor

// 1
struct CategoriesController: RouteCollection {
  // 2
  func boot(router: Router) throws {
    // 3
    let categoriesRoute = router.grouped("api", "categories")
    // 4
    categoriesRoute.post(Category.self, use: createHandler)
    categoriesRoute.get(use: getAllHandler)
    categoriesRoute.get(Category.parameter, use: getHandler)
  }

  // 5
  func createHandler(
    _ req: Request,
    category: Category
  ) throws -> Future<Category> {
    // 6
    return category.save(on: req)
  }

  // 7
  func getAllHandler(
    _ req: Request
  ) throws -> Future<[Category]> {
    // 8
    return Category.query(on: req).all()
  }

  // 9
  func getHandler(_ req: Request) throws -> Future<Category> {
    // 10
    return try req.parameters.next(Category.self)
  }
}
```

Here's what the controller does:

1. Define a new `CategoriesController` type that conforms to `RouteCollection`.

2. Implement `boot(router:)` as required by `RouteCollection`. This is where you register route handlers.

3. Create a new route group for the path **/api/categories**.

4. Register the route handlers to their routes.

5. Define `createHandler(_:category:)` that creates a category.

6. Save the decoded category from the request.

7. Define `getAllHandler(_:)` that returns all the categories.

8. Perform a Fluent query to retrieve all the categories from the database.

9. Define `getHandler(_:)` that returns a single category.

10. Return the category extracted from the request's parameters.

Finally, open **routes.swift** and register the controller by adding the following to the end of `routes(_:)`:

```
// 1
let categoriesController = CategoriesController()
// 2
try router.register(collection: categoriesController)
```

Here's what this does:

1. Create a `CategoriesController` instance.

2. Register the new instance with the router to hook up the routes.

Build and run the application, then create a new request in RESTed. Configure the request as follows:

- **URL**: http://localhost:8080/api/categories

- **method**: POST

- **Parameter encoding**: JSON-encoded

Add a single parameter with name and value:

- **name**: Teenager

Send the request and you'll see the saved category in the response:

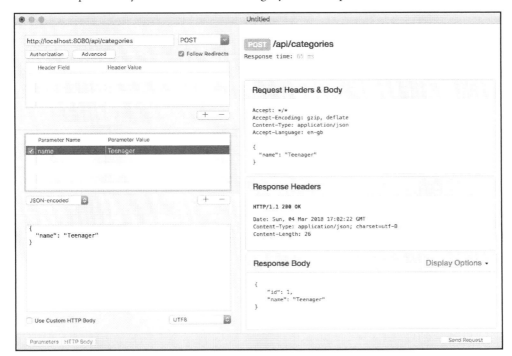

Creating a pivot

In Chapter 9, "Parent Child Relationships", to create the relationship between an acronym and a user, you added a reference to the user in the acronym. However, you can't model a sibling relationship like this as it would be too inefficient to query. If you had an array of acronyms inside a category, to search for all categories of an acronym you'd have to inspect every category. If you had an array of categories inside an acronym, to search for all acronyms in a category you'd have to inspect every acronym. You need a separate model to hold on to this relationship. In Fluent, this is a **pivot**.

A pivot is another model type in Fluent that contains the relationship. In Terminal, create this new model file:

```
touch Sources/App/Models/AcronymCategoryPivot.swift
vapor xcode -y
```

AcronymCategoryPivot.swift will contain the pivot model to manage the sibling relationship.

Open **AcronymCategoryPivot.swift** and add the following to create the pivot:

```swift
import FluentPostgreSQL
import Foundation

// 1
final class AcronymCategoryPivot: PostgreSQLUUIDPivot,
                                  ModifiablePivot {
  // 2
  var id: UUID?
  // 3
  var acronymID: Acronym.ID
  var categoryID: Category.ID

  // 4
  typealias Left = Acronym
  typealias Right = Category
  // 5
  static let leftIDKey: LeftIDKey = \.acronymID
  static let rightIDKey: RightIDKey = \.categoryID

  // 6
  init(_ acronym: Acronym, _ category: Category) throws {
    self.acronymID = try acronym.requireID()
    self.categoryID = try category.requireID()
  }
}

// 7
extension AcronymCategoryPivot: Migration {}
```

Here's what this model does:

1. Define a new object `AcronymCategoryPivot` that conforms to
   `PostgreSQLUUIDPivot`. This is a helper protocol on top of Fluent's `Pivot` protocol.
   Also conform to `ModifiablePivot`. This allows you to use the syntactic sugar Vapor
   provides for adding and removing the relationships.

2. Define an `id` for the model. Note this is a `UUID` type so you must import the
   Foundation module in the file.

3. Define two properties to link to the IDs of `Acronym` and `Category`. This is what
   holds the relationship.

4. Define the `Left` and `Right` types required by `Pivot`. This tells Fluent what the two
   models in the relationship are.

5. Tell Fluent the key path of the two ID properties for each side of the relationship.

6. Implement the throwing initializer, as required by `ModifiablePivot`.

7. Conform to `Migration` so Fluent can set up the table.

Finally, open **configure.swift** and add the `AcronymCategoryPivot` model to the migration list, after `migrations.add(model: Category.self, database: .psql)`:

```
migrations.add(
    model: AcronymCategoryPivot.self,
    database: .psql)
```

This adds the new pivot model to the `MigrationConfig` so that Fluent prepares the table in the database at the next application start. To actually create a relationship between two models you need to use the pivot. Fluent provides convenience functions for creating and removing relationships. First, open **Acronym.swift** and add a new computed property in the extension that contains the `user` computed property:

```
// 1
var categories: Siblings<Acronym,
                         Category,
                         AcronymCategoryPivot> {
  // 2
  return siblings()
}
```

Here's what this does:

1. Add a computed property to `Acronym` to get an acronym's categories. This returns Fluent's generic `Sibling` type. It returns the siblings of an `Acronym` that are of type `Category` and held using the `AcronymCategoryPivot`.

2. Use Fluent's `siblings()` function to retrieve all the categories. Fluent handles everything else.

Open **AcronymsController.swift** and add the following route handler below `getUserHandler(_:)` to set up the relationship between an acronym and a category:

```
// 1
func addCategoriesHandler(
  _ req: Request
) throws -> Future<HTTPStatus> {
  // 2
  return try flatMap(
    to: HTTPStatus.self,
    req.parameters.next(Acronym.self),
    req.parameters.next(Category.self)) { acronym, category in
      // 3
      return acronym.categories
        .attach(category, on: req)
        .transform(to: .created)
  }
}
```

Here's what the route handler does:

1. Define a new route handler, `addCategoriesHandler(_:)`, that returns a `Future<HTTPStatus>`.

2. Use `flatMap(to:_:_:)` to extract both the acronym and category from the request's parameters.

3. Use `attach(_:on:)` to set up the relationship between `acronym` and `category`. This creates a pivot model and saves it in the database. Transform the result into a `201 Created` response.

Register this route handler at the bottom of `boot(router:)`:

```
acronymsRoutes.post(
    Acronym.parameter,
    "categories",
    Category.parameter,
    use: addCategoriesHandler)
```

This routes an HTTP POST request to **/api/acronyms/<ACRONYM_ID>/categories/<CATEGORY_ID>** to `addCategoriesHandler(_:)`.

Build and run the application and launch RESTed. If you do not have any acronyms in the database, create one now. Then, create a new request configured as follows:

- **URL**: http://localhost:8080/api/acronyms/1/categories/1

- **method**: POST

This creates a sibling relationship between the acronym with ID **1** and the category with ID **1**, which you created earlier in the chapter.

Click **Send Request** and you'll see a **201 Created** response:

Querying the relationship

Acronyms and categories are now linked with a sibling relationship. But this isn't very useful if you can't view these relationships! Fluent provides functions that allow you to query these relationships. You've already used one above to create the relationship.

Acronym's categories

Open **AcronymsController.swift** and add a new route handler after `addCategoriesHandler(:_):`

```
// 1
func getCategoriesHandler(
  _ req: Request
) throws -> Future<[Category]> {
  // 2
  return try req.parameters.next(Acronym.self)
    .flatMap(to: [Category].self) { acronym in
      // 3
      try acronym.categories.query(on: req).all()
  }
}
```

Here's what this does:

1. Defines route handler `getCategoriesHandler(_:)` returning `Future<[Category]>`.

2. Extract the acronym from the request's parameters and unwrap the returned future.

3. Use the new computed property to get the categories. Then use a Fluent query to return all the categories.

Register this route handler at the bottom of `boot(router:)`:

```
acronymsRoutes.get(
  Acronym.parameter,
  "categories",
  use: getCategoriesHandler)
```

This routes an HTTP GET request to **/api/acronyms/<ACRONYM_ID>/categories** to `getCategoriesHandler(:_)`.

Build and run the application and launch RESTed. Create a request with the following properties:

• **URL**: http://localhost:8080/api/acronyms/1/categories

- **method**: GET

Send the request and you'll receive the array of categories that acronym's in:

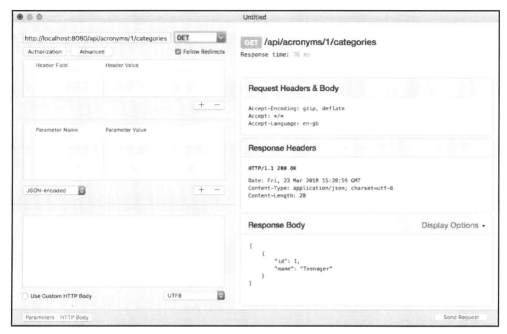

Category's acronyms

Open **Category.swift** and add an extension at the bottom of the file to get the category's acronyms:

```
extension Category {
  // 1
  var acronyms: Siblings<Category,
                         Acronym,
                         AcronymCategoryPivot> {
    // 2
    return siblings()
  }
}
```

Here's what this does:

1. Add a computed property to `Category` to get its acronyms. This returns Fluent's generic `Sibling` type. It returns the siblings of a `Category` that are of type `Acronym` and held using the `AcronymCategoryPivot`.

2. Use Fluent's `siblings()` function to retrieve all the acronyms. Fluent handles everything else.

Open **CategoriesController.swift** and add a new route handler after `getHandler(:_)`:

```
// 1
func getAcronymsHandler(
  _ req: Request) throws -> Future<[Acronym]> {
  // 2
  return try req.parameters.next(Category.self)
    .flatMap(to: [Acronym].self) { category in
      // 3
      try category.acronyms.query(on: req).all()
  }
}
```

Here's what this does:

1. Define a new route handler, `getAcronymsHandler(_:)`, that returns `Future<[Acronym]>`.

2. Extract the category from the request's parameters and unwrap the returned future.

3. Use the new computed property to get the acronyms. Then use a Fluent query to return all the acronyms.

Register this route handler at the bottom of `boot(router:)`:

```
categoriesRoute.get(
  Category.parameter,
  "acronyms",
  use: getAcronymsHandler)
```

This routes an HTTP GET request to **/api/categories/<CATEGORY_ID>/acronyms** to `getAcronymsHandler(:_)`.

Build and run the application and launch RESTed. Create a request as follows:

• **URL**: http://localhost:8080/api/categories/1/acronyms

• **method**: GET

Send the request and you'll receive an array of the acronyms in that category:

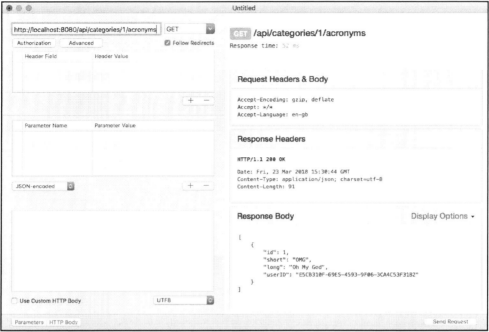

Removing the relationship

Removing a relationship between an acronym and a category is very similar to adding the relationship. Open **AcronymsController.swift** and add the following below `getCategoriesHandler(req:)`:

```
// 1
func removeCategoriesHandler(
  _ req: Request) throws -> Future<HTTPStatus> {
    // 2
    return try flatMap(
      to: HTTPStatus.self,
      req.parameters.next(Acronym.self),
      req.parameters.next(Category.self)
    ) { acronym, category in
        // 3
        return acronym.categories
          .detach(category, on: req)
          .transform(to: .noContent)
    }
}
```

Here's what the new route handler does:

1. Define a new route handler, `removeCategoriesHandler(_:)`, that returns a `Future<HTTPStatus>`.

2. Use `flatMap(to:_:_:)` to extract both the acronym and category from the request's parameters.

3. Use `detach(_:on:)` to remove the relationship between `acronym` and `category`. This finds the pivot model in the database and deletes it. Transform the result into a `204 No Content` response.

Finally, register the route at the bottom of `boot(router:)`:

```
acronymsRoutes.delete(
  Acronym.parameter,
  "categories",
  Category.parameter,
  use: removeCategoriesHandler)
```

This routes an HTTP DELETE request to **/api/acronyms/<ACRONYM_ID>/ categories/<CATEGORY_ID>** to `removeCategoriesHandler(_:)`. Build and run the application and launch RESTed. Create a request with the following properties:

- **URL**: http://localhost:8080/api/acronyms/1/categories/1

- **method**: DELETE

Send the request and you'll receive a **204 No Content** response:

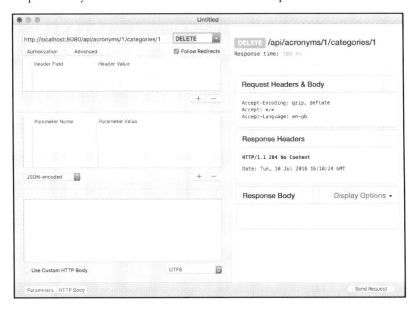

If you send the request to get the acronym's categories again, you'll receive an empty array.

Foreign key constraints

As in Chapter 9, "Parent Child Relationships," it's good practice to use foreign key constraints with sibling relationships. The current `AcronymCategoryPivot` does not check the IDs for the acronyms and categories. At this point, you can delete acronyms and categories that are still linked by the pivot and the relationship will remain, without flagging an error.

Open **AcronymCategoryPivot.swift** and replace the current `Migration` conformance extension. In the new migration, add foreign key constraints to the pivot:

```
// 1
extension AcronymCategoryPivot: Migration {
  // 2
  static func prepare(
    on connection: PostgreSQLConnection
  ) -> Future<Void> {
    // 3
    return Database.create(self, on: connection) { builder in
      // 4
      try addProperties(to: builder)
      // 5
      builder.reference(
        from: \.acronymID,
        to: \Acronym.id,
        onDelete: .cascade)
      // 6
      builder.reference(
        from: \.categoryID,
        to: \Category.id,
        onDelete: .cascade)
    }
  }
}
```

Here's what the new migration does:

1. Conform `AcronymCategoryPivot` to `Migration`.

2. Implement `prepare(on:)` as defined by `Migration`. This overrides the default implementation.

3. Create the table for `AcronymCategoryPivot` in the database.

4. Use `addProperties(to:)` to add all the fields to the database.

5. Add a reference between the `acronymID` property on `AcronymCategoryPivot` and the `id` property on `Acronym`. This sets up the foreign key constraint. `.cascade` sets a cascade schema reference action when you delete the acronym. This means that the relationship is automatically removed instead of an error being thrown.

6. Add a reference between the `categoryID` property on `AcronymCategoryPivot` and the `id` property on `Category`. This sets up the foreign key constraint. Also set the schema reference action for deletion when deleting the category.

Stop the application in Xcode. Because the migration has changed, you need to reset the database so Fluent runs the new migration.

In Terminal, type:

```
# 1
docker stop postgres
# 2
docker rm postgres
# 3
docker run --name postgres -e POSTGRES_DB=vapor \
  -e POSTGRES_USER=vapor -e POSTGRES_PASSWORD=password \
  -p 5432:5432 -d postgres
```

Here's what this does:

1. Stop the running Docker container called postgres. This is the container currently running the database.

2. Remove the Docker container called postgres to delete any existing data.

3. Start a new Docker container running PostgreSQL. For more information, see Chapter 6, "Configuring a Database."

Build and run the application. Create a user, acronym and category in RESTed. Then, set the URL to **http://localhost:8080/api/acronyms/1/categories/100** and the method to **POST**.

Send the request and you'll get an error back because there's no category with ID **100**:

Set the URL to **http://localhost:8080/api/acronyms/1/categories/1** and send the request to add the acronym to the category. You'll see a **201 Created** status in the response headers.

Set the URL to **http://localhost:8080/api/acronyms/1/** and the method to **DELETE**. Send the request and you'll get an error back because you can't delete the acronym while it's linked in a sibling relationship to a category:

Deploy to Vapor Cloud

> **Note**: This section requires that you have followed through Chapter 5, "Fluent and Persisting Models," to set up Vapor Cloud. It also requires that you have configured a database as shown in Chapter 6, "Configuring a Database."

This chapter has added two new models, a category and a pivot between categories and acronyms. However because no existing models have changed, deploying to Vapor Cloud is simple. In Terminal, commit and push your code:

```
# 1
git add .
# 2
git commit -m "Add sibling relationships"
# 2
git push
```

Here's what these commands do:

1. Tell Git to track your new files.

2. Commit your changes with the message "Add sibling relationships".

3. Push your local commits to the remote repository on GitHub.

Now that you have committed and pushed, deploy your updated application. In Terminal, run:

```
vapor cloud deploy --env=production --build=incremental -y
```

This command is the same as previous **vapor cloud deploy** commands, but with extra parameters:

- Deploy the application to the **production** environment.

- Use the **incremental** build type since you have included no new packages.

- Automatically deploy without waiting at the confirmation screen.

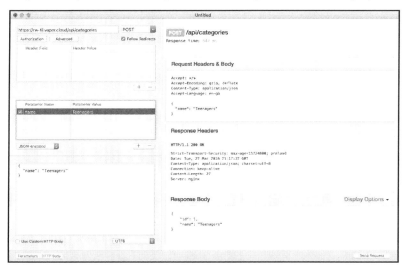

When this has finished, create a new request in RESTed:

- **URL**: https://<YOUR_URL>/api/categories

- **method**: POST

- **Parameter encoding**: JSON-encoded

Add a parameter, **name**, with the value **Teenager**.

Send the request and you'll see the response containing the created category:

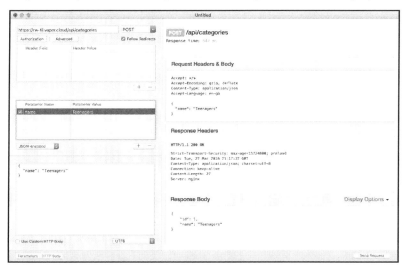

Next, assign that category to an existing acronym. In RESTed, remove the existing parameter and create a new request:

- **URL**: https://<YOUR_URL>/api/acronyms/1/categories/1

- **method**: POST

Send the request and you'll receive a `201 Created` response:

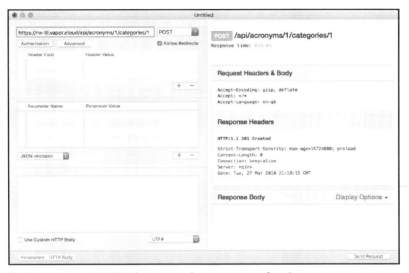

Create a final request in RESTed to view the categories for the acronym:

- **URL**: https://<YOUR_URL>/api/acronyms/1/categories

- **method**: GET

Send the request and you'll receive the category created earlier:

Where to go from here?

In this chapter, you've learned how to implement sibling relationships in Vapor using Fluent. Over the course of this section, you've learned how to use Fluent to model all types of relationships and perform advanced queries. The TIL API is fully featured and ready for use by clients.

In the next chapter, you'll learn how to write tests for the application to ensure that your code is correct. Then, the next section of this book shows you how to create powerful clients to interact with the API — both on iOS and on the web.

Chapter 11: Testing

By Tim Condon

Testing is an important part of the software development process. Writing unit tests and automating them as much as possible allows you to develop and evolve your applications quickly.

In this chapter, you'll learn how to write tests for your Vapor applications. You'll learn why testing is important and how it works with Swift Package Manager. Then, you'll learn how to write tests for the TIL application from the previous chapters. Finally, you'll see why testing matters on Linux and how to test your code on Linux using Docker.

Why should you write tests?

Software testing is as old as software development itself. Modern server applications are deployed many times *a day* so it's important that you're sure everything works as expected. Writing tests for your application gives you confidence the code is sound.

Testing also gives you confidence when you refactor your code. Over the last several chapters, you've evolved and changed the TIL application. Testing every part of the application manually is slow and laborious, and this application is small! To develop new features quickly, you want to ensure the existing features don't break. Having an expansive set of tests allows you to verify everything still works as you change your code.

Testing can also help you design your code. Test-driven development is a popular development process in which you write tests before writing code. This helps ensure you have full test coverage of your code. Test-driven development also helps you design your code and APIs.

Writing tests with SPM

On iOS, Xcode links tests to a specific test target. Xcode configures a scheme to use that target and you run your tests from within Xcode. The Objective-C runtime scans your `XCTestCase`s and picks out the methods whose names begin with `test`. On Linux, and with SPM, there's no Objective-C runtime. There's also no Xcode project to remember schemes and which tests belong where.

Open **Package.swift** in your project. There's a test target defined in the `targets` array:

```
.testTarget(name: "AppTests", dependencies: ["App"]),
```

This defines a `testTarget` type with a dependency on `App`. Tests must live in the **Tests/** directory. In this case, that's **Tests/AppTests**.

Generate an Xcode project and open it with **vapor xcode -y**. If you select the **TILApp-Package** scheme, it'll be set up with `AppTests` as a test target. You can run these tests as normal with **Command-U**, or **Product\Test**:

Testing users

Writing your first test

Close your project in Xcode, then in Terminal, create a file for user-related tests:

```
touch Tests/AppTests/UserTests.swift
vapor xcode -y
```

This adds the file in the correct place in the directory hierarchy and regenerates the Xcode project to ensure the new file builds correctly. In Xcode, open **UserTests.swift** and add the following:

```
@testable import App
import Vapor
import XCTest
import FluentPostgreSQL

final class UserTests: XCTestCase {

}
```

This creates the XCTestCase you'll use to test your users and imports the necessary modules to make everything work.

Next, add the following inside UserTests to test getting the users from the API:

```swift
func testUsersCanBeRetrievedFromAPI() throws {
  // 1
  let expectedName = "Alice"
  let expectedUsername = "alice"

  // 2
  var config = Config.default()
  var services = Services.default()
  var env = Environment.testing
  try App.configure(&config, &env, &services)
  let app = try Application(
    config: config,
    environment: env,
    services: services)
  try App.boot(app)

  // 3
  let conn = try app.newConnection(to: .psql).wait()

  // 4
  let user = User(
    name: expectedName,
    username: expectedUsername)
  let savedUser = try user.save(on: conn).wait()
  _ = try User(
    name: "Luke",
    username: "lukes").save(on: conn).wait()

  // 5
  let responder = try app.make(Responder.self)

  // 6
  let request = HTTPRequest(
    method: .GET,
    url: URL(string: "/api/users")!)
  let wrappedRequest = Request(http: request, using: app)

  // 7
  let response = try responder
    .respond(to: wrappedRequest)
    .wait()

  // 8
  let data = response.http.body.data
  let users = try JSONDecoder().decode([User].self, from: data!)

  // 9
  XCTAssertEqual(users.count, 2)
```

```
    XCTAssertEqual(users[0].name, expectedName)
    XCTAssertEqual(users[0].username, expectedUsername)
    XCTAssertEqual(users[0].id, savedUser.id)

    // 10
    conn.close()
}
```

There's a lot going on in this test; here's the breakdown:

1. Define some expected values for the test: a user's name and username.

2. Create an `Application`, as in **main.swift**. This creates an entire `Application` object but doesn't start running the application. This helps ensure you configure your real application correctly as your test calls the same `App.configure(_:_:_:)`. Note, you're using the `.testing` environment here.

3. Create a database connection to perform database operations. Note the use of `.wait()` here and throughout the test. As you aren't running the test on an `EventLoop`, you can use `wait()` to wait for the future to return. This helps simplify the code.

4. Create a couple of users and save them in the database.

5. Create a `Responder` type; this is what responds to your requests.

6. Send a GET `HTTPRequest` to **/api/users**, the endpoint for getting all the users. A `Request` object wraps the `HTTPRequest` so there's a `Worker` to execute it. Since this is a test, you can force unwrap variables to simplify the code.

7. Send the request and get the response.

8. Decode the response data into an array of `Users`.

9. Ensure there are the correct number of users in the response and the users match those created at the start of the test.

10. Close the connection to the database once the test has finished.

Next, you must update your app's configuration to support testing. Open **configure.swift** and replace:

```
let databaseName = Environment.get("DATABASE_DB") ?? "vapor"
```

with the following:

```
let databaseName: String
let databasePort: Int
// 1
if (env == .testing) {
```

```
    databaseName = "vapor-test"
    databasePort = 5433
} else {
    databaseName = Environment.get("DATABASE_DB") ?? "vapor"
    databasePort = 5432
}
```

Next, replace the call to `PostgreSQLDatabaseConfig` with the following:

```
let databaseConfig = PostgreSQLDatabaseConfig(
    hostname: hostname,
    // 2
    port: databasePort,
    username: username,
    database: databaseName,
    password: password)
```

The following changes were made:

1. If you're running in the `.testing` environment, set the database name and port to different values.

2. Configure the database port in the `PostgreSQLDatabaseConfig`.

These changes allow you to run your tests on a database other than your production database. This ensures you start each test in a known state and don't destroy live data. Since you're using Docker to host your database, setting up another database on the same machine is simple. In Terminal, type the following:

```
docker run --name postgres-test -e POSTGRES_DB=vapor-test \
    -e POSTGRES_USER=vapor -e POSTGRES_PASSWORD=password \
    -p 5433:5432 -d postgres
```

This is similar to the command you used in Chapter 6, "Configuring a Database", but it changes the container name and database name. The Docker container is also mapped to host port 5433 to avoid conflicting with the existing database.

Run the tests and they should pass. However, if you run the tests again, they'll fail. The first test run added two users to the database and the second test run now has four users since the database wasn't reset.

You already know how to reset a database as you've done it with Vapor Cloud. You can revert your database in test in a similar fashion. Open **UserTests.swift** and, at the start of `testUsersCanBeRetrievedFromAPI()`, add the following:

```
// 1
let revertEnvironmentArgs = ["vapor", "revert", "--all", "-y"]
// 2
```

```
var revertConfig = Config.default()
var revertServices = Services.default()
var revertEnv = Environment.testing
// 3
revertEnv.arguments = revertEnvironmentArgs
// 4
try App.configure(&revertConfig, &revertEnv, &revertServices)
let revertApp = try Application(
  config: revertConfig,
  environment: revertEnv,
  services: revertServices)
try App.boot(revertApp)
// 5
try revertApp.asyncRun().wait()

// 6
let migrateEnvironmentArgs = ["vapor", "migrate", "-y"]
var migrateConfig = Config.default()
var migrateServices = Services.default()
var migrateEnv = Environment.testing
migrateEnv.arguments = migrateEnvironmentArgs
try App.configure(&migrateConfig, &migrateEnv, &migrateServices)
let migrateApp = try Application(
  config: migrateConfig,
  environment: migrateEnv,
  services: migrateServices)
try App.boot(migrateApp)
try migrateApp.asyncRun().wait()
```

Here's what this does:

1. Set the arguments the `Application` should execute.

2. Set up the services, configuration and testing environment.

3. Set the arguments in the environment.

4. Set up the application as earlier in the test. This creates a different `Application` object that executes the revert command.

5. Call `asyncRun()` which starts the application and execute the revert command.

6. Repeat the process again to run the migrations. This sets up the database on a separate connection, similar to how Vapor does it.

Build and run the tests again and this time they'll pass!

Test extensions

The first test contains a lot of code that all tests need. Extract the common parts to make the tests easier to read and to simplify future tests. Close your project in Xcode then, in Terminal, create two new files for these extensions:

```
touch Tests/AppTests/Application+Testable.swift
touch Tests/AppTests/Models+Testable.swift
vapor xcode -y
```

When the project has regenerated, open **Application+Testable.swift** and add the following:

```swift
import Vapor
import App
import FluentPostgreSQL

extension Application {
  static func testable(envArgs: [String]? = nil) throws
    -> Application {
    var config = Config.default()
    var services = Services.default()
    var env = Environment.testing

    if let environmentArgs = envArgs {
      env.arguments = environmentArgs
    }

    try App.configure(&config, &env, &services)
    let app = try Application(
      config: config,
      environment: env,
      services: services)

    try App.boot(app)
    return app
  }
}
```

This function allows you to create a testable `Application` object. You can specify environment arguments, if required. This removes several lines of duplicated code in your test. Underneath `testable(envArgs:)` add the following function to reset the database:

```swift
static func reset() throws {
  let revertEnvironment = ["vapor", "revert", "--all", "-y"]
  try Application.testable(envArgs: revertEnvironment)
    .asyncRun()
    .wait()
```

```
    let migrateEnvironment = ["vapor", "migrate", "-y"]
    try Application.testable(envArgs: migrateEnvironment)
      .asyncRun()
      .wait()
}
```

This uses the function above to create an application that runs the revert command and then runs the migrate command. This simplifies resetting the database in each test. Next, add the following at the bottom of the file:

```
struct EmptyContent: Content {}
```

This defines an empty `Content` type to use when there's no body to send in a request. Since you can't define `nil` for a generic type, `EmptyContent` allows you to provide an type to satisfy the compiler. Next, under `reset()`, add the following:

```
// 1
func sendRequest<T>(
  to path: String,
  method: HTTPMethod,
  headers: HTTPHeaders = .init(),
  body: T? = nil
) throws -> Response where T: Content {
  let responder = try self.make(Responder.self)
  // 2
  let request = HTTPRequest(
    method: method,
    url: URL(string: path)!,
    headers: headers)
  let wrappedRequest = Request(http: request, using: self)
  // 3
  if let body = body {
    try wrappedRequest.content.encode(body)
  }
  // 4
  return try responder.respond(to: wrappedRequest).wait()
}

// 5
func sendRequest(
  to path: String,
  method: HTTPMethod,
  headers: HTTPHeaders = .init()
) throws -> Response {
  // 6
  let emptyContent: EmptyContent? = nil
  // 7
  return try sendRequest(
    to: path,
    method: method,
```

```
        headers: headers,
        body: emptyContent)
  }

  // 8
  func sendRequest<T>(
    to path: String,
    method: HTTPMethod,
    headers: HTTPHeaders,
    data: T
  ) throws where T: Content {
    // 9
    _ = try self.sendRequest(
      to: path,
      method: method,
      headers: headers,
      body: data)
  }
}
```

Here's what the code does:

1. Define a method that sends a request to a `path` and returns a `Response`. Allow the HTTP method and headers to be set; this is for later tests. Also allow an optional, generic `Content` to be provided for the body.

2. Create a responder, request and wrapped request as before.

3. If the test contains a body, encode the body into the request's `content`. Using Vapor's `encode(_:)` allows you to take advantage of any custom encoders you set.

4. Send the request and return the response.

5. Define a convenience method that sends a request to a `path` without a body.

6. Create an `EmptyContent` to satisfy the compiler for a body parameter.

7. Use the method created previously to send the request.

8. Define a method that sends a request to a `path` and accepts a generic `Content` type. This convenience method allows you to send a request when you don't care about the response.

9. Use the first method created above to send the request and ignore the response.

Next, underneath these helpers, add the following methods to get responses from a request:

```
// 1
func getResponse<C, T>(
  to path: String,
  method: HTTPMethod = .GET,
```

```
        headers: HTTPHeaders = .init(),
        data: C? = nil,
        decodeTo type: T.Type
    ) throws -> T where C: Content, T: Decodable {
        // 2
        let response = try self.sendRequest(
            to: path,
            method: method,
            headers: headers,
            body: data)
        // 3
        return try response.content.decode(type).wait()
    }

    // 4
    func getResponse<T>(
        to path: String,
        method: HTTPMethod = .GET,
        headers: HTTPHeaders = .init(),
        decodeTo type: T.Type
    ) throws -> T where T: Decodable {
        // 5
        let emptyContent: EmptyContent? = nil
        // 6
        return try self.getResponse(
            to: path,
            method: method,
            headers: headers,
            data: emptyContent,
            decodeTo: type)
    }
```

Here's what's going on:

1. Define a generic method that accepts a `Content` type and `Decodable` type to get a response to a request.

2. Use the method created above to send the request.

3. Decode the response body to the generic type and return the result.

4. Define a generic convenience method that accepts a `Decodable` type to get a response to a request without providing a body.

5. Create an empty `Content` to satisfy the compiler.

6. Use the previous method to get the response to the request.

Next, open **Models+Testable.swift** and create an extension to create a `User`:

```
@testable import App
import FluentPostgreSQL
```

```
extension User {
  static func create(
    name: String = "Luke",
    username: String = "lukes",
    on connection: PostgreSQLConnection
  ) throws -> User {
    let user = User(name: name, username: username)
    return try user.save(on: connection).wait()
  }
}
```

This function saves a user, created with the supplied details, in the database. It has default values so you don't have to provide any if you don't care about them.

With all this created, you can now rewrite your user test. Open **UserTests.swift** and delete `testUsersCanBeRetrievedFromAPI()`.

Next, in `UserTests` create the common properties for all the tests:

```
let usersName = "Alice"
let usersUsername = "alicea"
let usersURI = "/api/users/"
var app: Application!
var conn: PostgreSQLConnection!
```

Next implement `setUp()` to run the code that must execute before each test:

```
override func setUp() {
  try! Application.reset()
  app = try! Application.testable()
  conn = try! app.newConnection(to: .psql).wait()
}
```

This reverts the database, generates an `Application` for the test, and creates a connection to the database.

Next, implement `teardown()` to close the connection to the database:

```
override func tearDown() {
  conn.close()
}
```

Finally, rewrite `testUsersCanBeRetrievedFromAPI()` to use all the new helper methods:

```
func testUsersCanBeRetrievedFromAPI() throws {
  let user = try User.create(
    name: usersName,
    username: usersUsername,
```

```
  on: conn)
  _ = try User.create(on: conn)

  let users = try app.getResponse(
    to: usersURI,
    decodeTo: [User].self)

  XCTAssertEqual(users.count, 2)
  XCTAssertEqual(users[0].name, usersName)
  XCTAssertEqual(users[0].username, usersUsername)
  XCTAssertEqual(users[0].id, user.id)
}
```

This test does exactly the same as before but is far more readable. It also makes the next tests much easier to write. Run the tests again to ensure they still work.

Testing the User API

Open **UserTests.swift** and using the test helper methods add the following to test saving a user via the API:

```
func testUserCanBeSavedWithAPI() throws {
  // 1
  let user = User(name: usersName, username: usersUsername)
  // 2
  let receivedUser = try app.getResponse(
    to: usersURI,
    method: .POST,
    headers: ["Content-Type": "application/json"],
    data: user,
    decodeTo: User.self)

  // 3
  XCTAssertEqual(receivedUser.name, usersName)
  XCTAssertEqual(receivedUser.username, usersUsername)
  XCTAssertNotNil(receivedUser.id)

  // 4
  let users = try app.getResponse(
    to: usersURI,
    decodeTo: [User].self)

  // 5
  XCTAssertEqual(users.count, 1)
  XCTAssertEqual(users[0].name, usersName)
  XCTAssertEqual(users[0].username, usersUsername)
  XCTAssertEqual(users[0].id, receivedUser.id)
}
```

Here's what the test does:

1. Create a `User` object with known values.

2. Use `getResponse(to:method:headers:data:decodeTo:)` to send a POST request to the API and get the response. Use the `user` object as the request body and set the headers correctly to simulate a JSON request. Convert the response into a `User` object.

3. Assert the response from the API matches the expected values.

4. Get all the users from API.

5. Ensure the response only contains the user you created in the first request.

Run the tests to ensure that the changes work!

Next, add the following test to retrieve a single user from the API:

```
func testGettingASingleUserFromTheAPI() throws {
  // 1
  let user = try User.create(
    name: usersName,
    username: usersUsername,
    on: conn)
  // 2
  let receivedUser = try app.getResponse(
    to: "\(usersURI)\(user.id!)",
    decodeTo: User.self)

  // 3
  XCTAssertEqual(receivedUser.name, usersName)
  XCTAssertEqual(receivedUser.username, usersUsername)
  XCTAssertEqual(receivedUser.id, user.id)
}
```

Here's what the test does:

1. Save a user in the database with known values.

2. Get the user at **/api/users/<USER ID>**.

3. Assert the values are the same as provided when creating the user.

The final part of the user's API to test retrieves a user's acronyms. Open **Models+Testable.swift** and, at the end of the file, create a new extension to create acronyms:

```
extension Acronym {
  static func create(
    short: String = "TIL",
    long: String = "Today I Learned",
```

```
    user: User? = nil,
    on connection: PostgreSQLConnection
) throws -> Acronym {
    var acronymsUser = user

    if acronymsUser == nil {
        acronymsUser = try User.create(on: connection)
    }

    let acronym = Acronym(
        short: short,
        long: long,
        userID: acronymsUser!.id!)
    return try acronym.save(on: connection).wait()
    }
}
```

This creates an acronym and saves it in the database with the provided values. If you don't provide any values, it uses defaults. If you don't provide a user for the acronym, it creates a user to use first.

Next, open **UserTests.swift** and create a method to test getting a user's acronyms:

```
func testGettingAUsersAcronymsFromTheAPI() throws {
  // 1
  let user = try User.create(on: conn)
  // 2
  let acronymShort = "OMG"
  let acronymLong = "Oh My God"
  // 3
  let acronym1 = try Acronym.create(
    short: acronymShort,
    long: acronymLong,
    user: user,
    on: conn)
  _ = try Acronym.create(
    short: "LOL",
    long: "Laugh Out Loud",
    user: user,
    on: conn)

  // 4
  let acronyms = try app.getResponse(
    to: "\(usersURI)\(user.id!)/acronyms",
    decodeTo: [Acronym].self)

  // 5
  XCTAssertEqual(acronyms.count, 2)
  XCTAssertEqual(acronyms[0].id, acronym1.id)
  XCTAssertEqual(acronyms[0].short, acronymShort)
  XCTAssertEqual(acronyms[0].long, acronymLong)
}
```

Here's what the test does:

1. Create a user for the acronyms.

2. Define some expected values for an acronym.

3. Create two acronyms in the database using the created user. Use the expected values for the first acronym.

4. Get the user's acronyms from the API by sending a request to **/api/users/<USER ID>/acronyms**.

5. Assert the response returns the correct number of acronyms and the first one matches the expected values.

Run the tests to ensure that the changes work!

Testing acronyms and categories

Open **Models+Testable.swift** and, at the bottom of the file, add a new extension to simplify creating categories:

```
extension App.Category {
  static func create(
    name: String = "Random",
    on connection: PostgreSQLConnection
  ) throws -> App.Category {
    let category = Category(name: name)
    return try category.save(on: connection).wait()
  }
}
```

Like the other model helper functions, `create(name:on:)` takes the `name` as a parameter and creates a category in the database. The tests for the acronyms API and categories API are part of the starter project for this chapter. Open **CategoryTests.swift** and uncomment all the code. The tests follow the same pattern as the user tests.

Open **AcronymTests.swift** and uncomment all the code. These tests also follow a similar pattern to before but there are some extra tests for the extra routes in the acronyms API. These include updating an acronym, deleting an acronym and the different Fluent query routes.

Run all the tests to make sure they all work. You should have a sea of green tests with every route tested!

Testing on Linux

Earlier in the chapter you learned why testing your application is important. For server-side Swift, testing on Linux is especially important. When you deploy your application to Vapor Cloud, for instance, you're deploying to an operating system different from the one you used for development. It's vital that you test your application on the same environment that you deploy it on.

Why is this so? Foundation on Linux isn't the same as Foundation on macOS. At the time of writing, Foundation on macOS still uses the Objective-C framework, which has been thoroughly tested over the years. Linux uses the pure-Swift Foundation framework, which isn't as robust. The <u>implementation status list</u> shows that many features remain unimplemented on Linux. If you use these features, your application may crash. While the situation improves constantly, you must still ensure everything works as expected on Linux.

Declaring tests on Linux

Running tests on Linux requires you to do things differently from running them on macOS. As mentioned earlier, the Objective-C runtime determines the test methods your XCTestCases provide.

On Linux there's no runtime to do this, so you must point Swift in the right direction.

On Linux, you declare test cases in **LinuxMain.swift** in the **Tests** directory. This file is not part of your Xcode project. You can open it in Xcode by double-clicking it in Finder or you may edit it using a different text editor. Add the following to **LinuxMain.swift**:

```
import XCTest
// 1
@testable import AppTests

// 2
XCTMain([
  testCase(AcronymTests.allTests),
  testCase(CategoryTests.allTests),
  testCase(UserTests.allTests)
])
```

This file is the test equivalent of **main.swift**. Here's what it does:

1. Import the `AppTests` module which contains your tests.

2. Provide an array of tests for each `XCTestCase` to `XCTMain(_:)`. These are executed when testing your application on Linux.

You must provide an array for each `XCTestCase`. By convention, you call this array `allTests`. It contains a list of tuples consisting of the name of the test and the test itself. For now, you must create and maintain this yourself.

`AcronymTests` and `CategoryTests` already include the `allTests` array. Open **UserTests.swift** in Xcode and add the array at the bottom of `UserTests`:

```
static let allTests = [
  ("testUsersCanBeRetrievedFromAPI",
   testUsersCanBeRetrievedFromAPI),
  ("testUserCanBeSavedWithAPI", testUserCanBeSavedWithAPI),
  ("testGettingASingleUserFromTheAPI",
   testGettingASingleUserFromTheAPI),
  ("testGettingAUsersAcronymsFromTheAPI",
   testGettingAUsersAcronymsFromTheAPI)
]
```

When you call `swift test` or `vapor test` on Linux, the test executable uses this array to determine which tests to run.

Running tests in Linux

Early feedback is always valuable in software development and running tests on Linux is no exception. Using a Continuous Integration system to automatically test on Linux is vital but what happens if you want to test on Linux on your Mac?

Well, you're already running Linux for the PostgreSQL database using Docker! So, you can also use Docker to run your tests in a Linux environment. In the project directory, create a new file called **Dockerfile** (with no extension). Open the file in a text editor and add the following:

```
# 1
FROM swift:4.1

# 2
WORKDIR /package
# 3
COPY . ./
# 4
RUN swift package resolve
RUN swift package clean
# 5
CMD ["swift", "test"]
```

Here's what the **Dockerfile** does:

1. Use the Swift 4.1 image.

2. Set the working directory to **/package**.

3. Copy the contents of the current directory into **/package** in the container.

4. Fetch the dependencies and clean up the project's build artifacts.

5. Set the default command to `swift test`. This is the command Docker executes when you run the Dockerfile.

The tests need a PostgreSQL database in order to run. By default, Docker containers can't see each other. However, Docker has a tool, Docker Compose, designed to link together different containers for testing and running applications. Create a new file called **docker-compose.yml** in the project directory. Open the file in an editor and add the following:

```
# 1
version: '3'
# 2
services:
  # 3
  til-app:
    # 4
    depends_on:
      - postgres
    # 5
    build: .
    # 6
    environment:
```

```
      - DATABASE_HOSTNAME=postgres
      - DATABASE_PORT=5432
  # 7
  postgres:
    # 8
    image: "postgres"
    # 9
    environment:
      - POSTGRES_DB=vapor-test
      - POSTGRES_USER=vapor
      - POSTGRES_PASSWORD=password
```

Here's what this does:

1. Specify the Docker Compose version.

2. Define the services for this application.

3. Define a service for the TIL application.

4. Set a dependency on the Postgres container, so Docker Compose starts the Postgres container first.

5. Build the Dockerfile in the current directory — the Dockerfile you created earlier.

6. Inject the DATABASE_HOSTNAME environment variable. Docker Compose has an internal DNS resolver. This allows the til-app container to connect to the postgres container with the hostname postgres. Also set the port for the database.

7. Define a service for the Postgres container.

8. Use the standard Postgres image.

9. Set the same environment variables as used at the start of the chapter for the test database.

Finally open **configure.swift** in Xcode and allow the database port to be set as an environment variable for testing. Replace the line databasePort = 5433 with:

```
if let testPort = Environment.get("DATABASE_PORT") {
  databasePort = Int(testPort) ?? 5433
} else {
  databasePort = 5433
}
```

This uses the DATABASE_PORT environment variable if set, otherwise defaults the port to 5433. This allows you to set the port in **docker-compose.yml**.

To test your application in Linux, open Terminal and type the following:

```
# 1
docker-compose build
# 2
docker-compose up --abort-on-container-exit
```

Here's what this does:

1. Build the different docker containers.

2. Spin up the different containers and run the tests. `--abort-on-container-exit` tells Docker Compose to stop the `postgres` container when the `til-app` container stops. The `postgres` container used for this test is different from, and doesn't conflict with, the one you've been using during development.

When the tests finish running, you'll see the output in Terminal with all tests passing:

Where to go from here?

In this chapter, you've learned how you to test your Vapor applications to ensure they work correctly. Writing tests for your application means you can run these tests on Linux. This gives you confidence the application will work when you deploy it. Having a good test suite allows you to evolve and adapt your applications quickly.

Vapor's architecture has a heavy reliance on protocols. This, combined with Vapor's dependency injection Service framework, makes testing simple and scalable. For large applications, you may even want to introduce a data abstraction layer so you aren't testing with a real database.

This means you don't have to connect to a database to test your main logic and will speed up the tests.

It's important you run your tests regularly. Using a continuous integration (CI) system such as Jenkins or Bitbucket Pipelines allows you to test every commit. You must also keep your tests up to date. In future chapters where the behavior changes, such as when authentication is introduced, you'll change the tests to work with these new features.

Chapter 12: Creating a Simple iPhone App, Part 1

By Tim Condon

In the previous chapters, you created an API and interacted with it using RESTed. However, users expect something a bit nicer to use TIL! The next two chapters show you how to build a simple iOS app that interacts with the API. In this chapter, you'll learn how to create different models and get models from the database.

> **Note**: This chapter expects you have a TIL application running in Vapor Cloud and have followed through Chapters 5-10.

At the end of the two chapters, you'll have an iOS application that can do everything you've learned up to this point. It will look similar to the following:

Getting started

To kick things off, download the materials for this chapter and open the **TILiOS** project. **TILiOS** contains a skeleton application that interacts with the TIL API. It's a tab bar application with three tabs:

- **Acronyms**: view all acronyms, view details about an acronym and add acronyms.

- **Users**: view all users and create users.

- **Categories**: view all categories and create categories.

The project contains several empty table views controllers, ready to be configured to display data from the TIL API.

Look at the **Models** group in the project; it provides three model classes:

- Acronym

- User

- Category

You may recognize the code — these are the same models found in the API application! This shows how powerful using the same language for both client and server can be. It's even possible to create a separate module both projects use so you don't have to duplicate code.

Viewing the acronyms

The first tab's table displays all the acronyms. Create a new **Swift** file in the **Utilities** group called **ResourceRequest.swift**. Open the file and create an enum to represent results from calling the TILApp API:

```
enum GetResourcesRequest<ResourceType> {
  // 1
  case success([ResourceType])
  // 2
  case failure
}
```

This enum represents a generic resource type and provides two cases:

1. A success case that stores an array of the resource type.

2. A failure case.

Underneath `GetResourcesRequest`, create a type to manage making resource requests:

```
// 1
struct ResourceRequest<ResourceType>
  where ResourceType: Codable {

  // 2
  let baseURL = "https://<YOUR_CLOUD_URL>/api/"
  let resourceURL: URL

  // 3
  init(resourcePath: String) {
    guard let resourceURL = URL(string: baseURL) else {
      fatalError()
    }
    self.resourceURL
      = resourceURL.appendingPathComponent(resourcePath)
  }

  // 4
  func getAll(
    completion: @escaping
      (GetResourcesRequest<ResourceType>) -> Void) {
    // 5
    let dataTask = URLSession.shared
                           .dataTask(with: resourceURL) {
      data, _, _ in
      // 6
      guard let jsonData = data else {
        completion(.failure)
        return
      }
      do {
        // 7
        let resources
          = try JSONDecoder().decode([ResourceType].self,
                                     from: jsonData)
        // 8
        completion(.success(resources))
      } catch {
        // 9
        completion(.failure)
      }
    }
    // 10
    dataTask.resume()
  }
}
```

Here's what this does:

1. Define a generic `ResourceRequest` type whose generic parameter must conform to `Codable`.

2. Set the base URL for the API. Update this with the URL of your Vapor Cloud API, for example **https://rw-til.vapor.cloud/api/**.

3. Initialize the URL for the particular resource.

4. Define a function to get all values of the resource type from the API. This takes a completion closure as a parameter.

5. Create a data task with the resource URL.

6. Ensure the response returns some data. Otherwise, call the `completion(_:)` closure with the `.failure` case.

7. Decode the response data into an array of `ResourceTypes`.

8. Call the `completion(_:)` closure with the `.success` case and return the array of `ResourceTypes`.

9. Catch any errors and return failure.

10. Start the `dataTask`.

Open **AcronymsTableViewController.swift** and add the following under `// MARK: -
Properties`:

```
// 1
var acronyms: [Acronym] = []
// 2
let acronymsRequest =
  ResourceRequest<Acronym>(resourcePath: "acronyms")
```

Here's what this does:

1. Declare an array of acronyms. These are the acronyms the table displays.

2. Create a `ResourceRequest` for acronyms.

Getting the acronyms

Whenever the view appears on screen, the table view controller calls `refresh(_:)`.
Replace the implementation of `refresh(_:)` with the following:

```
// 1
acronymsRequest.getAll { [weak self] acronymResult in
  // 2
  DispatchQueue.main.async {
    sender?.endRefreshing()
  }

  switch acronymResult {
  // 3
```

```
  case .failure:
    ErrorPresenter.showError(message:
      "There was an error getting the acronyms", on: self)
  // 4
  case .success(let acronyms):
    DispatchQueue.main.async { [weak self] in
      self?.acronyms = acronyms
      self?.tableView.reloadData()
    }
  }
}
```

Here's what this does:

1. Call `getAll(completion:)` to get all the acronyms. This returns a result in the completion closure.

2. As the request is complete, call `endRefreshing()` on the refresh control.

3. If the fetch fails, use the `ErrorPresenter` utility to display an alert view with an appropriate error message.

4. If the fetch succeeds, update the `acronyms` array from the result and reload the table.

Displaying acronyms

Still in **AcronymsTableViewController.swift**, update `tableView(_:numberOfRowsInSection:)` to return the correct number of acronyms by replacing `return 1` with the following:

```
return acronyms.count
```

Next, update `tableView(_:cellForRowAt:)` to display the acronyms in the table. Add the following before `return cell`:

```
let acronym = acronyms[indexPath.row]
cell.textLabel?.text = acronym.short
cell.detailTextLabel?.text = acronym.long
```

This sets the title and subtitle text to the acronym short and long properties for each cell.

Build and run and you'll see your table populated with acronyms from Vapor Cloud:

Viewing the users

Viewing all the users follows a similar pattern. Most of the view controller is already set up. Open **UsersTableViewController.swift** and under `var users: [User] = []` add the following:

```
let usersRequest = ResourceRequest<User>(resourcePath: "users")
```

This creates a `ResourceRequest` to get the users from the API. Next, replace the implementation of `refresh(_:)` with the following:

```
// 1
usersRequest.getAll { [weak self] result in
  // 2
  DispatchQueue.main.async {
    sender?.endRefreshing()
  }
  switch result {
  // 3
  case .failure:
    ErrorPresenter.showError(
      message: "There was an error getting the users",
      on: self)
  // 4
  case .success(let users):
```

```
    DispatchQueue.main.async { [weak self] in
      self?.users = users
      self?.tableView.reloadData()
    }
  }
}
```

Here's what this does:

1. Call `getAll(completion:)` to get all the users. This returns a result in the completion closure.

2. As the request is complete, call `endRefreshing()` on the refresh control.

3. If the fetch fails, use the `ErrorPresenter` utility to display an alert view with an appropriate error message.

4. If the fetch succeeds, update the `users` array from the result and reload the table.

Build and run. Go to the **Users** tab and you'll see table table populated with users from Vapor Cloud:

Viewing the categories

Follow a similar pattern to view all the categories. Open **CategoriesTableViewController.swift** and under `var categories: [Category] = []` add the following:

```
let categoriesRequest =
  ResourceRequest<Category>(resourcePath: "categories")
```

This sets up a ResourceRequest to get the categories from the API. Next, replace the implementation of refresh(_:) with the following:

```
// 1
categoriesRequest.getAll { [weak self] result in
  // 2
  DispatchQueue.main.async {
    sender?.endRefreshing()
  }
  switch result {
  // 3
  case .failure:
    let message = "There was an error getting the categories"
    ErrorPresenter.showError(message: message, on: self)
  // 4
  case .success(let categories):
    DispatchQueue.main.async { [weak self] in
      self?.categories = categories
      self?.tableView.reloadData()
    }
  }
}
```

Here's what this does:

1. Call getAll(completion:) to get all the categories. This returns a result in the completion closure.

2. As the request is complete, call endRefreshing() on the refresh control.

3. If the fetch fails, use the ErrorPresenter utility to display an alert view with an appropriate error message.

4. If the fetch succeeds, update the categories array from the result and reload the table.

Build and run. Go to the **Categories** tab and you'll see the table populated with categories from Vapor Cloud:

Creating users

In the TIL API, you must have a user to create acronyms, so set up that flow first. Open **ResourceRequest.swift** and create a new enum underneath GetResourcesRequest to represent a save result:

```
enum SaveResult<ResourceType> {
  case success(ResourceType)
  case failure
}
```

The enum has two cases: a success, which contains the result from the API, and a failure. Add a new method at the bottom of ResourceRequest to save a model:

```
// 1
func save(_ resourceToSave: ResourceType,
        completion:
            @escaping (SaveResult<ResourceType>) -> Void) {
  do {
    // 2
    var urlRequest = URLRequest(url: resourceURL)
    // 3
    urlRequest.httpMethod = "POST"
    // 4
```

```
        urlRequest.addValue("application/json",
                         forHTTPHeaderField: "Content-Type")
        // 5
        urlRequest.httpBody =
          try JSONEncoder().encode(resourceToSave)
        // 6
        let dataTask = URLSession.shared
                          .dataTask(with: urlRequest) {
          data, response, _ in
          // 7
          guard let httpResponse = response as? HTTPURLResponse,
            httpResponse.statusCode == 200,
            let jsonData = data else {
              completion(.failure)
              return
          }

          do {
            // 8
            let resource =
              try JSONDecoder().decode(ResourceType.self,
                                    from: jsonData)
            completion(.success(resource))
          } catch {
            // 9
            completion(.failure)
          }
        }
        // 10
        dataTask.resume()
      // 11
      } catch {
        completion(.failure)
      }
    }
```

Here's what the new method does:

1. Declare a method save(_:completion:) that takes the resource to save and a completion handler that takes the save result.

2. Create a URLRequest for the save request.

3. Set the HTTP method for the request to **POST**.

4. Set the **Content-Type** header for the request to **application/json** so the API knows there's JSON data to decode.

5. Set the request body as the encoded resource type.

6. Create a data task with the request.

7. Ensure there's an HTTP response. Check the response status is 200 OK, the code returned by the API upon a successful save. Ensure there's data in the response body.

8. Decode the response body into the resource type. Call the completion handler with a success result.

9. Catch a decode error and call the completion handler with a failure result.

10. Start the data task.

11. Catch any errors and call the completion handler with a failure result.

Next, open **CreateUserTableViewController.swift** and replace the implementation of save(_:) with the following:

```swift
// 1
guard let name = nameTextField.text,
  !name.isEmpty else {
    ErrorPresenter
      .showError(message: "You must specify a name", on: self)
    return
}

// 2
guard let username = usernameTextField.text,
  !username.isEmpty else {
    ErrorPresenter
      .showError(message: "You must specify a username",
                 on: self)
    return
}

// 3
let user = User(name: name, username: username)
// 4
ResourceRequest<User>(resourcePath: "users")
  .save(user) { [weak self] result in
  switch result {
  // 5
  case .failure:
    let message = "There was a problem saving the user"
    ErrorPresenter.showError(message: message, on: self)
  // 6
  case .success:
    DispatchQueue.main.async { [weak self] in
      self?.navigationController?
          .popViewController(animated: true)
    }
  }
}
```

Here's what this does:

1. Ensure the name text field contains a non-empty string.

2. Ensure the username text field contains a non-empty string.

3. Create a new user from the provided data.

4. Create a `ResourceRequest` for a user and call `save(_:completion:)`.

5. If the save fails, display an error message.

6. If the save succeeds, return to the previous view: the users table.

Build and run. Go to the **Users** tab and tap the **+** button to open the **Create User** screen. Fill in the two fields and tap **Save**. If the save succeeds, the screen closes and the new user appears in the table:

Creating acronyms

Selecting users

When you create an acronym with the API, you must provide a user ID. Asking a user to remember and input a UUID isn't a good user experience! The iOS app should allow a user to select a user by name.

Open **CreateAcronymTableViewController.swift** and create a new method under
viewDidLoad() to populate the User cell in the create acronym table with a default
user:

```
func populateUsers() {
  // 1
  let usersRequest =
    ResourceRequest<User>(resourcePath: "users")

  usersRequest.getAll { [weak self] result in
    switch result {
    // 2
    case .failure:
      let message = "There was an error getting the users"
      ErrorPresenter.showError(message: message,
                                   on: self) { _ in
        self?.navigationController?
             .popViewController(animated: true)
      }
    // 3
    case .success(let users):
      DispatchQueue.main.async { [weak self] in
        self?.userLabel.text = users[0].name
      }
      self?.selectedUser = users[0]
    }
  }
}
```

Here's what this does:

1. Get all users from the API.

2. Show an error if the request fails. Return from the create acronym view when the
    user dismisses the alert view. This uses the dismissAction on
    showError(message:on:dismissAction:).

3. If the request succeeds, set the user field to the first user's name and update
    selectedUser.

At the end of viewDidLoad() add the following:

```
populateUsers()
```

Your app's user can tap the **USER** cell to select a different user for creating an acronym.
This gesture opens the **Select A User** screen.

Open **SelectUserTableViewController.swift**. Under `var users: [User] = []` add the following:

```
var selectedUser: User!
```

This property holds the selected user. Next, add the following implementation to `loadData()` so the table displays the users when the view loads:

```
// 1
let usersRequest =
  ResourceRequest<User>(resourcePath: "users")

usersRequest.getAll { [weak self] result in
  switch result {
  // 2
  case .failure:
    let message = "There was an error getting the users"
    ErrorPresenter.showError(message: message,
                             on: self) { _ in
      self?.navigationController?
          .popViewController(animated: true)
    }
  // 3
  case .success(let users):
    self?.users = users
    DispatchQueue.main.async { [weak self] in
      self?.tableView.reloadData()
    }
  }
}
```

Here's what this does:

1. Get all the users from the API.

2. If the request fails, show an error message. Return to the previous view once a user taps dismiss on the alert.

3. If the request succeeds, save the users and reload the table data.

In `tableView(_:cellForRowAt:)` before `return cell` add the following:

```
if user.name == selectedUser.name {
  cell.accessoryType = .checkmark
} else {
  cell.accessoryType = .none
}
```

This compares the current cell against the currently selected user. If they are the same, set a checkmark on that cell.

`SelectUserTableViewController` uses an unwind segue to navigate back to the `CreateAcronymTableViewController` when a user taps a cell.

Add the following implementation of `prepare(for:)` in `SelectUserTableViewController` to set the selected user for the segue:

```
// 1
if segue.identifier == "UnwindSelectUserSegue" {
  // 2
  guard
    let cell = sender as? UITableViewCell,
    let indexPath = tableView.indexPath(for: cell)
    else {
      return
  }
  // 3
  selectedUser = users[indexPath.row]
}
```

Here's what this does:

1. Verify this is the expected segue.

2. Get the index path of the cell that triggered the segue.

3. Update `selectedUser` to the user for the tapped cell.

The unwind segue calls `updateSelectedUser(_:)` in `CreateAcronymTableViewController`. Open **CreateAcronymTableViewController.swift** and add the following implementation to the `updateSelectedUser(_:)`:

```
// 1
guard let controller =
  segue.source as? SelectUserTableViewController else {
  return
}
// 2
selectedUser = controller.selectedUser
userLabel.text = selectedUser?.name
```

Here's what this does:

1. Ensure the segue came from `SelectUserTableViewController`.

2. Update `selectedUser` with the new value and update the user label.

Finally, add the following implementation to prepare(for:sender:) in CreateAcronymTableViewController to set the selected user on SelectUserTableViewController:

```
// 1
if segue.identifier == "SelectUserSegue" {
  // 2
  guard
    let destination =
      segue.destination as? SelectUserTableViewController,
    let user = selectedUser else {
      return
  }
  // 3
  destination.selectedUser = user
}
```

Here's what this does:

1. Verify this is the expected segue.

2. Get the destination from the segue and ensure a user has been selected.

3. Set the selected user on SelectUserTableViewController.

Build and run. In the Acronyms tab, tap **+** to bring up the **Create An Acronym** view. Tap the user row and the application opens the **Select A User** view, allowing you to select a user. When you tap a user, that user is the set on the **Create An Acronym** page:

Saving acronyms

Finally, replace the implementation of save(_:) in
CreateAcronymTableViewController.swift to save the acronym in the database:

```
// 1
guard
  let shortText = acronymShortTextField.text,
  !shortText.isEmpty else {
    ErrorPresenter
      .showError(message: "You must specify an acronym!",
                 on: self)
    return
}
guard
  let longText = acronymLongTextField.text,
  !longText.isEmpty else {
    ErrorPresenter
      .showError(message: "You must specify a meaning!",
                 on: self)
    return
}
guard let userID = selectedUser?.id else {
  let message = "You must have a user to create an acronym!"
  ErrorPresenter.showError(message: message, on: self)
  return
}

// 2
let acronym = Acronym(short: shortText,
                      long: longText,
                      userID: userID)
// 3
ResourceRequest<Acronym>(resourcePath: "acronyms")
  .save(acronym) { [weak self] result in
    switch result {
    // 4
    case .failure:
      let message = "There was a problem saving the acronym"
      ErrorPresenter.showError(message: message, on: self)
    // 5
    case .success:
      DispatchQueue.main.async { [weak self] in
        self?.navigationController?
          .popViewController(animated: true)
      }
    }
  }
}
```

Here are the steps to save the acronym:

1. Ensure the user has filled in the acronym and meaning. Check the selected user is not `nil` and the user has a valid ID.

2. Create a new `Acronym` from the supplied data.

3. Create a `ResourceRequest` for an acronym and call `save(_:)`.

4. If the save request fails, show an error message.

5. If the save request succeeds, return to the previous view: the acronyms table.

Build and run. On the **Acronyms** tab, tap **+**. Fill in the fields to create an acronym and tap **Save**. The saved acronym appears in the table:

Where to go from here?

In this chapter, you've learned how to interact with the API with an iOS application. You've learned how to create different models and retrieve them from the API. You've also learned how to manage the required relationships in a user-friendly way.

The next chapter builds upon this to view details about a single acronym. You'll also learn how to implement the rest of the CRUD operations. Finally, you'll see how to set up relationships between categories and acronyms.

Chapter 13: Creating a Simple iPhone App, Part 2

By Tim Condon

In the previous chapter, you created an iPhone application that can create users and acronyms. In this chapter, you'll expand the app to include viewing details about a single acronym. You'll also learn how to perform the final CRUD operations: edit and delete. Finally, you'll learn how to add acronyms to categories.

> **Note**: This chapter expects you have a TIL application running in Vapor Cloud and have followed through Chapters 5-10. It also expects you've completed the iOS application from the previous chapter. If not, grab the starter project and pick up from there.

Getting started

In the previous chapter, you learned how to view all the acronyms in a table. Now you want to show all the information about a single acronym when a user taps on a table cell. The starter project contains the necessary plumbing; you simply need to implement the details.

Open **AcronymsTableViewController.swift**. After viewWillAppear(_:) add the following:

```
// MARK: - Navigation
override func prepare(for segue: UIStoryboardSegue,
                      sender: Any?) {
  // 1
  if segue.identifier == "AcronymsToAcronymDetail" {
    // 2
```

```
guard
  let destination =
    segue.destination as? AcronymDetailTableViewController,
  let indexPath = tableView.indexPathForSelectedRow else {
    return
}

// 3
destination.acronym = acronyms[indexPath.row]
  }
}
```

Here's what this does:

1. Verify the expected segue identifier.

2. Ensure the destination view controller is an
   `AcronymDetailTableViewController`.

3. Set the `acronym` property in `AcronymDetailTableViewController` to the selected
   acronym.

Create a new Swift file called **AcronymRequest.swift** in the **Utilities** group. Open the
new file and add an enum for the acronym's user request:

```
enum AcronymUserRequestResult {
  case success(User)
  case failure
}
```

This defines a success case that stores the creating user and a failure case. Since categories
are represented by an array, the acronym's categories request will use the existing
`GetResourcesRequest`. At the bottom of the file create a new type to represent an
acronym resource request:

```
struct AcronymRequest {
  let resource: URL

  init(acronymID: Int) {
    let resourceString =
      "https://<YOUR_CLOUD_URL>/api/acronyms/\(acronymID)"
    guard let resourceURL = URL(string: resourceString) else {
      fatalError()
    }
    self.resource = resourceURL
  }
}
```

This sets the `resource` property to the URL for that acronym. **Be sure to update the
string to use your Vapor Cloud URL.**

At the bottom of `AcronymRequest` add a method to get the acronym's user:

```swift
func getUser(completion:
  @escaping (AcronymUserRequestResult) -> Void) {
  // 1
  let url = resource.appendingPathComponent("user")

  // 2
  let dataTask = URLSession.shared
                          .dataTask(with: url) { data, _, _ in
    // 3
    guard let jsonData = data else {
      completion(.failure)
      return
    }
    do {
      // 4
      let user = try JSONDecoder().decode(User.self,
                                          from: jsonData)
      completion(.success(user))
    } catch {
      // 5
      completion(.failure)
    }
  }
  // 6
  dataTask.resume()
}
```

Here's what this does:

1. Create the URL to get the acronym's user.

2. Create a data task using the shared `URLSession`.

3. Check the response contains a body, otherwise fail.

4. Decode the response body into a `User` object and call the completion handler with the success result.

5. Catch any decoding errors and call the completion handler with the failure result.

6. Start the network task.

Below `getUser(completion:)` add the following method to get the user's categories:

```swift
func getCategories(completion:
  @escaping (GetResourcesRequest<Category>) -> Void) {
  let url = resource.appendingPathComponent("categories")
  let dataTask = URLSession.shared
                          .dataTask(with: url) { data, _, _ in
    guard let jsonData = data else {
      completion(.failure)
```

```
      return
    }
    do {
      let categories = try JSONDecoder().decode([Category].self,
                                                from: jsonData)
      completion(.success(categories))
    } catch {
      completion(.failure)
    }
  }
  dataTask.resume()
}
```

This works exactly like the other request methods in the project, decoding the response body into [Category].

Open **AcronymDetailTableViewController.swift** and add the following implementation to getAcronymData():

```
// 1
guard let id = acronym?.id else {
  return
}

// 2
let acronymDetailRequester = AcronymRequest(acronymID: id)
// 3
acronymDetailRequester.getUser { [weak self] result in
  switch result {
  case .success(let user):
    self?.user = user
  case .failure:
    let message =
      "There was an error getting the acronym's user"
    ErrorPresenter.showError(message: message, on: self)
  }
}

// 4
acronymDetailRequester.getCategories { [weak self] result in
  switch result {
  case .success(let categories):
    self?.categories = categories
  case .failure:
    let message =
      "There was an error getting the acronym's categories"
    ErrorPresenter.showError(message: message, on: self)
  }
}
```

Here's the play by play:

1. Ensure the acronym has a non-nil ID.

2. Create an `AcronymRequest` to gather information.

3. Get the acronym's user. If the request succeeds, update the `user` property. Otherwise, display an appropriate error message.

4. Get the acronym's categories. If the request succeeds, update the `categories` property. Otherwise, display an appropriate error message.

The project displays acronym data in a table view with four sections. These are:

- the acronym

- its meaning

- its user

- its categories

Build and run. Tap an acronym in the Acronyms table and the application will show the detail view with all the information:

Editing acronyms

To edit an acronym, users tap the **Edit** button in the Acronym detail view. Open **CreateAcronymTableViewController.swift**. The `acronym` property exists to store the current acronym. If this property is set — by `prepare(for:sender:)` in **AcronymDetailTableViewController.swift** — then the user is editing the acronym. Otherwise, a new acronym is being created.

In `viewDidLoad()`, replace `populateUsers()` with:

```
if let acronym = acronym {
  acronymShortTextField.text = acronym.short
  acronymLongTextField.text = acronym.long
  userLabel.text = selectedUser?.name
  navigationItem.title = "Edit Acronym"
} else {
  populateUsers()
}
```

If the acronym is set, you're in edit mode. Populate the display fields with the correct values and update the view's title. If you're in create mode, call `populateUsers()` as before.

To update an acronym, you make a PUT request to the acronym's resource in the API. Open **AcronymRequest.swift** and add a method at the bottom of `AcronymRequest` to update an acronym:

```
func update(with updateData: Acronym,
            completion:
              @escaping (SaveResult<Acronym>) -> Void) {
  do {
    // 1
    var urlRequest = URLRequest(url: resource)
    urlRequest.httpMethod = "PUT"
    urlRequest.httpBody = try JSONEncoder().encode(updateData)
    urlRequest.addValue("application/json",
                        forHTTPHeaderField: "Content-Type")
    let dataTask = URLSession.shared
                              .dataTask(with: urlRequest) {
      data, response, _ in
      // 2
      guard
        let httpResponse = response as? HTTPURLResponse,
        httpResponse.statusCode == 200,
        let jsonData = data else {
          completion(.failure)
          return
      }
      do {
        // 3
        let acronym = try JSONDecoder().decode(Acronym.self,
                                               from: jsonData)
        completion(.success(acronym))
      } catch {
        completion(.failure)
      }
    }
    dataTask.resume()
  } catch {
```

```
      completion(.failure)
    }
  }
```

This method works like other requests you have built. The differences are:

1. Create and configure a `URLRequest`. The method must be **PUT** and the body contains the encoded `Acronym` data. Set the correct header so the Vapor application knows the request contains JSON.

2. Ensure the response is an HTTP response, the status code is 200 and the response has a body.

3. Decode the response body into an `Acronym` and call the completion handler with a success result.

Return to **CreateAcronymTableViewController.swift**. Inside `save(_:)` after `let acronym = Acronym(short: shortText, long: longText, userID: userID)`, replace the rest of the function with the following:

```
if self.acronym != nil {
  // update code goes here
} else {
  ResourceRequest<Acronym>(resourcePath: "acronyms")
    .save(acronym) { [weak self] result in
    switch result {
    case .failure:
      let message = "There was a problem saving the acronym"
      ErrorPresenter.showError(message: message, on: self)
    case .success:
      DispatchQueue.main.async { [weak self] in
        self?.navigationController?
            .popViewController(animated: true)
      }
    }
  }
}
```

This checks the class's `acronym` property to see if it has been set. If the property is `nil`, then the user is saving a new acronym so the function performs the same save request as before.

Inside the `if` block after `// update code goes here`, add the following code to update an acronym:

```
// 1
guard let existingID = self.acronym?.id else {
  let message = "There was an error updating the acronym"
  ErrorPresenter.showError(message: message, on: self)
```

```
    return
}
// 2
AcronymRequest(acronymID: existingID)
  .update(with: acronym) { result in
  switch result {
  // 3
  case .failure:
    let message = "There was a problem saving the acronym"
    ErrorPresenter.showError(message: message, on: self)
  case .success(let updatedAcronym):
    self.acronym = updatedAcronym
    DispatchQueue.main.async { [weak self] in
      // 4
      self?.performSegue(withIdentifier: "UpdateAcronymDetails",
                         sender: nil)
    }
  }
}
```

Here's what the update code does:

1. Ensure the acronym has a valid ID.

2. Create an `AcronymRequest` and call `update(with:completion:)`.

3. If the update fails, display an error message.

4. If the update succeeds, store the updated acronym and trigger an unwind segue to the `AcronymsDetailTableViewController`.

Next, open **AcronymsDetailTableViewController.swift** and add the following implementation to `prepare(for:sender:)`:

```
if segue.identifier == "EditAcronymSegue" {
  // 1.
  guard
    let destination = segue.destination
      as? CreateAcronymTableViewController else {
    return
  }

  // 2.
  destination.selectedUser = user
  destination.acronym = acronym
}
```

Here's what this does:

1. Ensure the destination is a `CreateAcronymTableViewController`.

2. Set the `selectedUser` and `acronym` properties on the destination.

Next, add the following implementation to the unwind segue's target,
updateAcronymDetails(_:):

```
guard let controller = segue.source
  as? CreateAcronymTableViewController else {
  return
}

user = controller.selectedUser
acronym = controller.acronym
```

This captures the updated acronym and user, triggering an update to its own view.

Build and run. Tap an acronym to open the acronym detail view and tap **Edit**. Change
the details and tap **Save**. The view will return to the acronyms details page with the
updated values:

Deleting acronyms

Open **AcronymRequest.swift** and add a method to delete an acronym and the end:

```
func delete() {
  // 1
  var urlRequest = URLRequest(url: resource)
  urlRequest.httpMethod = "DELETE"
  // 2
  let dataTask = URLSession.shared.dataTask(with: urlRequest)
  dataTask.resume()
}
```

Here's what `delete()` does:

1. Create a `URLRequest` and set the HTTP method to **DELETE**.

2. Create a data task for the request using the shared `URLSession` and send the request. This ignores the result of the request.

Open **AcronymsTableViewController.swift**. To enable deletion of a table row, add the following after `tableView(_:cellForRowAt:)`:

```
override func tableView(
  _ tableView: UITableView,
  commit editingStyle: UITableViewCellEditingStyle,
  forRowAt indexPath: IndexPath) {
  if let id = acronyms[indexPath.row].id {
    // 1
    let acronymDetailRequester = AcronymRequest(acronymID: id)
    acronymDetailRequester.delete()
  }

  // 2
  acronyms.remove(at: indexPath.row)
  // 3
  tableView.deleteRows(at: [indexPath], with: .automatic)
}
```

This enables "swipe-to-delete" functionality on the table view. Here's how it works:

1. If the acronym has a valid ID, create an `AcronymRequest` for the acronym and call `delete()` to delete the acronym in the API.

2. Remove the acronym from the local array of acronyms.

3. Remove the acronym's row from the table view.

Build and run. Swipe left on an acronym and the **Delete** button will appear. Tap **Delete** to remove the acronym.

If you pull-to-refresh the table view, the acronym doesn't reappear as the application has deleted it in the API:

Creating categories

Setting up the create category table is like setting up the create users table. Open **CreateCategoryTableViewController.swift** and replace the implementation of save(_:) with:

```
// 1
guard
    let name = nameTextField.text,
    !name.isEmpty else {
        ErrorPresenter
            .showError(message: "You must specify a name",
                       on: self)
        return
}

// 2
let category = Category(name: name)
```

```
// 3
ResourceRequest<Category>(resourcePath: "categories")
  .save(category) { [weak self] result in
  switch result {
  // 5
  case .failure:
    let message = "There was a problem saving the category"
    ErrorPresenter.showError(message: message, on: self)
  // 6
  case .success:
    DispatchQueue.main.async { [weak self] in
      self?.navigationController?
          .popViewController(animated: true)
    }
  }
}
```

This is just like the save(_:) method for saving a user. Build and run. On the Categories tab, tap the + button to open the **Create Category** screen. Fill in a name and tap **Save**. If the save is successful, the screen will close and the new category will appear in the table:

Adding acronyms to categories

The finish up, you must implement the ability to add acronyms to categories. Add a new table row section to the acronym detail view that contains a button to add the acronym to a category.

Open **AcronymsDetailTableViewController.swift**. Change the `return` statement in `numberOfSections(in:)` to:

```
return 5
```

In `tableView(_:cellForRowAt:)`, add a new case to the `switch` before `default`:

```
// 1
case 4:
   cell.textLabel?.text = "Add To Category"
```

Next, add the following just before `return cell`:

```
// 2
if indexPath.section == 4 {
   cell.selectionStyle = .default
   cell.isUserInteractionEnabled = true
} else {
   cell.selectionStyle = .none
   cell.isUserInteractionEnabled = false
}
```

1. Set the table cell title to "Add To Category" if the cell is in the new section.

2. If the cell is in the new section, enable selection on the cell, otherwise disable selection. This allows a user to select the new row but no others.

The starter project already contains the view controller for this new table view: **AddToCategoryTableViewController.swift**. The class defines three key properties:

- `categories`: an array for all the categories retrieved from the API.

- `selectedCategories`: the categories selected for the acronym.

- `acronym`: the acronym to add to categories.

The class also contains an extension for the `UITableViewDataSource` methods. `tableView(_:cellForRowAt:)` sets the `accessoryType` on the cell if the category is in the `selectedCategories` array.

Open, **AddToCategoryTableViewController.swift** and add the following
implementation to `loadData()` to get all the categories from the API:

```
// 1
let categoriesRequest =
  ResourceRequest<Category>(resourcePath: "categories")
// 2
categoriesRequest.getAll { [weak self] result in
  switch result {
  // 3
  case .failure:
    let message =
      "There was an error getting the categories"
    ErrorPresenter.showError(message: message, on: self)
  // 4
  case .success(let categories):
    self?.categories = categories
    DispatchQueue.main.async { [weak self] in
      self?.tableView.reloadData()
    }
  }
}
```

Here's what this does:

1. Create a `ResourceRequest` for categories.

2. Get all the categories from the API.

3. If the fetch fails, show an error message.

4. If the fetch succeeds, populate the categories array and reload the table data.

Open **AcronymRequest.swift** and add a new enum under
`AcronymUserRequestResult` to represent the result of adding an acronym to a
category:

```
enum CategoryAddResult {
  case success
  case failure
}
```

This just defines success and failure cases. Next, add the following method at the bottom
of `AcronymRequest`:

```
func add(category: Category,
         completion: @escaping (CategoryAddResult) -> Void) {
  // 1
  guard let categoryID = category.id else {
    completion(.failure)
    return
```

```
  }
  // 2
  let url = resource.appendingPathComponent("categories")
                    .appendingPathComponent("\(categoryID)")
  // 3
  var urlRequest = URLRequest(url: url)
  urlRequest.httpMethod = "POST"
  // 4
  let dataTask = URLSession.shared
                        .dataTask(with: urlRequest) {
    _, response, _ in
    // 5
    guard let httpResponse = response as? HTTPURLResponse,
      httpResponse.statusCode == 201 else {
        completion(.failure)
        return
    }
    // 6
    completion(.success)
  }
  dataTask.resume()
}
```

Here's what this does:

1. Ensure the category has a valid ID, otherwise call the completion handler with a failure case.

2. Build the URL for the request.

3. Create a URLRequest and set the HTTP method to **POST**.

4. Create a data task from the shared URLSession.

5. Ensure the response is an HTTP response and the response status is 201 Created. Otherwise, call the completion handler with a failure case.

6. Call the completion handler with the success case.

Open **AddToCategoryTableViewController.swift** and add the following extension at the end of the file:

```
// MARK: - UITableViewDelegate
extension AddToCategoryTableViewController {
  override func tableView(_ tableView: UITableView,
                    didSelectRowAt indexPath: IndexPath) {
    // 1
    let category = categories[indexPath.row]
    // 2
    guard let acronymID = acronym.id else {
      let message = """
        There was an error adding the acronym
```

```
        to the category — the acronym has no ID
      """
    ErrorPresenter.showError(message: message, on: self)
    return
  }
  // 3
  let acronymRequest = AcronymRequest(acronymID: acronymID)
  acronymRequest.add(category: category) {
    [weak self] result in

    switch result {
    // 4
    case .success:
      DispatchQueue.main.async { [weak self] in
        self?.navigationController?
            .popViewController(animated: true)
      }
    // 5
    case .failure:
      let message = """
        There was an error adding the acronym
        to the category
      """
      ErrorPresenter.showError(message: message, on: self)
    }
  }
 }
}
```

Here's what this function does:

1. Get the category the user has selected.

2. Ensure the acronym has a valid ID; otherwise, show an error message.

3. Create an `AcronymRequest` to add the acronym to the category.

4. If the request succeeds, return to the previous view.

5. If the request fails, show an error message.

Finally, open **AcronymDetailTableViewController.swift** to set up
`AddToCategoryTableViewController`. At the end of `prepare(for:sender:)`, add a
new segue identifier case:

```
else if segue.identifier == "AddToCategorySegue" {
  // 1
  guard let destination = segue.destination
    as? AddToCategoryTableViewController else {
    return
  }
  // 2
```

```
    destination.acronym = acronym
    destination.selectedCategories = categories
}
```

Here's what this does:

1. Ensure the destination is an `AddToCategoryTableViewController`.

2. Set the `acronym` and `selectedCategories` properties on the destination.

Build and run. Tap an acronym and, in the detail view, a new row labeled **Add To Category** now appears. Tap this cell and the categories list appears with already selected categories marked.

Select a new category and the view closes. The acronym detail view will now have the new category in its list:

Where to go from here?

This chapter has shown you how to build an iOS application that interacts with the Vapor API. The application isn't fully-featured, however, and you could improve it. For example, you could add a category information view that displays all the acronyms for a particular category.

The next section of the book shows you how to build another client: The website.

Section II: Making a Simple Web App

This section teaches you how to build a front-end web site for your Vapor application. You'll learn to use Leaf, Vapor's templating engine, to generate dynamic web pages to display your app's data. You'll also learn how to accept data from a browser so that users can create and edit your models.

Specifically, you'll learn:

- **Chapter 14: Templating with Leaf:** In this chapter, you'll learn how to use **Leaf** Vapor's templating language to make simple and dynamic websites using Vapor. **Leaf** allows you to pass information to a webpage so it can generate the final HTML without knowing everything up front.

- **Chapter 15: Beautifying Pages:** In this chapter, you'll learn how to use the Bootstrap framework to add styling to your pages. You'll also learn how to embed templates so you only have to make changes in one place. Next, you'll also see how to serve files with Vapor.

- **Chapter 16: Making a Simple Web App, Part I:** In this chapter, you'll learn how to create different models and how to edit acronyms.

- **Chapter 17: Making a Simple Web App, Part II:** In this chapter, you'll learn how to allow users to add categories to acronyms in a user-friendly way. Finally, you'll deploy your completed web application to Vapor Cloud.

These chapters will provide you the necessary building blocks to build a full website with Vapor.

Chapter 14: Templating with Leaf

By Tim Condon

In a previous section of the book, you learned how to create an API using Vapor and Fluent. This section explains how to use Leaf to create dynamic websites in Vapor applications. Just like the previous section, you'll deploy the website to Vapor Cloud.

Leaf

Leaf is Vapor's **templating language**. A templating language allows you to pass information to a page so that it can generate the final HTML without knowing everything up front. For example, in the TIL application, you don't know every acronym that users will create when you deploy your application. Templating allows you handle this with ease.

Templating languages also allow you to reduce duplication in your webpages. Instead of multiple pages for acronyms, you create a single template and set the properties specific to displaying a particular acronym. If you decide to change the way you display an acronym, you only need change your code in one place and all acronym pages will show the new format.

Finally, templating languages allow you to embed templates into other templates. For example, if you have navigation on your website, you can create a single template that generates the code for your navigation. You embed the navigation template in all templates that need navigation rather than duplicating code.

Configuring Leaf

To use Leaf, you need to add it to your project as a dependency. Using the TIL application from Chapter 10, "Sibling Relationships", open **Package.swift**. Replace its contents with the following:

```swift
// swift-tools-version:4.0
import PackageDescription

let package = Package(
  name: "TILApp",
  dependencies: [
    .package(url: "https://github.com/vapor/vapor.git",
             from: "3.0.0"),
    .package(
      url: "https://github.com/vapor/fluent-postgresql.git",
      from: "1.0.0-rc"),
    .package(url: "https://github.com/vapor/leaf.git",
             from: "3.0.0-rc")
  ],
  targets: [
    .target(name: "App",
            dependencies: ["FluentPostgreSQL",
                           "Vapor",
                           "Leaf"]),
    .target(name: "Run", dependencies: ["App"]),
    .testTarget(name: "AppTests", dependencies: ["App"]),
  ]
)
```

The changes made were:

• Make the TILApp package depend upon the Leaf package.

• Make the App target depend upon the Leaf target to ensure it links properly.

By default, Leaf expects templates to be in the **Resources/Views** directory. In Terminal, type the following to create these directories:

```
mkdir -p Resources/Views
```

Finally, you must create new routes for the website. Create a new controller to contain these routes. In Terminal, type the following:

```
touch Sources/App/Controllers/WebsiteController.swift
```

With everything configured, regenerate the Xcode project to start using Leaf. In Terminal, type the following:

```
vapor xcode -y
```

Rendering a page

Open **WebsiteController.swift** and create a new type to hold all the website routes and a route that returns an index template:

```swift
import Vapor
import Leaf

// 1
struct WebsiteController: RouteCollection {
  // 2
  func boot(router: Router) throws {
    // 3
    router.get(use: indexHandler)
  }

  // 4
  func indexHandler(_ req: Request) throws -> Future<View> {
    // 5
    return try req.view().render("index")
  }
}
```

Here's what this does:

1. Declare a new `WebsiteController` type that conforms to `RouteCollection`.

2. Implement `boot(router:)` as required by `RouteCollection`.

3. Register `indexHandler(_:)` to process GET requests to the router's root path, i.e., a request to `/`.

4. Implement `indexHandler(_:)` that returns `Future<View>`.

5. Render the **index** template and return the result. You'll learn about `req.view()` in a moment.

Leaf generates a page from a template called **index.leaf** inside the **Resources/Views** directory.

Note that the file extension's not required by the render(_:) call. Create this file and insert the following:

```
<!DOCTYPE html>
#// 1
<html lang="en">
<head>
  <meta charset="utf-8" />
  #// 2
  <title>Hello World</title>
</head>
<body>
  #// 3
  <h1>Hello World</h1>
</body>
</html>
```

Here's what this file does:

1. Declare a basic HTML 5 page with a <head> and <body>.

2. Set the page title to **Hello World** — this is the title displayed in a browser's tab.

3. Set the body to be a single <h1> title that says **Hello World**.

> **Note**: You can create your **.leaf** files using any text editor you choose, including Xcode. If you use Xcode, choose **Editor\Syntax Coloring\HTML** in order to get proper highlighting of elements and indentation support.

You must register your new WebsiteController. Open **routes.swift** and add the following to the end of routes(_:):

```
let websiteController = WebsiteController()
try router.register(collection: websiteController)
```

Next, you must register the Leaf service. Open **configure.swift** and add the following to the imports section below import Vapor:

```
import Leaf
```

Next, after try services.register(FluentPostgreSQLProvider()), add the following:

```
try services.register(LeafProvider())
```

Using the generic `req.view()` to obtain a renderer allows you to switch to different templating engines easily. While this may not be useful when running your application, it's extremely useful for testing. For example, it allows you to use a test renderer to produce plain text to verify against, rather than parsing HTML output in your test cases.

`req.view()` asks Vapor to provide a type that conforms to `ViewRenderer`. TemplateKit — the module that Leaf is built upon — provides `PlaintextRenderer` and Leaf provides `LeafRenderer`. In **configure.swift** add the following to the end of `configure(_:_:_:)`:

```
config.prefer(LeafRenderer.self, for: ViewRenderer.self)
```

This tells Vapor to use `LeafRenderer` when asked for a `ViewRenderer` type.

Build and run, then open your browser. Enter the URL **http://localhost:8080** and you'll receive the page generated from the template:

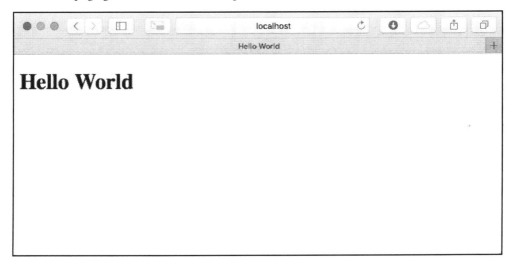

Injecting variables

The template is currently just a static page and not at all impressive! Make the page more dynamic, open **index.leaf** and change the `<title>` line to the following:

```
<title>#(title) | Acronyms</title>
```

This extracts a parameter called `title` using the `#()` Leaf function. Like a lot of Vapor, Leaf uses `Codable` to handle data.

At the bottom of **WebsiteController.swift**, add the following, to create a new type to contain the title:

```
struct IndexContext: Encodable {
  let title: String
}
```

As data only flows to Leaf, you only need to conform to `Encodable`. `IndexContext` is the data for your view, similar to a view model in the MVVM design pattern. Next, change the `indexHandler(_:)` to pass an `IndexContext` to the template. Replace the implementation with the following:

```
func indexHandler(_ req: Request) throws -> Future<View> {
  // 1
  let context = IndexContext(title: "Homepage")
  // 2
  return try req.view().render("index", context)
}
```

Here's what the new code does:

1. Create an `IndexContext` containing the desired title.

2. Pass the `context` to Leaf as the second parameter to `render(_:_:)`.

Build and run, then refresh the page in the browser. You'll see the updated title:

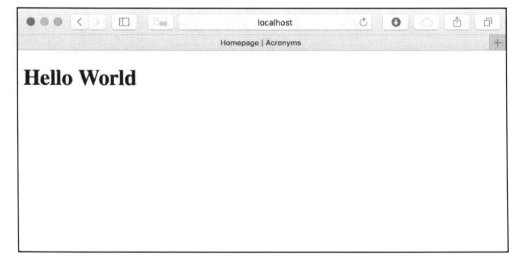

Using tags

The homepage of the TIL website should display a list of all the acronyms. Still in **WebsiteController.swift** , add a new property to IndexContext underneath title:

```
let acronyms: [Acronym]?
```

This is an optional array of acronyms; it can be nil as there may be no acronyms in the database.

Next, change indexHandler(_:) to get all the acronyms and insert them in the IndexContext.

Replace the implementation once more with the following:

```
func indexHandler(_ req: Request) throws -> Future<View> {
  // 1
  return Acronym.query(on: req)
    .all()
    .flatMap(to: View.self) { acronyms in
      // 2
      let acronymsData = acronyms.isEmpty ? nil : acronyms
      let context = IndexContext(
        title: "Homepage",
        acronyms: acronymsData)
      return try req.view().render("index", context)
  }
}
```

Here's what this does:

1. Use a Fluent query to get all the acronyms from the database.

2. Add the acronyms to IndexContext if there are any, otherwise set the variable to nil. This is easier for Leaf to manage than an empty array.

Finally open **index.leaf** and change the parts between the <body> tags to the following:

```
#// 1
<h1>Acronyms</h1>

#// 2
#if(acronyms) {
  #// 3
  <table>
    <thead>
      <tr>
        <th>Short</th>
        <th>Long</th>
```

```
      </tr>
    </thead>
    <tbody>
      #// 4
      #for(acronym in acronyms) {
        <tr>
          #// 5
          <td>#(acronym.short)</td>
          <td>#(acronym.long)</td>
        </tr>
      }
    </tbody>
  </table>
#// 6
} else {
  <h2>There aren't any acronyms yet!</h2>
}
```

Here's what the new code does:

1. Declare a new heading, "Acronyms".

2. Use Leaf's `#if()` tag to see if the `acronyms` variable is set. `#if()` can validate variables for nullability, work on booleans or even evaluate expressions.

3. If `acronyms` is set, create an HTML table. The table has a header row — `<thead>` — with two columns, **Short** and **Long**.

4. Use Leaf's `#for()` tag to loop through all the acronyms. This works in a similar way to Swift's `for` loop.

5. Create a row for each acronym. Use Leaf's `#()` function to extract the variable. Since everything is `Encodable`, you can use dot notation to access properties on acronyms, just like Swift!

6. If there are no acronyms, print a suitable message.

Build and run, then refresh the page in the browser.

If you have no acronyms in the database, you'll see the correct message:

If there are acronyms in the database, you'll see them in the table:

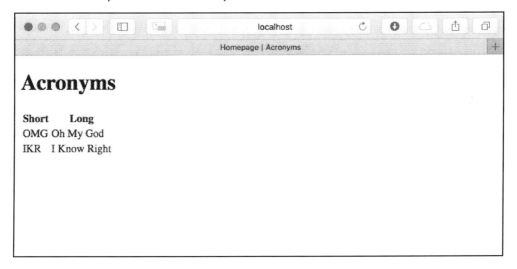

Acronym detail page

Now, you need a page to show the details for each acronym. At the end of **WebsiteController.swift**, create a new type to hold the context for this page:

```
struct AcronymContext: Encodable {
    let title: String
```

```
    let acronym: Acronym
    let user: User
}
```

This `AcronymContext` contains a title for the page, the acronym itself and the user who created the acronym. Create the following route handler for the acronym detail page under `indexHandler(_:)`:

```
// 1
func acronymHandler(_ req: Request) throws -> Future<View> {
  // 2
  return try req.parameters.next(Acronym.self)
    .flatMap(to: View.self) { acronym in
      // 3
      return acronym.user
        .get(on: req)
        .flatMap(to: View.self) { user in
          // 4
          let context = AcronymContext(
            title: acronym.short,
            acronym: acronym,
            user: user)
          return try req.view().render("acronym", context)
      }
  }
}
```

Here's what this route handler does:

1. Declare a new route handler, `acronymHandler(_:)`, that returns `Future<View>`.

2. Extract the acronym from the request's parameters and unwrap the result.

3. Get the user for acronym and unwrap the result.

4. Create an `AcronymContext` that contains the appropriate details and render the page using the **acronym.leaf** template.

Finally register the route at the bottom of `boot(router:)`:

```
router.get("acronyms", Acronym.parameter, use: acronymHandler)
```

This registers the `acronymHandler` route for **/acronyms/<ACRONYM ID>**, similar to the API. Create the **acronym.leaf** template inside the **Resources/Views** directory and open the new file and add the following:

```
<!DOCTYPE html>
#// 1
<html lang="en">
<head>
```

```
    <meta charset="utf-8" />
    #// 2
    <title>#(title) | Acronyms</title>
</head>
<body>
    #// 3
    <h1>#(acronym.short)</h1>
    #// 4
    <h2>#(acronym.long)</h2>

    #// 5
    <p>Created by #(user.name)</p>
</body>
</html>
```

Here's what this template does:

1. Declare an HTML5 page like **index.leaf**.

2. Set the title to the value that's passed in.

3. Print the acronym's short property in an <h1> heading.

4. Print the acronym's long property in an <h2> heading.

5. Print the acronym's user in a <p> block

Finally, change **index.leaf** so you can navigate to the page. Replace the first column in the table for each acronym (<td>#(acronym.short)</td>) with:

```
<td><a href="/acronyms/#(acronym.id)">#(acronym.short)</a></td>
```

This wraps the acronym's short property in an HTML <a> tag, which is a link. The link sets the URL for each acronym to the route registered above. Build and run, then refresh the page in the browser:

You'll see that each acronym's short form is now a link. Click the link and the browser navigates to the acronym's page:

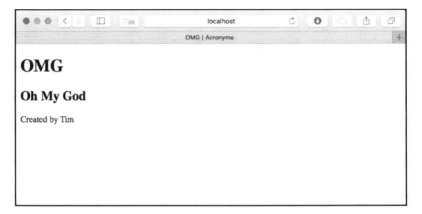

Deploying to Vapor Cloud

> **Note**: This section requires that you have followed through Chapter 5, "Fluent and Persisting Models" to set up Vapor Cloud. It also requires that you have configured a PostgreSQL database as shown in Chapter 6, "Configuring a Database."

Since this section doesn't change any model structures, deploying the new code from this chapter to Vapor Cloud is simple.

You must commit your new code first, however. In Terminal, type:

```
# 1
git add .
# 2
git commit -m "Add basic website"
# 3
git push
```

```
                         TILApp — -bash — 100×17
Tims-MBP:TILApp timc$ git add .
Tims-MBP:TILApp timc$ git commit -m "Add basic website"
[master c5ceb55] Add basic website
 7 files changed, 141 insertions(+), 27 deletions(-)
 create mode 100644 Resources/Views/acronym.leaf
 create mode 100644 Resources/Views/index.leaf
 create mode 100644 Sources/App/Controllers/WebsiteController.swift
Tims-MBP:TILApp timc$ git push
Counting objects: 14, done.
Delta compression using up to 4 threads.
Compressing objects: 100% (13/13), done.
Writing objects: 100% (14/14), 2.35 KiB | 1.17 MiB/s, done.
Total 14 (delta 7), reused 0 (delta 0)
remote: Resolving deltas: 100% (7/7), completed with 6 local objects.
To github.com:raywenderlich/vapor-til.git
   b1d37af..c5ceb55  master -> master
Tims-MBP:TILApp timc$
```

Here's what these commands do:

1. Tell Git to track your new files and add any changes to the Git staging area.

2. Commit your changes with the message "Add basic website".

3. Push your local commits to the remote repository on GitHub.

Now that you have committed and pushed, deploy your updated application. In Terminal, run:

```
vapor cloud deploy --env=production --build=update -y
```

This command deploys the application to Vapor Cloud with the following options:

• Deploy the application to the **production** environment.

• Use the **update** build type since you have included Leaf as a new package.

• Automatically deploy without waiting at the confirmation screen.

```
                         TILApp — -bash — 100×28
Tims-MBP:TILApp timc$ vapor cloud deploy --env=production --build=update -y
app: TIL
git: git@github.com:raywenderlich/vapor-til.git
env: production
db: yes
replicas: 1
replica size: free
branch: master
build: update
Creating deployment [Done]
Connecting to build logs ...
Waiting in Queue [Done]
Starting deployment: 'rw-til' [Done]
Getting project from Git 'git@github.com:raywenderlich/vapor-til.git' [Done]
Checkout branch 'master' [Done]
Verifying base folder [Done]
Selected swift version: 4.1.0-beta [Done]
Running swift package update [Done]
Building vapor (release) [Done]
Trying to find executable [Done]
Found executable: Run [Done]
Creating container registry [Done]
Building container [Done]
Pushing container to registry [Done]
Updating replicas [Done]
Deployment succeeded: https://rw-til.vapor.cloud [Done]
Successfully deployed.
Tims-MBP:TILApp timc$
```

When this has finished, open your browser and enter the URL **https://<YOUR_URL>/**. You'll see the homepage of the application with acronyms created from previous chapters:

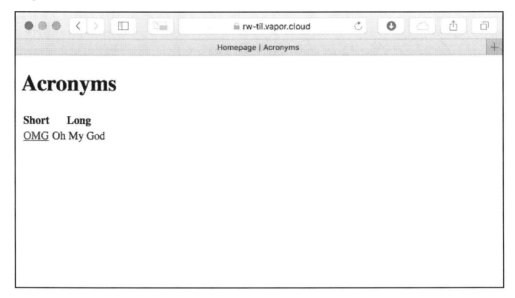

Where to go from here?

This chapter introduced Leaf and showed you how to start building a dynamic website. The next chapters in this section show you how to embed templates into other templates, beautify your application and create acronyms from the website.

Chapter 15: Beautifying Pages

By Tim Condon

In the previous chapter, you started building a powerful, dynamic website with Leaf. The web pages, however, only use simple HTML and aren't styled — they don't look great!

In this chapter, you'll learn how to use the Bootstrap framework to add styling to your pages. You'll also learn how to embed templates so you only have to make changes in one place. Next, you'll also see how to serve files with Vapor. Finally, like every chapter in this section, you'll deploy the new website to Vapor Cloud.

Embedding templates

Currently, if you change the index page template to add styling, you'll affect only that page. You'd have to duplicate the styling in the acronym detail page, and any other future pages.

Leaf allows you to embed templates into other templates. This enables you to create a "base" template that contains the code common to all pages and use that across your site.

In **Resources/Views** create a new file, **base.leaf**. Copy the contents of **index.leaf** into **base.leaf**. Remove everything between the <body> and </body> tags. This remaining code looks similar to the following:

```
<!DOCTYPE html>
<html lang="en">
<head>
  <meta charset="utf-8" />
  <title>#(title) | Acronyms</title>
</head>
<body>
```

```
        </body>
        </html>
```

This forms your base template and will be the same for all pages. Between the `<body>` and `</body>` tags add:

```
    #get(content)
```

This uses Leaf's `#get()` tag to retrieve the `content` variable. To create this variable, open **index.leaf** replace its contents with:

```
#set("content") {
  <h1>Acronyms</h1>

  #if(acronyms) {
    <table>
      <thead>
        <tr>
          <th>
            Short
          </th>
          <th>
            Long
          </th>
        </tr>
      </thead>
      <tbody>
        #for(acronym in acronyms) {
          <tr>
            <td>
              <a href="/acronyms/#(acronym.id)">
                #(acronym.short)
              </a>
            </td>
            <td>#(acronym.long)</td>
          </tr>
        }
      </tbody>
    </table>
  } else {
    <h2>There aren't any acronyms yet!</h2>
  }
}
```

The changes made were:

• Remove the HTML that now lives in **base.leaf**.

- Wrap the remaining HTML with Leaf's `#set()` tag and call the created variable `content`. You **must** wrap the variable name in `#set()` with quotations for Leaf to register it.

Finally at the bottom of the **index.leaf** add:

```
#embed("base")
```

This embeds the **base.leaf** template into the page and renders it. The **base.leaf** template uses `#get()` to get the content that's set above. Save the files, then build and run. Open your browser and enter the URL **http://localhost:8080/**. The page renders as before:

Next, open **acronym.leaf** and change it to use the base template by replacing its contents with the following:

```
#set("content") {
  <h1>#(acronym.short)</h1>
  <h2>#(acronym.long)</h2>

  <p>Created by #(user.name)</p>
}

#embed("base")
```

Again, the changes made were:

- Remove all the HTML that now lives in the base template.

- Store the remaining HTML in the `content` variable, using Leaf's `#set()` tag.

- Embed the base template to bring in the common code and render `content`.

Save the file and, in your browser, navigate to an acronym page. The page renders as before with the new base template:

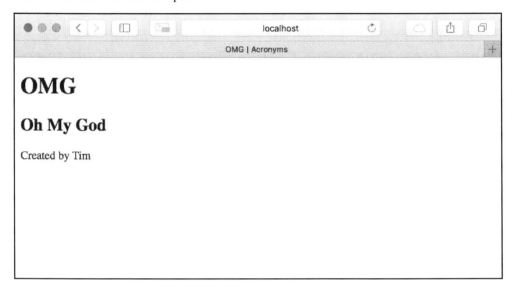

> **Note**: In debug mode, you can refresh pages to pick up Leaf changes. In release mode, Leaf caches the pages for performance so you must restart your application to see changes.

Bootstrap

Bootstrap is an open-source, front-end framework for websites, originally built by Twitter. It provides easy-to-use components that you add to webpages. It's a mobile-first library and makes it simple to build a site that works on screens of all sizes.

To use Bootstrap go to getbootstrap.com and click **Get Started**. Bootstrap provides a CSS file to provide the styling and Javascript files that provide functionality for Bootstrap components. You need to include these files need to in all pages. Since you've created a **base.leaf** template, this is easy to do!

On the **Get Started** page, find the **Starter template** section.

In the starter template's `<head>` section, copy the two `<meta>` tags — labeled "Required meta tags" — and the `<link>` tag for the CSS — labeled "Bootstrap CSS." Replace the current `<meta>` tag in **base.leaf** with the new tags.

At the bottom of the starter template, copy the three `<script>` tags. Put them in the **base.leaf** template, under `#get(content)` and before the `</body>` tag.

Save the file then, in your browser, visit **http://localhost:8080**. You'll notice the page looks a bit different. The page is now using Bootstrap's styling, but you need to add Bootstrap-specific components to make your page really shine.

Open **base.leaf** and replace `#get(content)` with the following:

```
<div class="container mt-3">
  #get(content)
</div>
```

This wraps the page's content in a **container**, which is a basic layout element in Bootstrap. The `<div>` also applies a margin at the top of the container. If you save the file and refresh your webpage, you'll see the page now has some space around the sides and top, and no longer looks cramped:

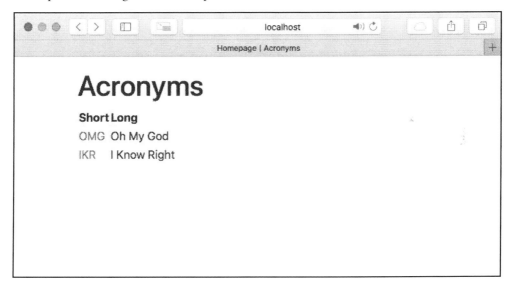

Navigation

The TIL website currently consists of two pages: a home page and an acronym detail page. As more and more pages are added, it can become difficult to find your way around the site. Currently, if you go to an acronym's detail page, there is no easy way to get back to the home page! Adding navigation to a website makes the site more friendly for users.

HTML defines a `<nav>` element to denote the navigation section of a page. Bootstrap supplies classes and utilities to extend this for styling and mobile support. Open **base.leaf** and add the following above `<div class="container mt-3">`:

```
#// 1
<nav class="navbar navbar-expand-md navbar-dark bg-dark">
  #// 2
  <a class="navbar-brand" href="/">TIL</a>
  #// 3
  <button class="navbar-toggler" type="button"
    data-toggle="collapse" data-target="#navbarSupportedContent"
    aria-controls="navbarSupportedContent" aria-expanded="false"
    aria-label="Toggle navigation">
    <span class="navbar-toggler-icon"></span>
  </button>
  #// 4
  <div class="collapse navbar-collapse"
    id="navbarSupportedContent">
    #// 5
    <ul class="navbar-nav mr-auto">
      #// 6
      <li class="nav-item #if(title == "Homepage"){active}">
        <a href="/" class="nav-link">Home</a>
      </li>
    </ul>
  </div>
</nav>
```

Here's what this new code does:

1. Define a `<nav>` element with some class names for styling. Bootstrap uses these classes to specify a Bootstrap navigation bar, allow the navigation bar to be full size in medium-sized screens, and apply a dark theme to the bar.

2. Specify a root link to the homepage.

3. Create a button that toggles the navigation bar for small screen sizes. This shows and hides the `navbarSupportedContent` section defined in the next element.

4. Create a collapsable section for small screens.

5. Define a list of navigation links to display. Bootstrap styles these `nav-item` list items for a navigation bar instead of a standard bulleted list.

6. Add a link for the homepage. This uses Leaf's `#if` tag to check the page title. If the title is set to "Homepage" then Leaf adds the `active` class to the item. This styles the link differently when on that page.

Save the file and refresh the page in the browser. The page is starting to look professional! For small screens you'll get a toggle button, which opens the navigation links:

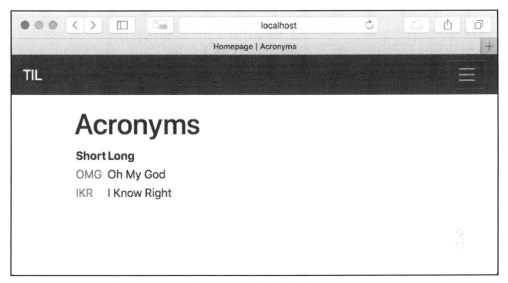

On larger screens, the navigation bar shows all the links:

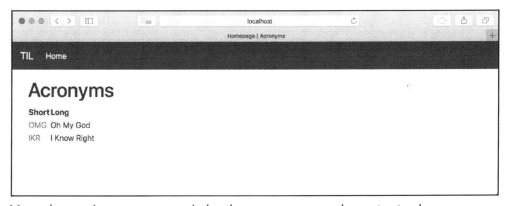

Now when you're on an acronym's detail page, you can use the navigation bar to return to the home screen!

Tables

Bootstrap provides classes to style tables with ease. Open **index.leaf** and replace the `<table>` tag with the following:

```
<table class="table table-bordered table-hover">
```

This adds the following Bootstrap classes to the table:

- `table`: apply standard Bootstrap table styling.
- `table-bordered`: add a border to the table and table cells.
- `table-hover`: enable a hover style on table rows so users can more easily see what row they are looking at.

Next, replace the `<thead>` tag with the following:

```
<thead class="thead-light">
```

This makes the table head stand out. Save the file and refresh the page. The home page now looks even more professional!

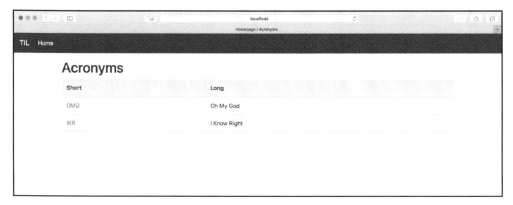

Serving files

Almost every website needs to be able to host static files, such as images or stylesheets. Most of the time, you'll do this using a CDN or a server such as Nginx or Apache. However, Vapor provides a `FileMiddleware` to serve files.

To enable this, open **configure.swift** in Xcode. Find the section that begins `// Register middleware` and there should be a commented-out line for the `FileMiddleware`. Uncomment this line to enable the middleware:

```
middlewares.use(FileMiddleware.self)
```

This adds the `FileMiddleware` to the `MiddlewareConfig` to serve files. By default, this serves files in the **Public** directory in your project. For example, if you had a file in **Public/styles** called **stylesheet.css** this would be accessible from the path **/styles/stylesheet.css**.

The starter project for this chapter contains an **images** directory in the **Public** folder, with a logo inside for the website. If you've continued with your own project from the previous chapters, copy the **images** folder into your existing **Public** folder. Build and run, then open **index.leaf**.

Above <h1>Acronyms</h1> add the following:

```
<img src="/images/logo.png"
  class="mx-auto d-block" alt="TIL Logo" />
```

This adds an <img> tag — for an image — to the page. The page loads the image from **/images/logo.png** which corresponds to **Public/images/logo.png** served by the FileMiddleware. The mx-auto and d-block classes tell Bootstrap to align the image centrally in the page. Finally the alt value provides an alternative title for the image. Screen readers uses this to help accessibility users.

Save the file and visit **http://localhost:8080** in the browser. The home page now displays the image, putting the final touches on the page:

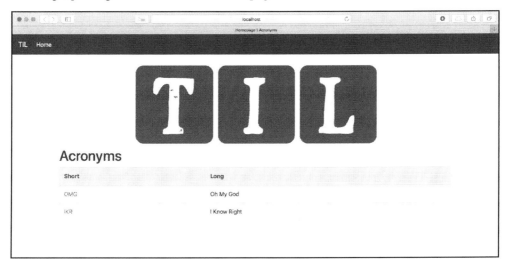

Users

The website now has a page that displays all the acronyms and a page that displays an acronym's details. Next, you'll add pages to view all the users and a specific user's information.

Create a new file in **Resources/Views** called **user.leaf**. Implement the template like so:

```
#// 1
#set("content") {
  #// 2
  <h1>#(user.name)</h1>
  #// 3
  <h2>#(user.username)</h2>

  #// 4
  #if(count(acronyms) > 0) {
    <table class="table table-bordered table-hover">
      <thead class="thead-light">
        <tr>
          <th>
            Short
          </th>
          <th>
            Long
          </th>
        </tr>
      </thead>
      <tbody>
        #// 5
        #for(acronym in acronyms) {
          <tr>
            <td>
              <a href="/acronyms/#(acronym.id)">
                #(acronym.short)</a>
            </td>
            <td>#(acronym.long)</td>
          </tr>
        }
      </tbody>
    </table>
  } else {
    <h2>There aren't any acronyms yet!</h2>
  }
}

#// 6
#embed("base")
```

Here's what the new page does:

1. Set the `content` variable for the base template.

2. Display the user's name in an `<h1>` heading.

3. Display the user's username in an `<h2>` heading.

4. Use a combination of Leaf's `#if` tag and `count` tag to see if the user has any acronyms.

5. Display a table of acronyms from the injected `acronyms` property. This table is identical to the one in the **index.leaf** template.

6. Embed the base template to bring in all the common HTML.

In Xcode, open **WebsiteController.swift**. At the bottom of the file create a new context for the user page:

```
struct UserContext: Encodable {
   let title: String
   let user: User
   let acronyms: [Acronym]
}
```

This context has properties for:

- The title of the page, which is the user's name.

- The user object to which the page refers.

- The acronyms created by this user.

Next, add the following handler below `acronymHandler(_:)` for this page:

```
// 1
func userHandler(_ req: Request) throws -> Future<View> {
   // 2
   return try req.parameters.next(User.self)
     .flatMap(to: View.self) { user in
        // 3
        return try user.acronyms
          .query(on: req)
          .all()
          .flatMap(to: View.self) { acronyms in
             // 4
             let context = UserContext(
               title: user.name,
               user: user,
               acronyms: acronyms)
             return try req.view().render("user", context)
        }
     }
}
```

Here's what the route handler does:

1. Define the route handler for the user page that returns `Future<View>`.

2. Get the user from the request's parameters and unwrap the future.

3. Get the user's acronyms using the computed property and unwrap the future.

4. Create a `UserContext`, then render the **user.leaf** template, returning the result. In this case, you're not setting the acronyms array to `nil` if it's empty. This is not required as you're checking the count in template.

Finally, add the following to register this route at the end of `boot(router:)`:

```
router.get("users", User.parameter, use: userHandler)
```

This registers the route for **/users/<USER ID>**, like the API. Build and run.

Next, open **acronym.leaf** to add a link to the new user page by replacing `<p>Created by #(user.name)</p>` with the following:

```
<p>Created by <a href="/users/#(user.id)/">#(user.name)</a></p>
```

Save the file and open your browser. Go to **http://localhost:8080** and click one of the acronyms. The page now displays a link to the creating user's page. Click the link visit your newly created page:

The final page for you to implement in this chapter displays a list of all users. Create a new file in **Resources/Views** called **allUsers.leaf**. Open the file and add the following:

```
#// 1
#set("content") {

  #// 2
  <h1>All Users</h1>
```

```
#// 3
#if(count(users) > 0) {
  <table class="table table-bordered table-hover">
    <thead class="thead-light">
      <tr>
        <th>
          Username
        </th>
        <th>
          Name
        </th>
      </tr>
    </thead>
    <tbody>
      #for(user in users) {
        <tr>
          <td>
            <a href="/users/#(user.id)">
              #(user.username)
            </a>
          </td>
          <td>#(user.name)</td>
        </tr>
      }
    </tbody>
  </table>
} else {
  <h2>There aren't any users yet!</h2>
}
}

#embed("base")
```

Here's what the new page does:

1. Set the `content` variable for the base template.

2. Display an `<h1>` heading for "All Users".

3. See if the context provides any users. If so, create a table that contains two columns: username and name. This is like the acronyms table.

Save the file and open **WebsiteController.swift** in Xcode. At the bottom of the file, create a new context for the page:

```
struct AllUsersContext: Encodable {
  let title: String
  let users: [User]
}
```

This context contains a title and an array of users. Next, add the following below userHandler(_:) to create a route handler for the new page:

```
// 1
func allUsersHandler(_ req: Request) throws -> Future<View> {
  // 2
  return User.query(on: req)
    .all()
    .flatMap(to: View.self) { users in
      // 3
      let context = AllUsersContext(
        title: "All Users",
        users: users)
      return try req.view().render("allUsers", context)
  }
}
```

Here's what the new route handler does:

1. Define a route handler for the "All Users" page that returns Future<View>.

2. Get the users from the database and unwrap the future.

3. Create an AllUsersContext and render the **allUsers.leaf** template, then return the result.

Next, register the route at the bottom of boot(router:):

```
router.get("users", use: allUsersHandler)
```

This registers the route for **/users/**, like the API. Build and run, then open **base.leaf**. Add a link to the new page in the navigation bar above the </ul> tag:

```
<li class="nav-item #if(title == "All Users"){active}">
  <a href="/users" class="nav-link">All Users</a>
</li>
```

This adds a link to **/users** and sets the link to active if the page title is "All Users".

Save the file and open your browser.

Go to **http://localhost:8080** and you'll see a new link in the navigation bar. Click **All Users** and you'll see your new "All Users" page:

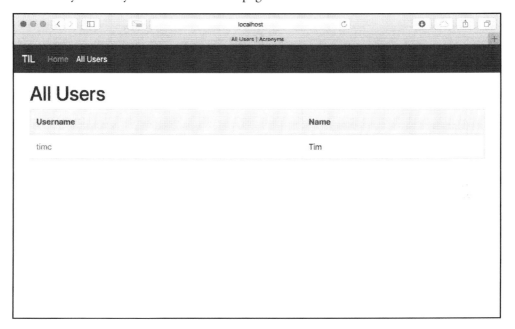

Deploying to Vapor Cloud

Like many of the previous chapters, deploying the changes from this chapter to Vapor Cloud is simple. In Terminal, type the following:

```
# 1
git add .
# 2
git commit -m "Beautify the pages and add navigation"
# 3
git push
```

Here's what these commands do:

1. Tell Git to track the new template files.

2. Commit your changes with the message "Beautify the pages and add navigation".

3. Push your local commits to the remote repository on GitHub.

```
● ● ●                      🗔 TILApp — -bash — 100×18
Tims-MBP:TILApp timc$ git add .
Tims-MBP:TILApp timc$ git commit -m "Beautify the pages and add navigation"
[master ed91790] Beautify the pages and add navigation
 8 files changed, 136 insertions(+), 22 deletions(-)
 create mode 100644 Public/images/logo.png
 create mode 100644 Resources/Views/allUsers.leaf
 create mode 100644 Resources/Views/base.leaf
 create mode 100644 Resources/Views/user.leaf
Tims-MBP:TILApp timc$ git push
Counting objects: 17, done.
Delta compression using up to 4 threads.
Compressing objects: 100% (15/15), done.
Writing objects: 100% (17/17), 10.20 KiB | 2.55 MiB/s, done.
Total 17 (delta 7), reused 0 (delta 0)
remote: Resolving deltas: 100% (7/7), completed with 5 local objects.
To github.com:raywenderlich/vapor-til.git
   89851a1..ed91790  master -> master
Tims-MBP:TILApp timc$ █
```

Now that you've committed and pushed, you can deploy your updated application to Vapor Cloud. In Terminal, type the following:

```
vapor cloud deploy --env=production --build=incremental -y
```

This command is the same as previous `vapor cloud deploy` commands, with parameters that:

• Deploy the application to the production environment.

• Use the incremental build type since you have included no new packages.

• Automatically deploy without waiting at the confirmation screen.

```
● ● ●                      🗔 TILApp — -bash — 100×25
git: git@github.com:raywenderlich/vapor-til.git
env: production
db: yes
replicas: 1
replica size: free
branch: master
build: incremental
Creating deployment [Done]
Connecting to build logs ...
Waiting in Queue [Done]
Starting deployment: 'rw-til' [Done]
Getting project from Git 'git@github.com:raywenderlich/vapor-til.git' [Done]
Checkout branch 'master' [Done]
Verifying base folder [Done]
Selected swift version: 4.1.0-beta [Done]
Building vapor (release) [Done]
Trying to find executable [Done]
Found executable: Run [Done]
Creating container registry [Done]
Building container [Done]
Pushing container to registry [Done]
Updating replicas [Done]
Deployment succeeded: https://rw-til.vapor.cloud [Done]
Successfully deployed.
Tims-MBP:TILApp timc$ █
```

When the application has deployed, go to **https://<YOUR_URL>**. You'll see your homepage updated with the new pages and links:

Where to go from here?

Now that you've completed the chapter, the website for the TIL application looks much better! Using the Bootstrap framework allows you to style the site easily. This makes a better impression on users visiting your application.

In the next chapters, you'll learn how to go from just displaying information on the page to implementing all the functionality to be able to create acronyms, categories and users.

Chapter 16: Making a Simple Web App, Part 1

By Tim Condon

In the previous chapters, you learned how to display data in a website and how to make the pages look nice with Bootstrap. In this chapter, you'll learn how to create different models and how to edit acronyms.

Categories

You've created pages for viewing acronyms and users. Now it's time to create similar pages for categories. Open **WebsiteController.swift**. At the bottom of the file, add a context for the "All Categories" page:

```
struct AllCategoriesContext: Encodable {
  // 1
  let title = "All Categories"
  // 2
  let categories: Future<[Category]>
}
```

Here's what this does:

1. Define the page's title for the template.

2. Define a future array of categories to display in the page.

Leaf knows how to handle futures. This helps tidy up your code when you don't need access to the resolved futures in your request handler.

Next, add the following under `allUsersHandler(_:)` to add new route handler for the "All Categories" page:

```
func allCategoriesHandler(_ req: Request) throws
  -> Future<View> {
  // 1
  let categories = Category.query(on: req).all()
  let context = AllCategoriesContext(categories: categories)
  // 2
  return try req.view().render("allCategories", context)
}
```

Here's what this route handler does:

1. Create an `AllCategoriesContext`. Notice that the context includes the query result directly, since Leaf can handle futures.

2. Render the **allCategories.leaf** template with the provided context.

Create a new file in **Resources/Views** called **allCategories.leaf** for the "All Categories" page. Open the new file and add the following:

```
#// 1
#set("content") {

  <h1>All Categories</h1>

  #// 2
  #if(count(categories) > 0) {
    <table class="table table-bordered table-hover">
      <thead class="thead-light">
        <tr>
          <th>
            Name
          </th>
        </tr>
      </thead>
      <tbody>
        #// 3
        #for(category in categories) {
          <tr>
            <td>
              <a href="/categories/#(category.id)">
                #(category.name)
              </a>
            </td>
          </tr>
        }
      </tbody>
    </table>
  } else {
    <h2>There aren't any categories yet!</h2>
```

```
    }
  }
  #embed("base")
```

This template is like those for the "All Users" and index pages, but the important points are:

1. Set the `content` variable for use by **base.leaf**.

2. See if any categories exist. You access future variables in the exact same way as non-futures. Leaf makes this transparent to the templates.

3. Loop through each category and add a row to the table with the name, linking to a category page.

Open, **WebsiteController.swift** and add the following context at the bottom of the file for the new category page:

```
struct CategoryContext: Encodable {
  // 1
  let title: String
  // 2
  let category: Category
  // 3
  let acronyms: Future<[Acronym]>
}
```

Here's what the context contains:

1. A title for the page; you'll set this as the category name.

2. The category for the page. This isn't `Future<Category>` since you need the category's name to set the title. This means you'll have to unwrap the future in your route handler.

3. The category's acronyms, provided as a future.

Next, add the following under `allCategoriesHandler(_:)` to create a route handler for the page:

```
func categoryHandler(_ req: Request) throws -> Future<View> {
  // 1
  return try req.parameters.next(Category.self)
    .flatMap(to: View.self) { category in
      // 2
      let acronyms = try category.acronyms.query(on: req).all()
      // 3
      let context = CategoryContext(
        title: category.name,
```

```
        category: category,
        acronyms: acronyms)
    // 4
    return try req.view().render("category", context)
  }
}
```

Here's what the route handler does:

1. Get the category from the request's parameters and unwrap the returned future.

2. Create a query to get all the acronyms for the category. This is a `Future<[Acronym]>`.

3. Create a context for the page.

4. Return a rendered view using the **category.leaf** template.

Create the new template, **category.leaf**, in **Resources/Views**. Open the new file and add the following:

```
#set("content") {
  <h1>#(category.name)</h1>

  #if(count(acronyms) > 0) {
    <table class="table table-bordered table-hover">
      <thead class="thead-light">
        <tr>
          <th>
            Short
          </th>
          <th>
            Long
          </th>
        </tr>
      </thead>
      <tbody>
        #for(acronym in acronyms) {
          <tr>
            <td>
              <a href="/acronyms/#(acronym.id)">
                #(acronym.short)
              </a>
            </td>
            <td>#(acronym.long)</td>
          </tr>
        }
      </tbody>
    </table>
  } else {
    <h2>There aren't any acronyms yet!</h2>
  }
```

```
    }
#embed("base")
```

This is almost the same as the user's page just with the category name for the title. Open **base.leaf** and add the following after the link to the all users page:

```
<li class="nav-item #if(title == "All Categories"){active}">
  <a href="/categories" class="nav-link">All Categories</a>
</li>
```

This adds a new link to the navigation on the site for the all categories page. Finally open **WebsiteController.swift** and at the end of boot(router:), add the following to register the new routes:

```
// 1
router.get("categories", use: allCategoriesHandler)
// 2
router.get(
  "categories", Category.parameter,
  use: categoryHandler)
```

Here's what this does:

1. Register a route at **/categories** that accepts GET requests and calls allCategoriesHandler(_:).

2. Register a route at **/categories/<CATEGORY ID>** that accepts GET requests and calls categoryHandler(_:).

Build and run, then go to **http://localhost:8080/** in your browser. Click the new **All Categories** link in the menu and you'll go to the new "All Categories" page:

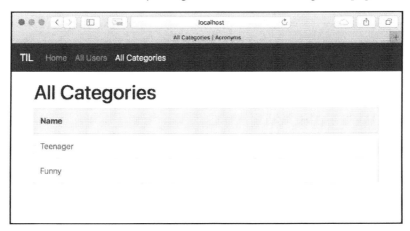

Click a category and you'll see the category information page with all the acronyms for that category:

Create acronyms

To create acronyms in a web application, you must actually implement *two* routes. You handle a GET request to display the form to fill in. Then, you handle a POST request to accept the data the form sends.

The page to create an acronym needs a list of all the users to permit selecting which user owns the acronym. Create a context at the bottom of **WebsiteController.swift** to represent this:

```
struct CreateAcronymContext: Encodable {
  let title = "Create An Acronym"
  let users: Future<[User]>
}
```

Again you're using a `Future` in the context. Next, create a route handler to present the "Create An Acronym" page under `categoryHandler(_:)`:

```
func createAcronymHandler(_ req: Request) throws
  -> Future<View> {
  // 1
  let context = CreateAcronymContext(
    users: User.query(on: req).all())
  // 2
  return try req.view().render("createAcronym", context)
}
```

Here's what this does:

1. Create a context by passing in a query to get all of the users.

2. Render the page using the **createAcronym.leaf** template.

Next, add the following below `createAcronymHandler(_:)` to create a route handler for the POST request:

```
// 1
func createAcronymPostHandler(
  _ req: Request,
  acronym: Acronym
) throws -> Future<Response> {
  // 2
  return acronym.save(on: req).map(to: Response.self) {
    acronym in
    // 3
    guard let id = acronym.id else {
      throw Abort(.internalServerError)
    }
    // 4
    return req.redirect(to: "/acronyms/\(id)")
  }
}
```

Here's what this does:

1. Declare a route handler that takes `Acronym` as a parameter. Vapor automatically decodes the form data to an `Acronym` object.

2. Save the provided acronym and unwrap the returned future.

3. Ensure that the ID has been set, otherwise throw a **500 Internal Server Error**.

4. Redirect to the page for the newly created acronym.

Next, register these routes, add the following to the bottom of `boot(router:)`:

```
// 1
router.get("acronyms", "create", use: createAcronymHandler)
// 2
router.post(
  Acronym.self, at: "acronyms", "create",
  use: createAcronymPostHandler)
```

Here's what the code does:

1. Register a route at **/acronyms/create** that accepts GET requests and calls `createAcronymHandler(_:)`.

2. Register a route at **/acronyms/create** that accepts POST requests and calls
    createAcronymPostHandler(_:acronym:). This also decodes the request's body
    to an Acronym.

You now need a template to display the create acronym form. Create a new file in
Resources/Views called **createAcronym.leaf**. Open the file and add the following:

```
#// 1
#set("content") {
  <h1>#(title)</h1>

  #// 2
  <form method="post">
    #// 3
    <div class="form-group">
      <label for="short">Acronym</label>
      <input type="text" name="short" class="form-control"
        id="short"/>
    </div>

    #// 4
    <div class="form-group">
      <label for="long">Meaning</label>
      <input type="text" name="long" class="form-control"
        id="long"/>
    </div>

    <div class="form-group">
      <label for="userID">User</label>
      #// 5
      <select name="userID" class="form-control" id="userID">
        #// 6
        #for(user in users) {
          <option value="#(user.id)">
            #(user.name)
          </option>
        }
      </select>
    </div>

    #// 7
    <button type="submit" class="btn btn-primary">
      Submit
    </button>
  </form>
}

#embed("base")
```

Here's what the template does:

1. Define the `content` variable used in the base template.

2. Create an HTML form. Set the method to POST. This means the browser sends the data to the same URL using a POST request when a user submits the form.

3. Create a group for the acronym's short value. Use HTML's `<input>` element to allow a user to insert text. The `name` property tells the browser what the key for this input should be when sending the data in the request.

4. Create a group for the acronym's long value using HTML's `<input>` element.

5. Create a group for the acronym's user. Use HTML's `<select>` element to display a drop-down menu of the different users.

6. Use Leaf's `#for()` loop to iterate through the provided users and add each as an option on the `<select>`.

7. Create a submit button the user can click to send the form to your web app.

Finally, add a link to the new page in **base.leaf** just before the `</ul>` tag:

```
#// 1
<li class="nav-item #if(title == "Create An Acronym"){active}">
  #// 2
  <a href="/acronyms/create" class="nav-link">
    Create An Acronym
  </a>
</li>
```

Here's what the code does:

1. Add a new navigation item to the nav bar. If you're on the "Create An Acronym" page, mark the item active.

2. Add a link to the create page.

Build and run, then open your browser. Navigate to **http://localhost:8080** and you'll see a new option, "Create An Acronym", in the navigation bar. Click the link to go to the new page. Fill in the form and click **Submit**.

The app redirects you to the new acronym's page:

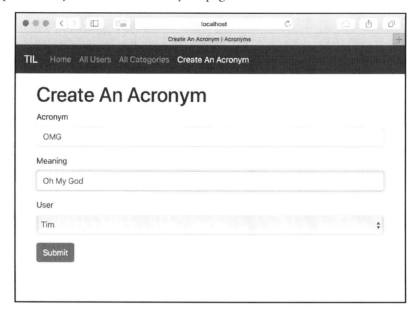

Editing acronyms

You now know how to create acronyms through the website. But what about editing an acronym? Thanks to Leaf, you can reuse many of the same components to allow users to edit acronyms. Open **WebsiteController.swift**.

At the end of the file, add the following context for editing an acronym:

```
struct EditAcronymContext: Encodable {
  // 1
  let title = "Edit Acronym"
  // 2
  let acronym: Acronym
  // 3
  let users: Future<[User]>
  // 4
  let editing = true
}
```

Here's what the context contains:

1. The title for the page: "Edit Acronym".

2. The acronym to edit.

3. A future array of users to display in the form.

4. A flag to tell the template that the page is for editing an acronym.

Next, add the following route handler below
`createAcronymPostHandler(_:acronymn:)` to show the edit acronym form:

```
func editAcronymHandler(_ req: Request) throws -> Future<View> {
  // 1
  return try req.parameters.next(Acronym.self)
    .flatMap(to: View.self) { acronym in
      // 2
      let context = EditAcronymContext(
        acronym: acronym,
        users: User.query(on: req).all())
      // 3
      return try req.view().render("createAcronym", context)
  }
}
```

Here's what this route does:

1. Get the acronym to edit from the request's parameter and unwrap the future.

2. Create a context to edit the acronym, passing in all the users.

3. Render the page using the **createAcronym.leaf** template, the same template used for the create page.

Next, add the following route handler for the POST request from the edit acronym page
below `editAcronymHandler(_:)`:

```
func editAcronymPostHandler(_ req: Request) throws
  -> Future<Response> {
  // 1
  return try flatMap(
    to: Response.self,
    req.parameters.next(Acronym.self),
    req.content.decode(Acronym.self)
  ) { acronym, data in
    // 2
    acronym.short = data.short
    acronym.long = data.long
    acronym.userID = data.userID

    // 3
    return acronym.save(on: req)
      .map(to: Response.self) { savedAcronym in
        // 4
        guard let id = savedAcronym.id else {
          throw Abort(.internalServerError)
        }
```

```
        // 5
        return req.redirect(to: "/acronyms/\(id)")
    }
  }
}
```

Here's what the route does:

1. Use the convenience form of `flatMap` to get the acronym from the request's parameter, decode the incoming data and unwrap both results.

2. Update the acronym with the new data.

3. Save the result and unwrap the returned future.

4. Ensure the ID has been set, otherwise throw a **500 Internal Server** error.

5. Return a redirect to the updated acronym's page.

Next, add the following to register the two new routes at the bottom of `boot(router:)`:

```
router.get(
  "acronyms", Acronym.parameter, "edit",
  use: editAcronymHandler)
router.post(
  "acronyms", Acronym.parameter, "edit",
  use: editAcronymPostHandler)
```

This registers a route at **/acronyms/<ACRONYM ID>/edit** to accept GET requests that calls `editAcronymHandler(_:)`. It also registers a route to handle POST requests to the same URL that calls `editAcronymPostHandler(_:)`.

Open **createAcronym.leaf** and change the template to accommodate editing an acronym. First, replace the input for the acronym short to accommodate editing:

```
<input type="text" name="short" class="form-control"
  id="short" #if(editing){value="#(acronym.short)"}/>
```

If the `editing` flag is set, this sets the `value` attribute of the `<input>` to the acronym's `short` property. This is how you pre-fill the form for editing. Do the same for the acronym's long input:

```
<input type="text" name="long" class="form-control"
  id="long" #if(editing){value="#(acronym.long)"}/>
```

Replace the users' `<select>` option for editing:

```
<option value="#(user.id)"
  #if(editing){#if(acronym.userID == user.id){selected}}>
```

```
    #(user.name)
</option>
```

This sets the `<option>`'s `selected` property if the user's ID matches the acronym's `userID`. This makes that option in the drop-down menu appear as the selected one. Next, replace the button for submitting the form:

```
<button type="submit" class="btn btn-primary">
  #if(editing){Update} else{Submit}
</button>
```

This uses Leaf's `#if()/else` tags to set the text of the button to "Update" or "Submit" depending on if the page's mode.

Finally, open **acronym.leaf** and add a button to edit that acronym at the bottom of `#set("content")`:

```
<a class="btn btn-primary" href="/acronyms/#(acronym.id)/edit"
  role="button">Edit</a>
```

This creates an HTML link to **/acronyms/<ACRONYM ID>/edit** and uses Bootstrap to style the link as a button. Build and run, then open **http://localhost:8080/** in your browser. Open an acronym page and there is now an **Edit** button at the bottom:

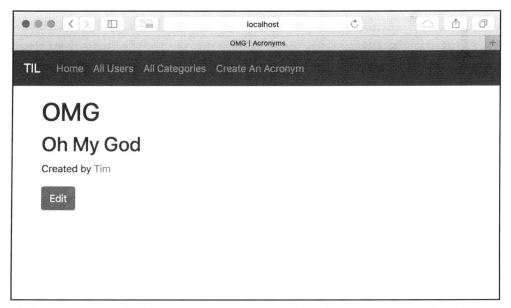

Click **Edit** to go to the edit acronym page with all the information pre-populated. The title and button are also different:

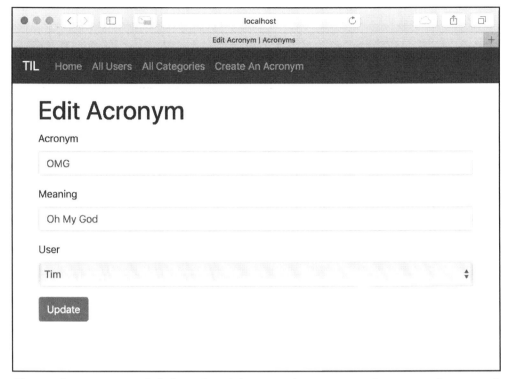

Change the acronym and click **Update**. The app redirects you to the acronym's page and you'll see the updated information.

Deleting acronyms

Unlike creating and editing acronyms, deleting an acronym only requires a single route. However, with web browsers there's no simple way to send a DELETE request. Browsers can only send GET requests to request a page and POST requests to send data with forms.

> It's possible to send a DELETE request with JavaScript, but that's outside the scope of this chapter.

To work around this, you'll send a POST request to a delete route. Open, **WebsiteController.swift** and add the following route handler below `editAcronymPostHandler(_:)` to delete an acronym:

```
func deleteAcronymHandler(_ req: Request) throws
  -> Future<Response> {
  return try req.parameters.next(Acronym.self).delete(on: req)
    .transform(to: req.redirect(to: "/"))
}
```

This route extracts the acronym from the request's parameter and calls `delete(on:)` on the acronym. The route then transforms the result to redirect the page to the home screen. Register the route at the bottom of `boot(router:)`:

```
router.post(
  "acronyms", Acronym.parameter, "delete",
  use: deleteAcronymHandler)
```

The registers a route at **/acronyms/<ACRONYM ID>/delete** to accept POST requests and call `deleteAcronymHandler(_:)`. Open **acronym.leaf** and replace the edit button with the following:

```
#// 1
<form method="post" action="/acronyms/#(acronym.id)/delete">
  #// 2
  <a class="btn btn-primary" href="/acronyms/#(acronym.id)/edit"
    role="button">Edit</a> 
  #// 3
  <input class="btn btn-danger" type="submit" value="Delete" />
</form>
```

Here's what the new code does:

1. Declare a form that sends a POST request. Set the `action` property to **/acronyms/<ACRONYM ID>/delete**. It's good practice to use a POST request for actions that modify the database, such as create or delete. This enables you to protect them with CSRF (Cross Site Request Forgery) tokens in the future, for example.

2. Incorporate the edit button that already exists on the page. This allows Bootstrap to align them.

3. Create a submit button for the delete form.

Build and run, then open **http://localhost:8080/** in the browser.

Open an acronym page and you'll see the delete button:

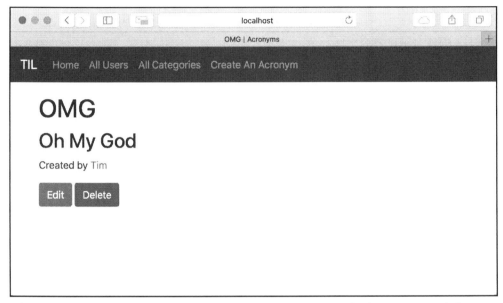

Click **Delete** to delete the acronym. The app redirects you to the homepage and the deleted acronym is no longer shown.

Where to go from here?

In this chapter, you learned how to display your categories and how to create, edit and delete acronyms. You still need to complete your support for categories, allowing your users to put acronyms into categories and remove them. You'll learn how to do that in the next chapter!

Chapter 17: Making a Simple Web App, Part 2

By Tim Condon

In the last chapter, you learned how to view categories and how to create, edit and delete acronyms. In this chapter, you'll learn how to allow users to add categories to acronyms in a user-friendly way. Finally, you'll deploy your completed web application to Vapor Cloud.

Adding categories to acronyms

Creating acronyms

The final implementation task for the web app is to allow users to manage categories on acronyms. When using the API with a REST client such as the iOS app, you send multiple requests, one per category. However, this isn't feasible with a web browser.

The web app must accept all the information in one request and translate the request into the appropriate Fluent operations. Additionally, having to create categories before a user can select them doesn't create a good user experience.

Open **Category.swift** and add the following function at the bottom of the extension below var acronyms:

```
static func addCategory(
  _ name: String,
  to acronym: Acronym,
  on req: Request
) throws -> Future<Void> {
  // 1
  return Category.query(on: req)
    .filter(\.name == name)
```

```
    .first()
    .flatMap(to: Void.self) { foundCategory in
      if let existingCategory = foundCategory {
        // 2
        return acronym.categories
          .attach(existingCategory, on: req)
          .transform(to: ())
      } else {
        // 3
        let category = Category(name: name)
        // 4
        return category.save(on: req)
          .flatMap(to: Void.self) { savedCategory in
          // 5
          return acronym.categories
            .attach(savedCategory, on: req)
            .transform(to: ())
        }
      }
    }
  }
}
```

Here's what this new function does:

1. Perform a query to search for a category with the provided name.

2. If the category exists, set up the relationship and transform to result to `Void`. `()` is shorthand for `Void()`.

3. If the category doesn't exist, create a new `Category` object with the provided name.

4. Save the new category and unwrap the returned future.

5. Set up the relationship and transform the result to `Void`.

Open **WebsiteController.swift** and add a new `Content` type at the bottom of the file to handle the new data:

```
struct CreateAcronymData: Content {
  let userID: User.ID
  let short: String
  let long: String
  let categories: [String]?
}
```

This takes the existing information required for an acronym and adds an optional array of `String`s to represent the categories. This allows users to submit existing *and* new categories instead of only existing ones.

Next, replace `createAcronymPostHandler(_:)` with the following:

```
// 1
func createAcronymPostHandler(
  _ req: Request,
  data: CreateAcronymData
) throws -> Future<Response> {
  // 2
  let acronym = Acronym(
    short: data.short,
    long: data.long,
    userID: data.userID)
  // 3
  return acronym.save(on: req)
    .flatMap(to: Response.self) { acronym in
      guard let id = acronym.id else {
        throw Abort(.internalServerError)
      }

      // 4
      var categorySaves: [Future<Void>] = []
      // 5
      for category in data.categories ?? [] {
        try categorySaves.append(
          Category.addCategory(category, to: acronym, on: req))
      }
      // 6
      let redirect = req.redirect(to: "/acronyms/\(id)")
      return categorySaves.flatten(on: req)
        .transform(to: redirect)
    }
}
```

Here's what you changed:

1. Change the `Content` type of route handler to accept `CreateAcronymData`.

2. Create an `Acronym` object to save as it's no longer passed into the route.

3. Call `flatMap(to:)` instead of `map(to:)` as you now return a `Future<Response>` in the closure.

4. Define an array of futures to store the save operations.

5. Loop through all the categories provided to the request and add the results of `Category.addCategory(_:to:on:)` to the array.

6. Flatten the array to complete all the Fluent operations and transform the result to a `Response`. Redirect the page to the new acronym's page.

Finally, in boot(router:), replace the create acronym POST route with the following:

```
router.post(
  CreateAcronymData.self,
  at: "acronyms", "create",
  use: createAcronymPostHandler)
```

This changes the content type to CreateAcronymData. Open **createAcronym.leaf** to allow a user to specify categories when they create an acronym. Just above the <button> section, add the following:

```
#// 1
<div class="form-group">
  #// 2
  <label for="categories">Categories</label>
  #// 3
  <select name="categories[]" class="form-control"
    id="categories" placeholder="Categories" multiple="multiple">
  </select>
</div>
```

Here's what this does:

1. Define a new <div> for categories that's styled with the form-group class.

2. Specify a label for the input.

3. Define a <select> input to allow a user to specify categories. The multiple attribute lets a user specify multiple options. The name categories[] allows the form to send the categories as a URL-encoded array.

Currently the form displays no categories. Using a <select> input only allows users to select pre-defined categories. To make this a nice user-experience, you'll use the Select2 JavaScript library.

Open **base.leaf** and under <link rel=stylesheet... for the Bootstrap stylesheet add the following:

```
#if(title == "Create An Acronym") {
  <link rel="stylesheet" href="https://cdnjs.cloudflare.com/
ajax/libs/select2/4.0.3/css/select2.min.css" integrity="sha384-
HIipfSYbpCkh5/1V87AWAeR5SUrNiewznrUrtNz1ux4uneLhsAKzv/
0FnMbj3m6g" crossorigin="anonymous">
}
#if(title == "Edit Acronym") {
  <link rel="stylesheet" href="https://cdnjs.cloudflare.com/
ajax/libs/select2/4.0.3/css/select2.min.css" integrity="sha384-
HIipfSYbpCkh5/1V87AWAeR5SUrNiewznrUrtNz1ux4uneLhsAKzv/
0FnMbj3m6g" crossorigin="anonymous">
}
```

This adds the stylesheet for Select2 to the create and edit acronym pages. At the bottom of **base.leaf**, remove the first `<script>` tag for jQuery and add the following:

```
#// 1
<script src="https://code.jquery.com/jquery-3.3.1.min.js"
integrity="sha384-tsQFqpEReu7ZLhBV2VZlAu7zcOV+rXbYlF2cqB8txI/
8aZajjp4Bqd+V6D5IgvKT" crossorigin="anonymous"></script>
#// 2
#if(title == "Edit Acronym") {
   <script src="https://cdnjs.cloudflare.com/ajax/libs/
select2/4.0.3/js/select2.min.js"
integrity="sha384-222hzbb8Z8ZKe6pzP18nTSltQM3PdcAwxWKzGOKOIF+Y3b
ROr5n9zdQ8yTRHgQkQ" crossorigin="anonymous"></script>
   #// 3
   <script src="/scripts/createAcronym.js"></script>
}
#if(title == "Create An Acronym") {
   <script src="https://cdnjs.cloudflare.com/ajax/libs/
select2/4.0.3/js/select2.min.js"
integrity="sha384-222hzbb8Z8ZKe6pzP18nTSltQM3PdcAwxWKzGOKOIF+Y3b
ROr5n9zdQ8yTRHgQkQ" crossorigin="anonymous"></script>
   <script src="/scripts/createAcronym.js"></script>
}
```

Here's what this does:

1. Include the full jQuery library. Bootstrap only requires the **slim** version, but Select2 requires functionality not included in the slim version, so the full library is required.

2. If the page is the create or edit acronym page, include the JavaScript for Select2.

3. Also include the local **createAcronym.js**.

In Terminal, enter the following commands to create your local JavaScript file.

```
mkdir Public/scripts
touch Public/scripts/createAcronym.js
```

Open the file and insert the following:

```
// 1
$.ajax({
  url: "/api/categories/",
  type: "GET",
  contentType: "application/json; charset=utf-8"
}).then(function (response) {
  var dataToReturn = [];
  // 2
  for (var i=0; i < response.length; i++) {
    var tagToTransform = response[i];
    var newTag = {
```

```
                       id: tagToTransform["name"],
                       text: tagToTransform["name"]
                    };
       dataToReturn.push(newTag);
    }
    // 3
    $("#categories").select2({
       // 4
       placeholder: "Select Categories for the Acronym",
       // 5
       tags: true,
       // 6
       tokenSeparators: [','],
       // 7
       data: dataToReturn
    });
 });
```

Here's what the script does:

1. On page load, send a GET request to **/api/categories**. This gets all the categories in the TIL app.

2. Loop through each returned category and turn it into a JSON object and add it to `dataToReturn`. The JSON object looks like:

```
{
  "id": <name of the category>,
  "text": <name of the category>
}
```

3. Get the HTML element with the ID `categories` and call `select2()` on it. This enables Select2 on the `<select>` in the form.

4. Set the placeholder text on the Select2 input.

5. Enable tags in Select2. This allows users to dynamically create new categories that don't exist in the input.

6. Set the separator for Select2. When a user types **,** Select2 creates a new category from the entered text. This allows users to categories with spaces.

7. Set the data — the options a user can choose from — to the existing categories.

Build and run, then navigate to the **Create An Acronym** page.

The categories list allows you to input existing categories or create new ones. The list also allows you to add and remove the "tags" in a user-friendly way:

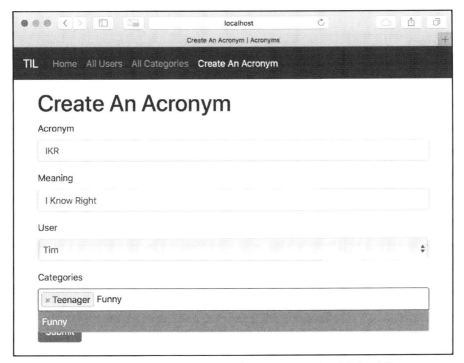

Now, open **acronym.leaf**. Under the "Created By" paragraph add the following:

```
#// 1
#if(count(categories) > 0) {
  #// 2
  <h3>Categories</h3>
  <ul>
    #// 3
    #for(category in categories) {
      <li>
        <a href="/categories/#(category.id)">
          #(category.name)
        </a>
      </li>
    }
  </ul>
}
```

Here's what this does:

1. Check if the template context has any categories.

2. If so, create a heading and a `<ul>` list.

3. Loop through the provided categories and add a link to each one.

Open **WebsiteController.swift** and at a new property at the bottom of
AcronymContext for the categories:

```
let categories: Future<[Category]>
```

In acronymHandler(_:), replace:

```
let context = AcronymContext(
  title: acronym.short,
  acronym: acronym,
  user: user)
```

With the following:

```
let categories = try acronym.categories.query(on: req).all()
let context = AcronymContext(
  title: acronym.short,
  acronym: acronym,
  user: user,
  categories: categories)
```

Again, this passes a Future to Leaf which it handles when required. Build and run, then
open the create acronym page in the browser. Create an acronym with categories in the
browser and head to the acronym's page. You'll see the acronym's categories on the page:

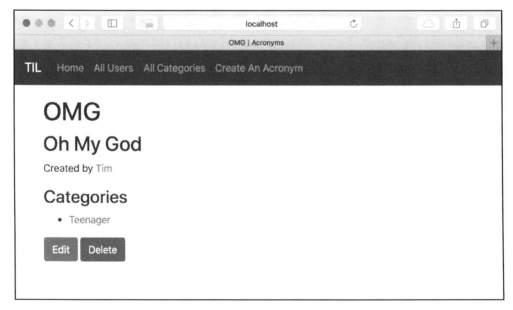

Editing acronyms

To allow adding and editing categories when editing an acronym, open
createAcronym.leaf. In the categories `<div>`, between the `<select>` and `</select>`
tags, add the following:

```
#if(editing) {
  #// 1
  #for(category in categories) {
    #// 2
    <option value="#(category.name)" selected="selected">
      #(category.name)
    </option>
  }
}
```

Here's what this does:

1. If the `editing` flag is set, loop through the array of provided categories.

2. Add each category as an `<option>` with the `selected` attribute set. This allows the
    category tags to be pre-populated when editing a form.

Open **WebsiteController.swift** and add a new property at the bottom of
`EditAcronymContext`:

```
let categories: Future<[Category]>
```

In `editAcronymHandler(_:)` replace:

```
let context = EditAcronymContext(
  acronym: acronym,
  users: User.query(on: req).all())
```

with the following:

```
let users = User.query(on: req).all()
let categories = try acronym.categories.query(on: req).all()
let context = EditAcronymContext(
  acronym: acronym,
  users: users,
  categories: categories)
```

This correctly constructs your new `EditAcronymContext`. To make the final step work,
add the following with the other imports at the beginning of the file:

```
import Fluent
```

Finally, replace `editAcronymPostHandler(_:)` with the following:

```
func editAcronymPostHandler(_ req: Request) throws
  -> Future<Response> {
  // 1
  return try flatMap(
    to: Response.self,
    req.parameters.next(Acronym.self),
    req.content
      .decode(CreateAcronymData.self)) { acronym, data in
      acronym.short = data.short
      acronym.long = data.long
      acronym.userID = data.userID

      // 2
      return acronym.save(on: req)
        .flatMap(to: Response.self) { savedAcronym in
        guard let id = savedAcronym.id else {
          throw Abort(.internalServerError)
        }

        // 3
        return try acronym.categories.query(on: req).all()
          .flatMap(to: Response.self) { existingCategories in
          // 4
          let existingStringArray =
            existingCategories.map { $0.name }

          // 5
          let existingSet = Set<String>(existingStringArray)
          let newSet = Set<String>(data.categories ?? [])

          // 6
          let categoriesToAdd = newSet.subtracting(existingSet)
          let categoriesToRemove =
            existingSet.subtracting(newSet)

          // 7
          var categoryResults: [Future<Void>] = []
          // 8
          for newCategory in categoriesToAdd {
            categoryResults.append(
              try Category.addCategory(
                newCategory,
                to: acronym,
                on: req))
          }

          // 9
          for categoryNameToRemove in categoriesToRemove {
            // 10
            let categoryToRemove = existingCategories.first {
              $0.name == categoryNameToRemove
```

```
      }
      // 11
      if let category = categoryToRemove {
        categoryResults.append(
          acronym.categories.detach(category, on: req))
      }
    }
    // 12
    return categoryResults
      .flatten(on: req)
      .transform(to: req.redirect(to: "/acronyms/\(id)"))
  }
  }
  }
}
```

The important points in this new version are:

1. Change the content type the request decodes to `CreateAcronymData`.

2. Use `flatMap(to:)` on `save(on:)` since the closure now returns a future.

3. Get all categories from the database.

4. Create an array of category names from the categories in the database.

5. Create a `Set` for the categories in the database and another for the categories supplied with the request.

6. Calculate the categories to add to the acronym and the categories to remove.

7. Create an array of category operation results.

8. Loop through all the categories to add and call `Category.addCategory(_:to:on:)` to set up the relationship. Add each result to the results array.

9. Loop through all the categories to remove from the acronym.

10. Get the `Category` object from the name of the category to remove.

11. If the `Category` object exists, use `detach(_:on:)` to remove the relationship and delete the pivot.

12. Flatten all the future category results. Transform the result to redirect to the updated acronym's page.

Build and run, then open an acronym page in the browser.

Click **Edit** and you'll see the form populated with the existing categories:

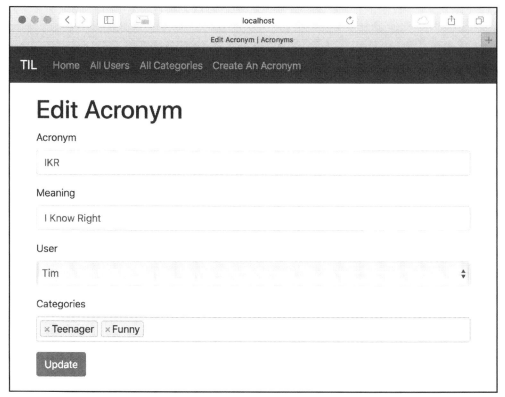

Add a new category and click **Update**. The page redirects to the acronym's page, with the updated acronym shown. Now try removing a category from an acronym.

Deploy to Vapor Cloud

Like many of the previous chapters, deploying the changes from this chapter to Vapor Cloud is simple. In Terminal, type the following:

```
# 1
git add .
# 2
git commit -m "Create and edit acronyms in web app"
# 3
git push
```

Here's what these commands do:

1. Tell Git to track the new template files.

2. Commit your changes with the message "Create and edit acronyms in web app".

3. Push your local commits to the remote repository on GitHub.

Now you've committed and pushed, you can deploy your updated application to Vapor Cloud. In Terminal, type the following:

```
vapor cloud deploy --env=production --build=incremental -y
```

This command is the same as previous Vapor Cloud deploy commands, with parameters:

• Deploy the application to the production environment.

• Use the incremental build type since you have included no new packages.

• Automatically deploy without waiting at the confirmation screen.

When the application has deployed, go to **https://<YOUR_URL>.vapor.cloud**. You'll see the option in the navigation bar to create an acronym. Click **Create An Acronym** and fill in the form to create an acronym:

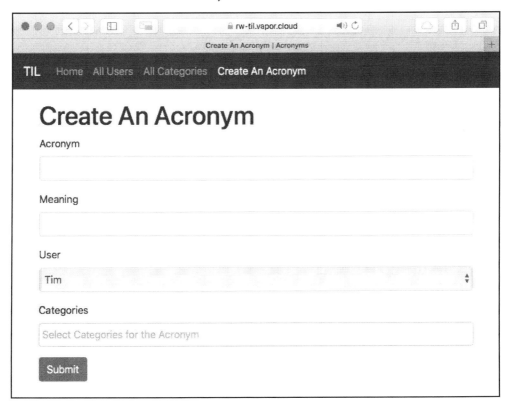

Where to go from here?

In this section, you've learned how to create a full-featured web app that performs the same functions as the iOS app. You've learned how to use Leaf to display different types of data and work with futures. You've also learned how to accept data from web forms and provide a good user-experience for handling data.

The TIL app contains both the API and the web app. This works well for small applications, but for very large applications you may consider splitting them up into their own apps. The web app then talks to the API like any other client would, such as the iOS app. This allows you to scale the different parts separately. Large applications may even be developed by different teams. Splitting them up lets the application grow and change, without reliance on the other team.

In the next section of the book, you'll learn how to apply authentication to your application. Currently anyone can create any acronyms in both the iOS app and the web app. This isn't desirable, especially for large systems. The next chapters show you how to protect both the API and web app with authentication.

Section III: Validation, Users & Authentication

This section shows you how to protect your Vapor application with authentication. You'll learn how to add password protection to both the API and the website, which lets you require users to log in. You'll learn about different types of authentication: HTTP Basic authentication and token-based authentication for the API, and cookie- and session-based authentication for the web site.Finally, you'll learn how to integrate with Google's OAuth provider. This allows you to delegate authentication and allow users to utilize their Google account credentials to access your site.

Specifically, you'll learn:

- **Chapter 18: API Authentication, Part I:** In this chapter, you'll learn how to protect your API with authentication. You'll learn how to implement both HTTP basic authentication and token authentication in your API. You'll also learn best-practices for storing passwords and authenticating users.

- **Chapter 19: API Authentication, Part II:** Now that you've implemented API authentication, neither your tests nor the iOS application work any longer. In this chapter, you'll learn the techniques needed to account for the new authentication requirements.

- **Chapter 20: Web Authentication, Cookies & Sessions:** In this chapter, you'll see how to implement authentication for the TIL website. You'll see how authentication works on the web and how Vapor's Authentication module provides all the necessary support. You'll then see how to protect different routes on the website. Next, you'll learn how to use cookies and sessions to your advantage.

- **Chapter 21: Validation:** In this chapter, you'll learn how to use Vapor's Validation library to verify some of the information users send the application. You'll create a registration page on the website for users to sign up. You'll validate the data from this form and display an error message if the data isn't correct.

- **Chapter 22: Facebook and Google Authentication:** In this chapter, you'll learn how to use OAuth 2.0 to delegate authentication to Google, so users can log in with their Google accounts instead.

These chapters will allow you to secure your important routes and keep only allowed routes as unauthenticated. You'll also learn how to delegate the authentication duties to third party vendors while still keeping your application secure.

Chapter 18: API Authentication, Part 1

By Tim Condon

The TILApp you've built so far has a ton of great features, but it also has one small problem: Anyone can create new users, categories or acronyms. There's no authentication on the API or the website to ensure only known users can change what's in the database. In this chapter, you'll learn how to protect your API with authentication. You'll learn how to implement both HTTP basic authentication and token authentication in your API. You'll also learn best-practices for storing passwords and authenticating users.

> **Note**: You must have PostgreSQL set up and configured in your project. If you still need to do this, follow the steps in Chapter 6, "Configuring a Database".

Passwords

Authentication is the process of verifying who someone is. This is different from **authorization**, which is verifying that a user has permission to perform a particular action. You commonly authenticate users with a username and password combination and TILApp will be no different.

Open the Vapor application in Xcode and open **User.swift**. Add the following property to User below `var username: String`:

```
var password: String
```

This property stores the user's password. Next, replace the initializer to account for the new property with the following:

```
init(name: String, username: String, password: String) {
    self.name = name
    self.username = username
    self.password = password
}
```

Password storage

Thanks to `Codable`, you don't have to make any additional changes to create users with passwords. The existing `UserController` now automatically expects to find the `password` property in the incoming JSON. However, without any changes, you'll be saving the user's password in plain text.

You should ***never*** store passwords in plain text. You should **always** store passwords in a secure fashion. `BCrypt` is an industry standard for hashing passwords and Vapor has it built in.

`BCrypt` is a one-way hashing algorithm. This means that you can turn a password into a hash, but can't convert a hash back into a password. Since `BCrypt` is designed to be slow, if someone steals a password hash, it takes a long time to brute-force the password. `BCrypt` hashes a **salt** with the password. A salt is a unique, random value to help defend against common attacks. `BCrypt` also provides a mechanism to verify a password using the password and a hash.

Open **UserController.swift** and add the following under `import Vapor`:

```
import Crypto
```

This brings in the Crypto module so you can use `BCrypt`. Next, in `createHandler(_:user:)` add the following before `return user.save(on:req)`:

```
user.password = try BCrypt.hash(user.password)
```

This hashes the user's password before saving it in the database.

Making usernames unique

In the coming sections of this chapter, you'll be using the username and password to uniquely identify users. At the moment, there's nothing to prevent multiple users from having the same username.

Open **User.swift** and replace the code below with the code on the next page:

```
extension User: Migration {}
```

Replace the previous code with the following:

```
extension User: Migration {
  static func prepare(on connection: PostgreSQLConnection)
    -> Future<Void> {
    // 1
    return Database.create(self, on: connection) { builder in
      // 2
      try addProperties(to: builder)
      // 3
      builder.unique(on: \.username)
    }
  }
}
```

This implements a custom migration, much like adding foreign key constraints in Chapter 9, "Parent Child Relationships". Here's what the custom migration does:

1. Create the User table.

2. Add all the columns to the User table using User's properties.

3. Add a unique index to username on User.

After the application has run the custom migration, any attempts to create duplicate usernames result in an error.

Returning users from the API

Since the model has changed you need to revert your database so Vapor can add the new column to the table. **Option-Click** the **Run** button in Xcode — or press **Option-Command-R** — to open the scheme editor.

On the **Arguments** tab, click **+** in the **Arguments Passed On Launch** section.

Enter:

```
revert --all --yes
```

You'll see the following:

Click **Run** and watch the reversion run in the Xcode console. **Option-Click** the **Run** button once more, clear the checkbox next to the arguments you entered, then click **Run**.

> **Note**: Entering **vapor run revert --all --yes** in Terminal is another way to revert your local database.

Launch RESTed, create a new request and configure it as follows:

- **URL**: http://localhost:8080/api/users/
- **method**: POST
- **Parameter encoding**: JSON-encoded

Add three parameters with names and values:

- **name**: your name
- **username**: a username of your choice
- **password**: a password of your choice

Click **Send Request**. Your application creates the requested user but the response returns the password hash:

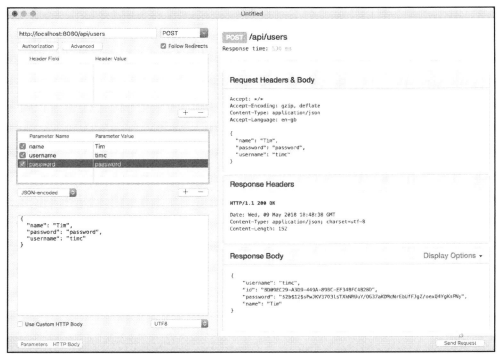

This isn't good! You should protect password hashes and never return them in responses. In fact, any user returned by the API includes the password hash, including listing all the users! This happens because you're returning User in all your routes. You should instead return a "public view" of User.

In Xcode, open **User.swift** and add the following below the User initializer:

```
final class Public: Codable {
  var id: UUID?
  var name: String
  var username: String

  init(id: UUID?, name: String, username: String) {
    self.id = id
    self.name = name
    self.username = username
  }
}
```

This creates an inner class to represent a public view of User. Next, add the following under `extension User: Parameter {}`:

```
extension User.Public: Content {}
```

This conforms `User.Public` to `Content`, allowing you to return the public view in responses. Next, add the following at the bottom of **User.swift**:

```
extension User {
  // 1
  func convertToPublic() -> User.Public {
    // 2
    return User.Public(id: id, name: name, username: username)
  }
}
```

Here's what the new method does:

1. Define a method on `User` that returns `User.Public`.

2. Create a public version of the current object.

Finally, add the following below the new extension:

```
// 1
extension Future where T: User {
  // 2
  func convertToPublic() -> Future<User.Public> {
    // 3
    return self.map(to: User.Public.self) { user in
      // 4
      return user.convertToPublic()
    }
  }
}
```

Here's what this does:

1. Define an extension for `Future<User>`.

2. Define a new method that returns a `Future<User.Public>`.

3. Unwrap the user contained in `self`.

4. Convert the `User` object to `User.Public`.

This extension allows you to call `convertToPublic()` on `Future<User>` which helps tidy up your code and reduce nesting. These new methods allow you to change your route handlers to return public users.

First, open **UsersController.swift** and change the return type of
createHandler(_:user:):

```
func createHandler(_ req: Request, user: User) throws
  -> Future<User.Public> {
```

Next, change your return to return a public user instead:

```
return user.save(on: req).convertToPublic()
```

This uses the extension for Future<User>. As a result, you don't need to unwrap the
result of the save yourself, making your code much cleaner!

Build and run, then create a new user in RESTed. You'll notice the user's password hash
is no longer returned:

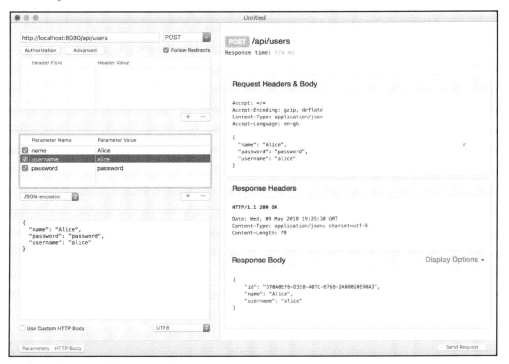

Update the rest of the routes that return User.

First, in **UsersController.swift** change the signature of getAllHandler(_:) to the
following:

```
func getAllHandler(_ req: Request) throws
  -> Future<[User.Public]> {
```

Next, change the body of `getAllHandler(_:)` to the following:

```
return User.query(on: req).decode(data: User.Public.self).all()
```

Instead of converting the `User` models to `User.Public`, this code decodes the data returned from the query into `User.Public`. This makes your code far simpler and more efficient. Next, change the signature of `getHandler(_:)` to return a public user:

```
func getHandler(_ req: Request) throws -> Future<User.Public> {
```

Next, change the body to return a public user:

```
return try req.parameters.next(User.self).convertToPublic()
```

Finally, open **AcronymsController.swift** and replace `getUserHandler(_:)` so it returns a public user:

```
// 1
func getUserHandler(_ req: Request) throws
  -> Future<User.Public> {
  // 2
  return try req.parameters.next(Acronym.self)
    .flatMap(to: User.Public.self) { acronym in
      // 3
      acronym.user.get(on: req).convertToPublic()
  }
}
```

Here's what changed:

1. Change the return type of the method to `Future<User.Public>`.

2. Change the parameter of `flatMap(to:)` to `User.Public.self`.

3. Call `convertToPublic()` on the acronym's user to return a public user.

Now, any calls to your API to retrieve a user won't return a password hash.

Basic authentication

HTTP basic authentication is a standardized method of sending credentials via HTTP and is defined by RFC 7617. You typically include the credentials in an HTTP request's **Authorization** header. To generate the token for this header, you combine the username and password, then base64-encode the result.

For example, for the username **timc** and password **password** the combined credential string is:

```
timc:password
```

You then base64-encode this which gives you:

```
dGltYzpwYXNzd29yZA==
```

The full header becomes:

```
Authorization: Basic dGltYzpwYXNzd29yZA==
```

Vapor has a package to help with handling many types of authentication, including HTTP basic authentication. Open **Package.swift** and replace `.package(url: "https://github.com/vapor/leaf.git", from: "3.0.0-rc")` with the following:

```
.package(url: "https://github.com/vapor/leaf.git",
         from: "3.0.0-rc"),
.package(url: "https://github.com/vapor/auth.git",
         from: "2.0.0-rc")
```

This adds the authentication package as a dependency to your project. Change the dependencies array for the App target to the following:

```
dependencies: ["FluentPostgreSQL",
               "Vapor",
               "Leaf",
               "Authentication"]
```

This adds the `Authentication` module as a dependency to the `App` target. In Terminal, regenerate the Xcode project to bring in the new dependency:

```
vapor xcode -y
```

Open **User.swift** and below `import FluentPostgreSQL` add the following:

```
import Authentication
```

This allows you to use the HTTP Basic helpers in the authentication module. At the bottom of the file, add the following:

```
// 1
extension User: BasicAuthenticatable {
  // 2
  static let usernameKey: UsernameKey = \User.username
  // 3
```

302   Server Side Swift with Vapor

```
    static let passwordKey: PasswordKey = \User.password
}
```

Here's what this does:

1. Conform `User` to `BasicAuthenticatable`.

2. Tell Vapor which property of `User` is the username.

3. Tell Vapor which property of `User` is the password.

Open **AcronymsController.swift** and, under `import Fluent`, add the following:

```
import Authentication
```

Next, add the following at the bottom of `boot(router:)`:

```
// 1
let basicAuthMiddleware =
  User.basicAuthMiddleware(using: BCryptDigest())
// 2
let guardAuthMiddleware = User.guardAuthMiddleware()
// 3
let protected = acronymsRoutes.grouped(
  basicAuthMiddleware,
  guardAuthMiddleware)
// 4
protected.post(Acronym.self, use: createHandler)
```

Here's what this does:

1. Instantiate a basic authentication middleware which uses `BCryptDigest` to verify passwords. Since `User` conforms to `BasicAuthenticatable`, this is available as a static function on the model.

2. Create an instance of `GuardAuthenticationMiddleware` which ensures that requests contain valid authorization.

3. Create a middleware group which uses `basicAuthMiddleware` and `guardAuthMiddleware`.

4. Connect the "create acronym" path to `createHandler(_:acronym:)` through this middleware group.

> **Middleware** allows you to intercept requests and responses in your application. In this example, `basicAuthMiddleware` intercepts the request and authenticates the user supplied. You can chain middleware together. In the above example,

> `basicAuthMiddleware` authenticates the user. Then `guardAuthMiddleware` ensures the request contains an authenticated user. If there's no authenticated user, `guardAuthMiddleware` throws an error. You can learn more about middleware in Chapter 25, "Middleware".

This ensures only requests authenticated using HTTP basic authentication can create acronyms.

Next, delete the following to remove the unauthenticated rout:

```
acronymsRoutes.post(Acronym.self, use: createHandler)
```

Next, open **configure.swift** and under `import Leaf`, add the following to import the authentication module:

```
import Authentication
```

Next, add the following under `try services.register(LeafProvider())`:

```
try services.register(AuthenticationProvider())
```

This registers the necessary services with your application to ensure authentication works. Build and run, then launch RESTed. Create a new request and configure it as follows:

- **URL**: http://localhost:8080/api/acronyms
- **method**: POST
- **Parameter encoding**: JSON-encoded

Add three parameters with names and values:

- **short**: OMG
- **long**: Oh My God
- **userID**: The ID of the user created earlier

Click **Send Request** and you'll receive a **401 Unauthorized** error response.

You should see the following:

In RESTed click **Authorization** and enter the username and password for the user created earlier. Check **Present Before Authentication Challenge** and click **OK**:

This sets the basic **Authorization** header as described above. Click **Send Request** again. This time the request succeeds:

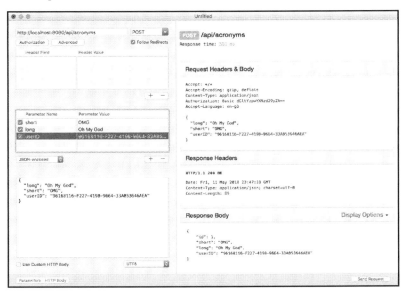

Token authentication

Getting a token

At this stage, only authenticated users can create acronyms. However, all other "destructive" routes are still unprotected. Asking a user to enter credentials with each request is impractical. You also don't want to store a user's password anywhere in your application since you'd have to store it in plain text. Instead, you'll allow users to log in to your API. When they log in, you exchange their credentials for a token the client can save.

In Terminal, type the following:

```
# 1
touch Sources/App/Models/Token.swift
# 2
vapor xcode -y
```

Here's what this does:

1. Create a new file for the Token model.

2. Regenerate the Xcode project to pick up the new file.

When the project regenerates, open **Token.swift** and add the following:

```swift
import Foundation
import Vapor
import FluentPostgreSQL
import Authentication

final class Token: Codable {
  var id: UUID?
  var token: String
  var userID: User.ID

  init(token: String, userID: User.ID) {
    self.token = token
    self.userID = userID
  }
}

extension Token: PostgreSQLUUIDModel {}

extension Token: Migration {
  static func prepare(on connection: PostgreSQLConnection) ->
Future<Void> {
    return Database.create(self, on: connection) { builder in
      try addProperties(to: builder)
      builder.reference(from: \.userID, to: \User.id)
    }
  }
}

extension Token: Content {}
```

This defines a model for Token that contains the following properties:

- id: the ID of the model.

- token: the token string provided to clients.

- userID: the token owner's user ID. The migration also creates a foreign key constraint with User.

In **configure.swift**, add the following before services.register(migrations):

```swift
migrations.add(model: Token.self, database: .psql)
```

This adds Token to the list of migrations so Vapor creates the table when the application next starts. When a user logs in, the application creates a token for that user. Open **Token.swift** and add the following at the bottom of the file:

```swift
extension Token {
  // 1
```

```
  static func generate(for user: User) throws -> Token {
    // 2
    let random = try CryptoRandom().generateData(count: 16)
    // 3
    return try Token(
      token: random.base64EncodedString(),
      userID: user.requireID())
  }
}
```

Here's what this extension does:

1. Define a static function to generate a token for a user.

2. Generate 16 random bytes to act as the token.

3. Create a `Token` using the base64-encoded representation of the random bytes and the user's ID.

Open **UsersController.swift** and add the following under `getAcronymsHandler(_:)`:

```
// 1
func loginHandler(_ req: Request) throws -> Future<Token> {
  // 2
  let user = try req.requireAuthenticated(User.self)
  // 3
  let token = try Token.generate(for: user)
  // 4
  return token.save(on: req)
}
```

Here's what this does:

1. Define a route handler for logging a user in.

2. Get the authenticated user from the request. You'll protect this route with the HTTP basic authentication middleware. This saves the user's identity in the request's authentication cache, allowing you to retrieve the user object later. `requireAuthenticated(_:)` throws an authentication error if there's no authenticated user.

3. Create a token for the user.

4. Save and return the token.

At the bottom of `boot(router:)` add the following:

```
// 1
let basicAuthMiddleware =
  User.basicAuthMiddleware(using: BCryptDigest())
let basicAuthGroup = usersRoute.grouped(basicAuthMiddleware)
```

```
// 2
basicAuthGroup.post("login", use: loginHandler)
```

Here's what this does:

1. Create a protected route group using HTTP basic authentication, as you did for creating an acronym. This doesn't use `GuardAuthenticationMiddleware` since `requireAuthenticated(_:)` throws the correct error if a user isn't authenticated.

2. Connect **/api/users/login** to `loginHandler(_:)` through the protected group.

Build and run, then head back to RESTed.

Ensure you've configured the HTTP basic authentication and set the URL to **http://localhost:8080/api/users/login**.

Click **Send Request** and you'll receive a token back:

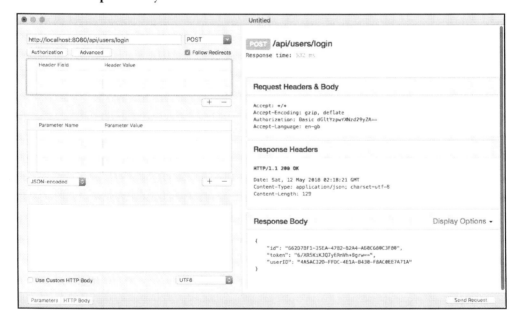

Using a token

Open **Token.swift** and add the following at the end of the file:

```
// 1
extension Token: Authentication.Token {
  // 2
  static let userIDKey: UserIDKey = \Token.userID
  // 3
  typealias UserType = User
```

```
  }

  // 4
  extension Token: BearerAuthenticatable {
    // 5
    static let tokenKey: TokenKey = \Token.token
  }
```

Here's what this does:

1. Conform `Token` to `Authentication`'s `Token` protocol.

2. Define the user ID key on `Token`.

3. Tell Vapor what type the user is.

4. Conform `Token` to `BearerAuthenticatable`. This allows you to use `Token` with bearer authentication.

5. Tell Vapor the key path to the token key, in this case, `Token`'s `token` string.

Bearer authentication is a mechanism for sending a token to authenticate requests. It uses the **Authorization** header, like HTTP basic authentication, but the header looks like **Authorization: Bearer <TOKEN STRING>**.

Open **User.swift** and add the following at the bottom of the file:

```
  // 1
  extension User: TokenAuthenticatable {
    // 2
    typealias TokenType = Token
  }
```

Here's what this does:

1. Conform `User` to `TokenAuthenticatable`. This allows a token to authenticate a user.

2. Tell Vapor what type a token is.

Currently when users create acronyms, they must send their ID in the request. However, because you're requiring authentication, you now know which user sent each request. At the bottom of **AcronymsController.swift**, add the following:

```
  struct AcronymCreateData: Content {
    let short: String
    let long: String
  }
```

This defines the request data that a user now has to send to create an acronym.

Replace `createHandler(_:acronym:)` with the following:

```
// 1
func createHandler(
  _ req: Request,
  data: AcronymCreateData) throws -> Future<Acronym> {
  // 2
  let user = try req.requireAuthenticated(User.self)
  // 3
  let acronym = try Acronym(
    short: data.short, long: data.long,
    userID: user.requireID())
  // 4
  return acronym.save(on: req)
}
```

Here's what the new function handler does:

1. Define a route handler that accepts `AcronymCreateData` as the request body.

2. Get the authenticated user from the request.

3. Create a new `Acronym` using the data from the request and the authenticated user.

4. Save and return the acronym.

In `boot(router:)`, remove the code you used earlier to protect the create an acronym route and replace it with the following:

```
// 1
let tokenAuthMiddleware = User.tokenAuthMiddleware()
let guardAuthMiddleware = User.guardAuthMiddleware()
// 2
let tokenAuthGroup = acronymsRoutes.grouped(
  tokenAuthMiddleware,
  guardAuthMiddleware)
// 3
tokenAuthGroup.post(AcronymCreateData.self, use: createHandler)
```

Here's what the new code does:

1. Create a `TokenAuthenticationMiddleware` for `User`. This uses `BearerAuthenticationMiddleware` to extract the bearer token out of the request. The middleware then converts this token into a logged in user.

2. Create a route group using `tokenAuthMiddleware` and `guardAuthMiddleware` to protect the route for creating an acronym with token authentication.

3. Connect the "create acronym" path to `createHandler(_:data:)` through this middleware group using the new `AcronymCreateData`.

Build and run, then head back to RESTed. Copy the token string returned from the user login. Configure a request like so:

- **URL**: http://localhost:8080/api/acronyms/

- **method**: POST

- **Parameter encoding**: JSON-encoded

Add two parameters with names and values:

- **short**: IKR

- **long**: I Know Right

Create a new header field for **Authorization** with the value **Bearer <TOKEN STRING>**, using the token string you copied earlier. Remove the HTTP basic authentication credentials you used for logging in. To do this, click **Authorization**, remove the username and password, and uncheck **Present Before Authentication Challenge**. Click **Send Request** and you'll see the created acronym returned:

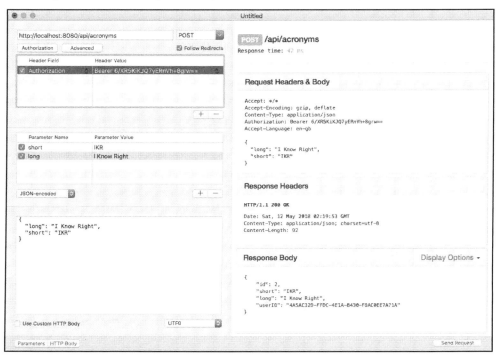

In **AcronymsController.swift** in boot(router:) delete the following lines:

```
acronymsRoutes.put(Acronym.parameter, use: updateHandler)
acronymsRoutes.delete(Acronym.parameter, use: deleteHandler)
acronymsRoutes.post(
```

```
    Acronym.parameter,
    "categories",
    Category.parameter,
    use: addCategoriesHandler)
  acronymsRoutes.delete(
    Acronym.parameter,
    "categories",
    Category.parameter,
    use: removeCategoriesHandler)
```

This is all of the original routes that are not `get()` routes. At the bottom of `boot(router:)` replace them with:

```
  tokenAuthGroup.delete(Acronym.parameter, use: deleteHandler)
  tokenAuthGroup.put(Acronym.parameter, use: updateHandler)
  tokenAuthGroup.post(
    Acronym.parameter,
    "categories",
    Category.parameter,
    use: addCategoriesHandler)
  tokenAuthGroup.delete(
    Acronym.parameter,
    "categories",
    Category.parameter,
    use: removeCategoriesHandler)
```

This ensures that only authenticated users can create, edit and delete acronyms, and add categories to acronyms. Unauthenticated users can still view details about acronyms.

Next, replace `updateHandler(_ req:)` with the following:

```
  func updateHandler(_ req: Request) throws -> Future<Acronym> {
    // 1
    return try flatMap(
      to: Acronym.self,
      req.parameters.next(Acronym.self),
      req.content.decode(AcronymCreateData.self)
    ) { acronym, updateData in
        acronym.short = updateData.short
        acronym.long = updateData.long
        // 2
        let user = try req.requireAuthenticated(User.self)
        acronym.userID = try user.requireID()
        return acronym.save(on: req)
    }
  }
```

Here's what changed:

1. Decode the request's data to `AcronymCreateData` since request no longer contains the user's ID in the post data.

2. Get the authenticated user from the request and use that to update the acronym.

Now, open **CategoriesController.swift** and in boot(router:) delete categoriesRoute.post(Category.self, use: createHandler).

Replace it with the following at the end of the method:

```
let tokenAuthMiddleware = User.tokenAuthMiddleware()
let guardAuthMiddleware = User.guardAuthMiddleware()
let tokenAuthGroup = categoriesRoute.grouped(
  tokenAuthMiddleware,
  guardAuthMiddleware)
tokenAuthGroup.post(Category.self, use: createHandler)
```

This uses the token middleware to protect category creation, just like creating an acronym, ensuring only authenticated users can create categories.

Finally, open **UsersController.swift** and delete usersRoute.post(User.self, use: createHandler). At the bottom of boot(router:), add the following:

```
let tokenAuthMiddleware = User.tokenAuthMiddleware()
let guardAuthMiddleware = User.guardAuthMiddleware()
let tokenAuthGroup = usersRoute.grouped(
  tokenAuthMiddleware,
  guardAuthMiddleware)
tokenAuthGroup.post(User.self, use: createHandler)
```

Again, using tokenAuthMiddleware and guardAuthMiddleware ensures only authenticated users can create other users. This stops anyone creating a user to be able to send requests to the routes you've just protected!

Now all API routes that can perform "destructive" actions — that is create, edit or delete resources — are protected. For those actions, the application only accept requests from authenticated users.

Database seeding

At this point the API is secure, but now there's another problem. When you deploy your application, you'll need to reset the database. Then, when you run your application, you won't have any users in the database.

But, you can't create a new user since that route requires authentication! One way to solve this is to seed the database and create a user when the application first boots up. In Vapor, you do this with a migration.

At the bottom of **User.swift**, add the following:

```
// 1
struct AdminUser: Migration {
  // 2
  typealias Database = PostgreSQLDatabase

  // 3
  static func prepare(on connection: PostgreSQLConnection)
    -> Future<Void> {
    // 4
    let password = try? BCrypt.hash("password")
    guard let hashedPassword = password else {
      fatalError("Failed to create admin user")
    }
    // 5
    let user = User(
      name: "Admin",
      username: "admin",
      password: hashedPassword)
    // 6
    return user.save(on: connection).transform(to: ())
  }

  // 7
  static func revert(on connection: PostgreSQLConnection)
    -> Future<Void> {
    return .done(on: connection)
  }
}
```

Here's what this does:

1. Define a new type that conforms to `Migration`.

2. Define which database type this migration is for.

3. Implement the required `prepare(on:)`.

4. Create a password hash and terminate with a fatal error if this fails.

5. Create a new user with the name **Admin**, username **admin** and the hashed password.

6. Save the user and transform to result to `Void`, the return type of `prepare(on:)`.

7. Implement the required `revert(on:)`. `.done(on:)` returns a pre-completed `Future<Void>`.

> **Note**: Obviously, in a production system, you shouldn't use **password** as the password for your admin user! You also don't want to hardcode the password in

> case it ends up in source control. You can either read an environment variable or generate a random password and print it out.

Open **configure.swift** and add the following before `services.register(migrations)`:

```
migrations.add(migration: AdminUser.self, database: .psql)
```

This adds `AdminUser` to the list of migrations so the app executes the migration at the next app launch. You use `add(migration:database:)` instead of `add(model:database:)` since this isn't a full model.

Build and run. Head to RESTed and try out all of your newly protected routes.

Where to go from here?

In this chapter, you learned about HTTP basic and bearer authentication. You saw how authentication middleware can simplify your code and do much of the heavy lifting for you. You saw how to modify your existing model to work with Vapor's authentication capabilities. You glued it all together to add authentication to your API.

But, there's much more to be done. Turn the page and get busy updating your test suite and your iOS app to work with the new authentication capabilities.

Chapter 19: API Authentication, Part 2

By Tim Condon

Now that you've implemented API authentication, neither your tests nor the iOS application work any longer. In this chapter, you'll learn the techniques needed to account for the new authentication requirements. Finally, you'll deploy the new code to Vapor Cloud.

> **Note**: You must have PostgreSQL set up and configured in your project. If you still need to do this, follow the steps in Chapter 6, "Configuring a Database".

Updating the tests

Now you've protected all the routes in your API, you need to update the tests. In Xcode, set the scheme to **TILApp-Package** and the deployment target to **My Mac**. Open **UserTests.swift**, find `testUserCanBeSavedWithAPI()` and replace:

```
let user = User(name: usersName, username: usersUsername)
```

with the following:

```
let user = User(
  name: usersName,
  username: usersUsername,
  password: "password")
```

This includes the password so the JSON body in the request is set properly. Next, open
Models+Testable.swift and under `import FluentPostgreSQL` add the following:

```
import Crypto
```

This imports the Crypto module to allow you to use BCrypt. Next, replace
`create(name:username:on:)` in the `User` extension with the following:

```
// 1
static func create(
  name: String = "Luke",
  username: String? = nil,
  on connection: PostgreSQLConnection
) throws -> User {
  var createUsername: String
  // 2
  if let suppliedUsername = username {
    createUsername = suppliedUsername
  // 3
  } else {
    createUsername = UUID().uuidString
  }

  // 4
  let password = try BCrypt.hash("password")
  let user = User(
    name: name,
    username: createUsername,
    password: password)
  return try user.save(on: connection).wait()
}
```

Here's what you changed:

1. Make the `username` parameter an optional string that defaults to `nil`.

2. If a username is supplied, use it.

3. If a username isn't supplied, create a new, random one using `UUID`. This ensures the
    username is unique as required by the migration.

4. Create a user.

In Terminal, run the following:

```
# 1
docker stop postgres-test
# 2
docker rm postgres-test
# 3
docker run --name postgres-test -e POSTGRES_DB=vapor-test \
```

```
    -e POSTGRES_USER=vapor -e POSTGRES_PASSWORD=password \
    -p 5433:5432 -d postgres
```

Here's what this does:

1. Stop the test PostgreSQL container.

2. Remove the test PostgreSQL container; this removes the existing database.

3. Run the test container again as described in Chapter 11, "Testing".

If you run the tests now, they crash since calls to any authenticated routes fail. You need to provide authentication for these requests.

Open **Application+Testable.swift** and replace

```
import App
```

with the following:

```
@testable import App
import Authentication
```

This enables you to use Token and imports the authentication module. Next, replace the signature of sendRequest<T>(to:method:headers:body:) with the following:

```
func sendRequest<T>(
  to path: String,
  method: HTTPMethod,
  headers: HTTPHeaders = .init(),
  body: T? = nil,
  loggedInRequest: Bool = false,
  loggedInUser: User? = nil
) throws -> Response where T: Content {
```

This adds loggedInRequest and loggedInUser as parameters. You use these to tell your tests to send an Authorization header or use a specified user, as required. Next, before let responder = try self.make(Responder.self) add the following:

```
var headers = headers
// 1
if (loggedInRequest || loggedInUser != nil) {
  let username: String
  // 2
  if let user = loggedInUser {
    username = user.username
  } else {
    username = "admin"
  }
  // 3
```

```
    let credentials = BasicAuthorization(
      username: username,
      password: "password")

    // 4
    var tokenHeaders = HTTPHeaders()
    tokenHeaders.basicAuthorization = credentials

    // 5
    let tokenResponse = try self.sendRequest(
      to: "/api/users/login",
      method: .POST,
      headers: tokenHeaders)
    // 6
    let token = try tokenResponse.content.syncDecode(Token.self)
    // 7
    headers.add(name: .authorization,
                value: "Bearer \(token.token)")
  }
```

Here's what the new code does:

1. Determine if this request requires authentication.

2. If a user is supplied, create a `BasicAuthorization` type using the user's details.
    Note: This requires you to know the user's password. As all the users in your tests
    have the password "password", this isn't an issue. If no user is specified, use "admin".

3. Create a `BasicAuthorization` credential.

4. Add the basic authorization header for the login request.

5. Send a request to log in the user and get the response.

6. Decode the `Token` from the login request.

7. Add the token to the authorization header for the request you're trying to send.

Change the remaining four request helpers in **Application+Testable.swift** to accept
`loggedInRequest` and `loggedInUser` parameters and pass them to
`sendRequest<T>(to:method:headers:body:loggedInRequest:loggedInUser:)`:

```
  func sendRequest(
    to path: String,
    method: HTTPMethod,
    headers: HTTPHeaders = .init(),
    loggedInRequest: Bool = false,
    loggedInUser: User? = nil
  ) throws -> Response {
    let emptyContent: EmptyContent? = nil
    return try sendRequest(
      to: path, method: method,
```

```
      headers: headers, body: emptyContent,
      loggedInRequest: loggedInRequest,
      loggedInUser: loggedInUser)
}

func getResponse<C, T>(
  to path: String,
  method: HTTPMethod = .GET,
  headers: HTTPHeaders = .init(),
  data: C? = nil, decodeTo type: T.Type,
  loggedInRequest: Bool = false,
  loggedInUser: User? = nil
) throws -> T where C: Content, T: Decodable {
  let response = try self.sendRequest(
    to: path, method: method,
    headers: headers, body: data,
    loggedInRequest: loggedInRequest,
    loggedInUser: loggedInUser)
  return try response.content.decode(type).wait()
}

func getResponse<T>(
  to path: String,
  method: HTTPMethod = .GET,
  headers: HTTPHeaders = .init(),
  decodeTo type: T.Type,
  loggedInRequest: Bool = false,
  loggedInUser: User? = nil
) throws -> T where T: Content {
  let emptyContent: EmptyContent? = nil
  return try self.getResponse(
    to: path, method: method,
    headers: headers, data: emptyContent,
    decodeTo: type,
    loggedInRequest: loggedInRequest,
    loggedInUser: loggedInUser)
}

func sendRequest<T>(
  to path: String,
  method: HTTPMethod,
  headers: HTTPHeaders,
  data: T,
  loggedInRequest: Bool = false,
  loggedInUser: User? = nil
) throws where T: Content {
  _ = try self.sendRequest(
    to: path, method: method,
    headers: headers, body: data,
    loggedInRequest: loggedInRequest,
    loggedInUser: loggedInUser)
}
```

Open **AcronymTests.swift** and, in `testAcronymCanBeSavedWithAPI()`, change the
call to `app.getResponse(to:method:headers:data:decodeTo:)` to set
`loggedInRequest`:

```
let receivedAcronym = try app.getResponse(
  to: acronymsURI,
  method: .POST,
  headers: ["Content-Type": "application/json"],
  data: acronym,
  decodeTo: Acronym.self,
  loggedInRequest: true)
```

In `testUpdatingAnAcronym()`, pass the user into the send request helper:

```
try app.sendRequest(
  to: "\(acronymsURI)\(acronym.id!)",
  method: .PUT,
  headers: ["Content-Type": "application/json"],
  data: updatedAcronym,
  loggedInUser: newUser)
```

In `testDeletingAnAcronym()` set `loggedInRequest` when sending the request:

```
_ = try app.sendRequest(
  to: "\(acronymsURI)\(acronym.id!)",
  method: .DELETE,
  loggedInRequest: true)
```

Next, in `testGettingAnAcronymsUser()` change the decoded user type to
`User.Public`:

```
let acronymsUser = try app.getResponse(
  to: "\(acronymsURI)\(acronym.id!)/user",
  decodeTo: User.Public.self)
```

Since the app no longer returns users' passwords in requests, you must change the decode
type to `User.Public`.

Next, in `testAcronymsCategories()` replace the two requests with the following:

```
let request1URL =
  "\(acronymsURI)\(acronym.id!)/categories/\(category.id!)"
_ = try app.sendRequest(
  to: request1URL,
  method: .POST,
  loggedInRequest: true)

let request2URL =
  "\(acronymsURI)\(acronym.id!)/categories/\(category2.id!)"
```

```
_ = try app.sendRequest(
    to: request2URL,
    method: .POST,
    loggedInRequest: true)
```

Finally, replace the request under the XCTAssertEqual statements with the following:

```
let request3URL =
    "\(acronymsURI)\(acronym.id!)/categories/\(category.id!)"
_ = try app.sendRequest(
    to: request3URL,
    method: .DELETE,
    loggedInRequest: true)
```

These requests now use an authenticated user.

Open **CategoryTests.swift** and change testCategoryCanBeSavedWithAPI() to use an authenticated request:

```
let receivedCategory = try app.getResponse(
    to: categoriesURI,
    method: .POST,
    headers: ["Content-Type": "application/json"],
    data: category,
    decodeTo: Category.self,
    loggedInRequest: true)
```

Next, in testGettingACategoriesAcronymsFromTheAPI(), replace the two POST requests with the following to use an authenticated user:

```
let acronym1URL =
    "/api/acronyms/\(acronym.id!)/categories/\(category.id!)"

_ = try app.sendRequest(
    to: acronym1URL,
    method: .POST,
    loggedInRequest: true)

let acronym2URL =
    "/api/acronyms/\(acronym2.id!)/categories/\(category.id!)"

_ = try app.sendRequest(
    to: acronym2URL,
    method: .POST,
    loggedInRequest: true)
```

Now, open **UserTests.swift**. First, change the request in
`testUsersCanBeRetrievedFromAPI` from:

```
let users = try app.getResponse(
  to: usersURI,
  decodeTo: [User].self)
```

to the following:

```
let users = try app.getResponse(
  to: usersURI,
  decodeTo: [User.Public].self)
```

This changes the decode type to `User.Public`. Update the assertions to account for the
admin user:

```
XCTAssertEqual(users.count, 3)
XCTAssertEqual(users[1].name, usersName)
XCTAssertEqual(users[1].username, usersUsername)
XCTAssertEqual(users[1].id, user.id)
```

Next, in `testUserCanBeSavedWithAPI` update the request:

```
let receivedUser = try app.getResponse(
  to: usersURI,
  method: .POST,
  headers: ["Content-Type": "application/json"],
  data: user,
  decodeTo: User.Public.self,
  loggedInRequest: true)
```

This changes the decode type to `User.Public` and sets the `loggedInRequest` flag.
Next, change the second request decode type:

```
let users = try app.getResponse(
  to: usersURI,
  decodeTo: [User.Public].self)
```

Then, update the assertions in `testUserCanBeSavedWithAPI()` to account for the
admin user:

```
XCTAssertEqual(users.count, 2)
XCTAssertEqual(users[1].name, usersName)
XCTAssertEqual(users[1].username, usersUsername)
XCTAssertEqual(users[1].id, receivedUser.id)
```

Finally, update the request in `testGettingASingleUserFromTheAPI()`:

```
let receivedUser = try app.getResponse(
  to: "\(usersURI)\(user.id!)",
  decodeTo: User.Public.self)
```

This changes the decode type to `User.Public` as the response no longer contains the user's password. Build and run the tests; they should all pass.

Deploying to Vapor Cloud

Commit your code

Like previous chapters, to deploy your new code to Vapor Cloud, type the following in Terminal:

```
#1
git add .
#2
git commit -m "Add API authentication"
#3
git push
```

Here's what these commands do:

1. Add all files so that Git picks up the new token file.

2. Commit your changes with the message "Add API authentication".

3. Push your local commits to the remote repository on GitHub.

Revert the database

Since you've changed the User model you need to revert your database in Vapor Cloud. This is just like Chapter 9, "Parent Child Relationships". In Terminal, type:

```
vapor cloud run "revert --all --yes"
```

Select the **Production** environment when Vapor Toolbox prompts you. This reverts your existing data in the database.

Since you've already deployed an application with the revert command, you don't need to deploy first:

> **WARNING**: DO NOT PROCEED until your revert has completed successfully. If you do, you'll have to delete your database entirely. You should see the following message in your Terminal window:

```
[ INFO ] Successfully reverted all migrations
(RevertCommand.swift:54)
```

Deploy

Finally, deploy your application. In Terminal, type:

```
vapor cloud deploy --env=production --build=update -y
```

As in previous chapters, this deploys your application. You use an **update** build because you've added new packages:

When the deployment finishes, open RESTed and create a new request:

- **URL**: https://<YOUR_URL>/api/users/login
- **method**: POST

Click **Authorization** and set the username and password to the admin username and password. Finally, check **Present Before Authentication Challenge** and click **OK**. Click **Send Request** and you'll receive a token.

You should see the following:

Updating the iOS application

> **Note**: You'll need to configure `AcronymRequest` and `ResourceRequest` to point to your Vapor Cloud API.

With the API in Vapor Cloud updated, the iOS Application can no longer create acronyms. Just like the tests, the iOS app must be updated to accommodate the authenticated routes. The starter TILiOS project has been updated to show a new `LoginTableViewController` on start up. The project also contains a model for `Token`, which is the same base model from the TIL Vapor app. Finally, the "create user" view now accepts a password.

Logging in

Open **AppDelegate.swift**. In application(_:didFinishLaunchingWithOptions:), the application checks the new Auth object for a token. If there's no token, it launches the login screen; otherwise, it displays the acronyms table as normal.

Open **Auth.swift**. The token check called from AppDelegate looks for a token in UserDefaults using the **TIL-API-KEY** key. When you set a token in Auth, it saves that token in UserDefaults.

At the bottom of Auth create a new method to log a user in:

```
// 1
func login(
  username: String,
  password: String,
  completion: @escaping (AuthResult) -> Void) {
  // 2
  let path = "https://<YOUR URL HERE>/api/users/login"
  guard let url = URL(string: path) else {
    fatalError()
  }
  // 3
  guard let loginString = "\(username):\(password)"
    .data(using: .utf8)?
    .base64EncodedString()
    else {
      fatalError()
  }

  // 4
  var loginRequest = URLRequest(url: url)
  // 5
  loginRequest.addValue(
    "Basic \(loginString)",
    forHTTPHeaderField: "Authorization")
  loginRequest.httpMethod = "POST"

  // 6
  let dataTask = URLSession.shared
    .dataTask(with: loginRequest) { data, response, _ in

    // 7
    guard
      let httpResponse = response as? HTTPURLResponse,
      httpResponse.statusCode == 200,
      let jsonData = data
      else {
        completion(.failure)
        return
    }
```

```
  do {
    // 8
    let token = try JSONDecoder()
      .decode(Token.self, from: jsonData)
    // 9
    self.token = token.token
    completion(.success)
  } catch {
    // 10
    completion(.failure)
  }
}
// 11
dataTask.resume()
}
```

Here's what the new method does:

1. Declare a method to log a user in. This takes the user's username, password and a completion handler as parameters.

2. Construct the URL for the login request. Don't forget to update this to point to your Vapor Cloud API.

3. Create the base64-encoded representation of the user's credentials for the header.

4. Create a `URLRequest` for the request to log a user in.

5. Add the necessary header for HTTP Basic authentication and set the HTTP method to **POST**.

6. Create a new `URLSessionDataTask` to send the request.

7. Ensure the response is valid, has a status code of 200 and contains a body.

8. Decode the response body into a `Token`.

9. Save the received token as the `Auth` token.

10. Catch any errors and call the completion handler with the `failure` case.

11. Start the data task to send the request.

Open **LoginTableViewController.swift**. When a user taps **Login**, the application calls `loginTapped(_:)`. At the end of `loginTapped(_:)`, add the following:

```
// 1
Auth().login(username: username, password: password) { result in
  switch result {
  case .success:
    DispatchQueue.main.async {
      let appDelegate =
```

```
      UIApplication.shared.delegate as? AppDelegate
    // 2
    appDelegate?.window?.rootViewController =
      UIStoryboard(name: "Main", bundle: Bundle.main)
        .instantiateInitialViewController()
  }
case .failure:
  let message =
    "Could not login. Check your credentials and try again"
  // 3
  ErrorPresenter.showError(message: message, on: self)
}
}
```

Here's what this does:

1. Create an instance of `Auth` and call `login(username:password:completion:)`.

2. If the login succeeds, load **Main.storyboard** to display the acronyms table.

3. If the login fails, show an alert using `ErrorPresenter`.

Build and run. When the application launches, it displays the login screen. Enter the admin credentials and tap **Login**:

The app logs you in and takes you to the main acronyms table.

Open **Auth.swift** and add the following implementation to `logout()`:

```
// 1
self.token = nil
DispatchQueue.main.async {
```

```
  // 2
  guard let applicationDelegate =
    UIApplication.shared.delegate as? AppDelegate else {
      return
  }
  let rootController =
    UIStoryboard(name: "Login", bundle: Bundle.main)
      .instantiateViewController(
        withIdentifier: "LoginNavigation")
  applicationDelegate.window?.rootViewController =
    rootController
}
```

Here's what this does:

1. Delete any existing token.

2. Load **Login.storyboard** and switch to the login screen.

Build and run. Switch to the **Users** tab and tap **Logout**. The app returns to the login screen.

Creating models

The starter project simplifies `CreateAcronymTableViewController` as you no longer have to provide a user when creating an acronym. Open **ResourceRequest.swift**. In `save(_:completion:)` before `var urlRequest = URLRequest(url: resourceURL)` add the following:

```
  // 1
  guard let token = Auth().token else {
    // 2
    Auth().logout()
    return
  }
```

Here's what this does:

1. Get the token from the `Auth` service.

2. If the token doesn't exist, call `logout()` since the user needs to log in again to get a new token.

Next, under `urlRequest.addValue("application/json", forHTTPHeaderField: "Content-Type")` add:

```
  urlRequest.addValue(
    "Bearer \(token)",
    forHTTPHeaderField: "Authorization")
```

This adds the token to the request using the **Authorization** header . Finally, inside `guard httpResponse.statusCode == 200, let jsonData = data else {`, before `completion(.failure)` add the following:

```
if httpResponse.statusCode == 401 {
  Auth().logout()
}
```

This checks the status code of the failure. If the response returns a **401 Unauthorized**, this means the token is invalid. Log the user out to trigger a new login sequence.

Build and run. Since you've already logged in, the app takes you to the main acronyms view. Click **+** and you'll see the new create acronym page, without a user option:

Fill in the form and click **Save** to create the acronym. You'll also be able to create users and categories. Note that the "create user" flow now includes a new model `CreateUser`. The app sends this model to the API as it contains the password property.

Acronym requests

You still need to add authentication to acronym requests. Open **AcronymRequest.swift** and in `update(with:completion:)`, before `var urlRequest = URLRequest(url: resource)` add the following:

```
guard let token = Auth().token else {
  Auth().logout()
  return
}
```

Like ResourceRequest, this gets the token from Auth and calls logout() if there's an error. After urlRequest.addValue("application/json", forHTTPHeaderField: "Content-Type") add:

```
urlRequest.addValue(
    "Bearer \(token)",
    forHTTPHeaderField: "Authorization")
```

This adds the token to the **Authorization** header. Next, in guard httpResponse.statusCode == 200 before completion(.failure) add:

```
if httpResponse.statusCode == 401 {
    Auth().logout()
}
```

This calls logout() if the token was invalid. Next change delete() to add authentication to the request. At the start of the function add:

```
guard let token = Auth().token else {
    Auth().logout()
    return
}
```

Next, after urlRequest.httpMethod = "DELETE" add the following:

```
urlRequest.addValue(
    "Bearer \(token)",
    forHTTPHeaderField: "Authorization")
```

Finally in add(category:completion:) before let url = ... get the token:

```
guard let token = Auth().token else {
    Auth().logout()
    return
}
```

Next, after urlRequest.httpMethod = "POST" add the token to the request:

```
urlRequest.addValue(
    "Bearer \(token)",
    forHTTPHeaderField: "Authorization")
```

Finally, inside guard httpResponse.statusCode == 201 else log the user out if the response returned a **401 Unauthorized**:

```
if httpResponse.statusCode == 401 {
    Auth().logout()
}
```

Build and run. You can now delete and edit acronyms and add categories to them.

Where to go from here?

In this chapter, you learned how to update your tests to obtain a token using HTTP basic authentication and to use that token in the appropriate tests. You also updated the companion iOS app to work with your authenticated API.

At the moment, only authenticated users can create acronyms in the API. However, the website is still open and anyone can do anything! In the next chapter, you'll learn how to apply authentication to the web front-end. You'll learn the differences between authenticating an API and a website and how to use cookies and sessions.

Chapter 20: Web Authentication, Cookies & Sessions

By Tim Condon

In the previous chapters, you learned how to implement authentication in the TIL app's API. In this chapter, you'll see how to implement authentication for the TIL website. You'll see how authentication works on the web and how Vapor's Authentication module provides all the necessary support. You'll then see how to protect different routes on the website. Next, you'll learn how to use cookies and sessions to your advantage. Finally, you'll deploy your code to Vapor Cloud.

Web authentication

How it works

Earlier, you learned how to use HTTP basic authentication and bearer authentication to protect the API. As you'll recall, this works by sending tokens and credentials in the request headers. However, this isn't possible in web browsers. There's no way to add headers to requests your browser makes with normal HTML.

To work around this, browsers and web sites use **cookies**. A cookie is a small bit of data your application sends to the browser to store on the user's computer. Then, when the user makes a request to your application, the browser attaches the cookies for your site.

You combine this with **sessions** to authenticate users. Sessions allow you to persist state across requests. In Vapor, when you have sessions enabled, the application provides a cookie to the user with a unique ID. This ID identifies the user's session. When the user logs in, Vapor saves the user in the session. When you need to ensure a user has logged in or get the current authenticated user, you query the session.

Implementing sessions

Vapor manages sessions using a middleware, `SessionsMiddleware`. Open the project in Xcode and open **configure.swift**. In the middleware configuration section, add the following below `middlewares.use(ErrorMiddleware.self)`:

```
middlewares.use(SessionsMiddleware.self)
```

This registers the sessions middleware as a global middleware for your application. It also enables sessions for all requests. Next, add the following at the bottom of `configure(_:_:_:)`:

```
config.prefer(MemoryKeyedCache.self, for: KeyedCache.self)
```

This tells your application to use `MemoryKeyedCache` when asked for the `KeyedCache` service. The `KeyedCache` service is a key-value cache that backs sessions. There are multiple implementations of `KeyedCache` and you can learn more in Chapter 24, "Caching".

Next, open **User.swift** and add the following at the bottom of the file:

```
// 1
extension User: PasswordAuthenticatable {}
// 2
extension User: SessionAuthenticatable {}
```

Here's what this does:

1. Conform `User` to `PasswordAuthenticatable`. This allows Vapor to authenticate users with a username and password when they log in. Since you've already implemented the necessary properties for `PasswordAuthenticatable` in `BasicAuthenticatable`, there's nothing to do here.

2. Conform `User` to `SessionAuthenticatable`. This allows the application to save and retrieve your user as part of a session.

Log in

To log a user in, you need two routes — one for showing the login page and one for accepting the POST request from that page. Open **WebsiteController.swift** and, add the following at the bottom of the file, to create a context for the login page:

```
struct LoginContext: Encodable {
    let title = "Log In"
    let loginError: Bool
```

```
    init(loginError: Bool = false) {
      self.loginError = loginError
    }
  }
```

This provides the title of the page and a flag to indicate a login error. At the bottom of `WebsiteController`, add a route handler for the page:

```
// 1
func loginHandler(_ req: Request) throws -> Future<View> {
  let context: LoginContext
  // 2
  if req.query[Bool.self, at: "error"] != nil {
    context = LoginContext(loginError: true)
  } else {
    context = LoginContext()
  }
  // 3
  return try req.view().render("login", context)
}
```

Here's what the route handler does:

1. Define a route handler for the login page that returns a future `View`.

2. If the request contains the **error** parameter, create a context with `loginError` set to true.

3. Render the **login.leaf** template, passing in the context.

Create the new template, **login.leaf**, in **Resources/Views** and open the file. Insert the following:

```
#// 1
#set("content") {
#// 2
<h1>#(title)</h1>

#// 3
#if(loginError) {
<div class="alert alert-danger" role="alert">
  User authentication error. Either your username or password
  was invalid.
</div>
}

#// 4
<form method="post">
  #// 5
  <div class="form-group">
    <label for="username">Username</label>
```

```
      <input type="text" name="username" class="form-control"
      id="username"/>
   </div>

   #// 6
   <div class="form-group">
     <label for="password">Password</label>
     <input type="password" name="password" class="form-control"
     id="password"/>
   </div>

   #// 7
   <button type="submit" class="btn btn-primary">Log In</button>
 </form>
 }

#embed("base")
```

Here's what's going on in the template:

1. Set content as required by **base.leaf**.

2. Set the title for the page using the provided title from the context.

3. If the context value for loginError is true, display a suitable message.

4. Define a <form> that sends a POST request to same URL when submitted.

5. Add an input for the user's username.

6. Add an input for the user's password. Note the type="password" — this tells the browser to render the input as a password field.

7. Add a submit button for the form.

Next, open **WebsiteController.swift**, and add the following at the bottom of the file:

```
struct LoginPostData: Content {
   let username: String
   let password: String
}
```

This new Content type defines the data you expect when you receive the login POST request. Next, at the top of **WebsiteController.swift**, all the following directly below import Fluent:

```
import Authentication
```

This allows you to see the `Crypto` module required for `BCrypt`. Next, below `loginHandler(_:)`, add the following route handler for this request:

```
// 1
func loginPostHandler(
  _ req: Request,
  userData: LoginPostData
) throws -> Future<Response> {
    // 2
    return User.authenticate(
      username: userData.username,
      password: userData.password,
      using: BCryptDigest(),
      on: req).map(to: Response.self) {
        user in
        // 3
        guard let user = user else {
          return req.redirect(to: "/login?error")
        }
        // 4
        try req.authenticateSession(user)
        // 5
        return req.redirect(to: "/")
    }
}
```

Here's what the route handler does:

1. Define the route handler that decodes `LoginPostData` from the request and returns `Future<Response>`.

2. Call `authenticate(username:password:using:on:)`. This checks the username and password against the database and verifies the BCrypt hash. This function returns a `nil` user in a future if there's an issue authenticating the user.

3. Verify `authenticate(username:password:using:on:)` returned an authenticated user; otherwise, redirect back to the login page to show an error.

4. Authenticate the request's session. This saves the authenticated `User` into the request's session so Vapor can retrieve it in later requests. This is how Vapor persists authentication when a user logs in.

5. Redirect to the homepage after the login succeeds.

Finally, at the bottom of `boot(router:)`, register the two routes:

```
// 1
router.get("login", use: loginHandler)
// 2
router.post(LoginPostData.self, at: "login",
            use: loginPostHandler)
```

Here's what this does:

1. Route GET requests for **/login** to `loginHandler(_:)`.

2. Route POST requests for **/login** to `loginPostHandler(_:userData:)`, decoding
    the request body into `LoginPostData`.

Build and run. In your browser, visit **http://localhost:8080/login**. Click **Log In** without
entering data to see the error handling.

Next, enter your credentials and click **Log In** again. After the app validates your
credentials, it redirects you to the main acronyms list.

Protecting routes

In the API, you used `GuardAuthenticationMiddleware` to assert that the request
contained an authenticated user. This middleware throws an authentication error if
there's no user, resulting in a `401 Unauthorized` response to the client.

On the web, this isn't the best user experience. Instead, you use `RedirectMiddleware`
to redirect users to the login page when they try to access a protected route without
logging in first. Before you can use this redirect, you must first translate the session
cookie, sent by the browser, into an authenticated user. In `WebsiteController`, replace
the entire contents of `boot(router:)`, including the new routes you just added with the
following:

```
let authSessionRoutes =
  router.grouped(User.authSessionsMiddleware())
```

This creates a route group that runs `AuthenticationSessionsMiddleware` before the route handlers. This middleware reads the cookie from the request and looks up the session ID in the application's session list. If the session contains a user, `AuthenticationSessionsMiddleware` adds it to the `AuthenticationCache`, making the user available later in the process.

Next, register all the public routes, including the new login routes, in this route group:

```
authSessionRoutes.get(use: indexHandler)
authSessionRoutes.get("acronyms", Acronym.parameter,
                      use: acronymHandler)
authSessionRoutes.get("users", User.parameter, use: userHandler)
authSessionRoutes.get("users", use: allUsersHandler)
authSessionRoutes.get("categories", use: allCategoriesHandler)
authSessionRoutes.get("categories", Category.parameter,
                      use: categoryHandler)
authSessionRoutes.get("login", use: loginHandler)
authSessionRoutes.post(LoginPostData.self, at: "login",
                       use: loginPostHandler)
```

This makes the user available to these pages, even though it's not required. This is useful for displaying user-specific content, such as a profile link, on any page you desire. Underneath these routes, add the following:

```
let protectedRoutes = authSessionRoutes
  .grouped(RedirectMiddleware<User>(path: "/login"))
```

This creates a new route group, extending from `authSessionRoutes`, that includes `RedirectMiddleware`. The application runs a request through `RedirectMiddleware` before it reaches the route handler, but *after* `AuthenticationSessionsMiddleware`. This allows `RedirectMiddleware` to check for an authenticated user. `RedirectMiddleware` requires you to specify the path for redirecting unauthenticated users and the `Authenticatable` type to check for. In this case, that's your `User` model.

Finally, register the routes that require protection — creating, editing and deleting acronyms — to this route group:

```
protectedRoutes.get("acronyms", "create",
                    use: createAcronymHandler)
protectedRoutes.post(CreateAcronymData.self, at: "acronyms",
                     "create", use: createAcronymPostHandler)
protectedRoutes.get("acronyms", Acronym.parameter, "edit",
                    use: editAcronymHandler)
protectedRoutes.post("acronyms", Acronym.parameter, "edit",
                     use: editAcronymPostHandler)
protectedRoutes.post("acronyms", Acronym.parameter, "delete",
                     use: deleteAcronymHandler)
```

Remember this includes both the GET requests and the POST requests. Build and run, then visit **http://localhost:8080** in your browser.

Click **Create An Acronym** in the navigation bar and, this time, the app redirects you to the login page:

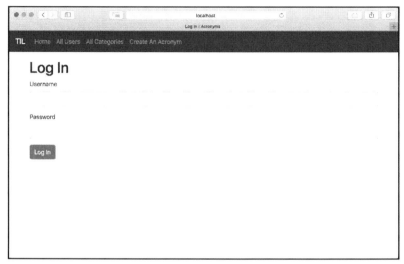

Enter the credentials for the seeded admin user and click **Log In**. The application redirects you to the main acronym list. If you click **Create An Acronym** again, the application lets you access the page.

Updating the site

Just like the API, now that users must login, the application knows which user is creating or editing an acronym. Still in **WebsiteController.swift**, find `CreateAcronymData` and remove the user ID:

```
let userID: User.ID
```

This is no longer required since you can get it from the authenticated user. Next, find `createAcronymPostHandler(_:data:)` and replace:

```
let acronym = Acronym(short: data.short, long: data.long,
                      userID: data.userID)
```

with the following:

```
let user = try req.requireAuthenticated(User.self)
let acronym = try Acronym(
  short: data.short,
```

```
    long: data.long,
    userID: user.requireID())
```

This gets the user from the request using `requireAuthenticated(_:)`, as in the API. Next, in `editAcronymPostHandler(_:)` add the following before `acronym.short = data.short`:

```
let user = try req.requireAuthenticated(User.self)
```

Again, this gets the authenticated user from the request. Finally, replace `acronym.userID = data.userID` with the following:

```
acronym.userID = try user.requireID()
```

This uses the authenticated user's ID for the updated acronym. Now, both creating and editing acronyms use the authenticated user. As a result, you no longer need to show the users in the form. Open **createAcronym.leaf** and remove the following code:

```
<div class="form-group">
  <label for="userID">User</label>
  <select name="userID" class="form-control" id="userID">
    #for(user in users) {
    <option value="#(user.id)"
      #if(editing){#if(acronym.userID == user.id){selected}}>
      #(user.name)
    </option>
    }
  </select>
</div>
```

As you use the same template for creating and editing acronyms, you only need to remove this from one place! Next, open **WebsiteController.swift** and remove the following from `CreateAcronymContext`:

```
let users: Future<[User]>
```

This is no longer required as the template doesn't use `users` anymore. In `createAcronymHandler(_:)`, address the change by replacing:

```
let context = CreateAcronymContext(
  users: User.query(on: req).all())
```

with the following:

```
let context = CreateAcronymContext()
```

Next, remove the following from `EditAcronymContext`:

```
let users: Future<[User]>
```

Next, in `editAcronymHandler(_:)` replace:

```
let context = EditAcronymContext(
  acronym: acronym,
  users: users,
  categories: categories)
```

with the following:

```
let context = EditAcronymContext(
  acronym: acronym,
  categories: categories)
```

Finally, delete the following from `editAcronymHandler(_:)` as you no longer use it:

```
let users = User.query(on: req).all()
```

Build and run, then visit **http://localhost:8080/** in your browser. Click **Create An Acronym** and log in again.

> **Note**: You need to log in again after restarting because the application keeps sessions in memory. For production applications, you can use Redis or a database to persist this information and share it across server instances.

Head back to **Create An Acronym** and the form no longer includes the list of users:

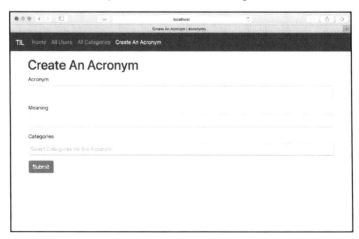

Create an acronym. When the application redirects you to the acronym's page, you'll see Vapor has used the authenticated user as the acronym's user:

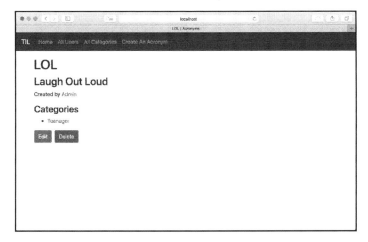

Log out

When you allow users to log in to your site, you should also allow them to logout. Still in **WebsiteController.swift**, add the following to the bottom of `WebsiteController`:

```
// 1
func logoutHandler(_ req: Request) throws -> Response {
  // 2
  try req.unauthenticateSession(User.self)
  // 3
  return req.redirect(to: "/")
}
```

Here's what this does:

1. Define a route handler that simply returns `Response`. There's no asynchronous work in this function so it doesn't need to return a future.

2. Call `unauthenticateSession(_:)` on the request. This deletes the user from the session so it can't be used to authenticate future requests.

3. Return a redirect to the index page.

Register the route inside boot(router:) after
authSessionRoutes.post(LoginPostData.self, at: "login", use:
loginPostHandler):

```
authSessionRoutes.post("logout", use: logoutHandler)
```

This connects POST requests for **/logout** to logoutHandler(). You should always use
POST requests for anything that changes application state. Moderns browsers prefetch
GET requests which could result in your users being unexpectedly logged out if you
don't use POST!

Open **base.leaf** and below </ul> in the navigation bar add the following:

```
#// 1
#if(userLoggedIn) {
  #// 2
  <form class="form-inline" action="/logout" method="POST">
    #// 3
    <input class="nav-link btn btn-link" type="submit"
      value="Log out">
  </form>
}
```

Here's what this does:

1. Check to see if userLoggedIn is set so you only display the logout option when a
    user's logged in.

2. Create a new form that sends a POST request to **/logout**.

3. Add a submit button to the form with the value **Log out** and style it like a
    navigation link.

Next, open **WebsiteController.swift** and at the bottom of IndexContext add the
following:

```
let userLoggedIn: Bool
```

This is the flag you set to tell the template that the request contains a logged in user.
Finally, in indexHandler(_:) replace let context = IndexContext(title:
"Homepage", acronyms: acronymsData) with the following:

```
// 1
let userLoggedIn = try req.isAuthenticated(User.self)
// 2
let context = IndexContext(
  title: "Homepage",
  acronyms: acronymsData,
  userLoggedIn: userLoggedIn)
```

Here's what this does:

1. Check if the request contains an authenticated user.

2. Pass the result to the new flag in `IndexContext`.

Build and run, then head to your browser. Click **Create An Acronym** and then log in. When the application redirects you to the homepage you'll see a new **Log out** option in the top right:

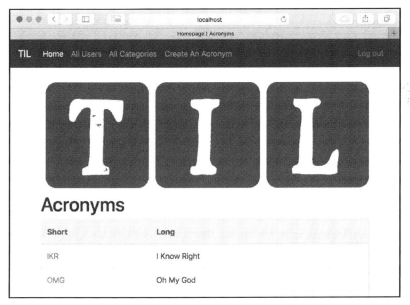

If you click this, then click **Create An Acronym** again, you'll need to sign in as the application has logged you out.

Cookies

Cookies are widely used on the web. Everyone's seen the cookie consent messages that pop up on a site when you first visit. You've already used cookies to implement authentication, but sometimes you want to set and read cookies manually.

A common way to handle the cookie consent message is to add a cookie when a user has accepted the notice (the irony!).

Open **base.leaf** and, above the script tag for jQuery, add the following:

```
#// 1
#if(showCookieMessage) {
```

```
#// 2
<footer id="cookie-footer">
  <div id="cookieMessage" class="container">
    <span class="muted">
      #// 3
      This site uses cookies! To accept this, click
      <a href="#" onclick="cookiesConfirmed()">OK</a>
    </span>
  </div>
</footer>
#// 4
<script src="/scripts/cookies.js"></script>
}
```

Here's what the code does:

1. Check whether a `showCookieMessage` flag has been set for the template.

2. If so, add a `<footer>` for the cookie message, styled using Bootstrap.

3. Add an **OK** link for users to click. This calls `cookiesConfirmed()`, a JavaScript function that dismisses the cookie message.

4. Add the JavaScript file for cookies.

Next, in **base.leaf** above `<title>#(title) | Acronyms</title>`, add the following:

```
<link rel="stylesheet" href="/styles/style.css">
```

This includes a new stylesheet for the website. You'll use this to add custom styling to your site. To create this stylesheet, enter the following in Terminal:

```
mkdir Public/styles
touch Public/styles/style.css
```

Next, open **style.css** and add the following:

```
#cookie-footer {
    position: absolute;
    bottom: 0;
    width: 100%;
    height: 60px;
    line-height: 60px;
    background-color: #f5f5f5;
}
```

This styling pins the cookie message to the bottom of the page. Next, enter the following into Terminal to create a new file in **Public/scripts** called **cookies.js** :

```
touch Public/scripts/cookies.js
```

Next, open **cookies.js** and add the following:

```
// 1
function cookiesConfirmed() {
  // 2
  $('#cookie-footer').hide();
  // 3
  var d = new Date();
  d.setTime(d.getTime() + (365*24*60*60*1000));
  var expires = "expires="+ d.toUTCString();
  // 4
  document.cookie = "cookies-accepted=true;" + expires;
}
```

Here's what the JavaScript does:

1. Define a function, `cookiesConfirmed()`, that the browser calls when the user clicks the OK link in the cookie message.

2. Hide the cookie message.

3. Create a date that's one year in the future. Then, create the **expires** string required for the cookie. By default, cookies are valid for the browser session — when the user closes the browser window or tab, the browser deletes the cookie. Adding the date ensures the browser persists the cookie for a year.

4. Add a cookie called `cookies-accepted` to the page using JavaScript. You'll check to see if this cookie exists when working out whether to show the cookie consent message.

Open **WebsiteController.swift** in Xcode and add the following to the bottom of `IndexContext`:

```
let showCookieMessage: Bool
```

This flag indicates to the template whether it should display the cookie consent message. In `indexHandler(_:)`, replace `let context = IndexContext...` with the following:

```
// 1
let showCookieMessage =
  req.http.cookies["cookies-accepted"] == nil
// 2
let context = IndexContext(
  title: "Homepage",
  acronyms: acronymsData,
  userLoggedIn: userLoggedIn,
  showCookieMessage: showCookieMessage)
```

Here's what this does:

1. See if a cookie called `cookies-accepted` exists. If it doesn't, set the `showCookieMessage` flag to `true`. You can read cookies from the request and set them on a response.

2. Pass the flag to `IndexContext` so the template knows whether to show the message.

Build and run, then go to **http://localhost:8080** in your browser. The site shows the cookie consent message on the page:

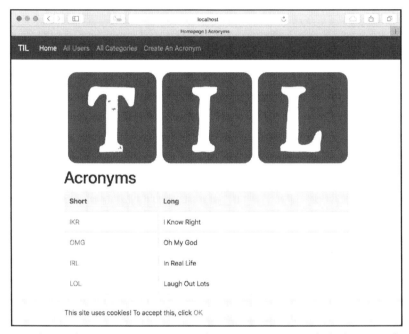

Click **OK** in the cookie consent message and your JavaScript code hides it. Refresh the page and the site won't show the message again.

Sessions

In addition to using cookies for web authentication, you've also made use of sessions. Sessions are useful in a number of scenarios, including authentication.

Another such scenario is Cross-Site Request Forgery (CSRF) prevention. CSRF is where an attacker tricks a user into sending an unexpected or unintended POST request, such as a request to a bank to transfer money. If the user is logged in, the site processes the request without any issue.

The same is possible with creating acronyms in the TIL website. If someone tricked an already-authenticated user into sending a POST request to **/acronyms/create**, the application would create the acronym!

A common approach to solving this problem involves including a CSRF token in the form. When the application receives the POST request, it verifies that the CSRF token matches the one issued to the form. If the tokens match, the application processes the request; otherwise, it rejects the request.

To add CSRF token support, begin by opening **WebsiteController.swift** and adding the following to the bottom of `CreateAcronymContext`:

```
let csrfToken: String
```

This is the CRSF token you'll pass into the template. In `createAcronymHandler(_:)` replace `let context = CreateAcronymContext()` with the following:

```
// 1
let token = try CryptoRandom()
  .generateData(count: 16)
  .base64EncodedString()
// 2
let context = CreateAcronymContext(csrfToken: token)
// 3
try req.session()["CSRF_TOKEN"] = token
```

Here's what the new code does:

1. Create a token using 16 bytes of randomly generated data, base64 encoded.

2. Initialize `CreateAcronymContext` with the created token.

3. Save the token into the request's session under the **CSRF_TOKEN** key.

Vapor persists the token in the session across different requests. When the user makes a new request and provides the cookie that identifies the session, all the session data is available. Open **createAcronym.leaf** and, underneath `<form method="post">`, add the following:

```
#if(csrfToken) {
  <input type="hidden" name="csrfToken" value="#(csrfToken)">
}
```

This checks to see if the context contains token. If so, the template adds a new input element to the form with the token as the value. Since this element is hidden, the browser doesn't display the token to the user.

Back in **WebsiteController.swift**, add the following to the bottom of
CreateAcronymData:

```
let csrfToken: String
```

This is the CSRF token that the form sends using the hidden input. Finally, at the
beginning of createAcronymPostHandler(_:data:), add the following:

```
// 1
let expectedToken = try req.session()["CSRF_TOKEN"]
// 2
try req.session()["CSRF_TOKEN"] = nil
// 3
guard expectedToken == data.csrfToken else {
  throw Abort(.badRequest)
}
```

Here's what this does:

1. Get the expected token from the request's session. This is the token you saved in
    createAcronymHandler(_:).

2. Clear the CSRF token now that you've used it. You generate a new token with each
    form.

3. Ensure the provided token matches the expected token; otherwise, throw a 400 Bad
    Request error.

Build and run, then visit **http://localhost:8080** in your browser. Go to the **Create An
Acronym** page once you've logged in and create a new acronym. The application creates
the acronym as the form provided the correct CSRF token. If you send a request without
the token, either by removing it from your page or using RESTed, you'll get a 400 Bad
Request response.

Deploying to Vapor Cloud

As in previous chapters, deploying the changes from this chapter to Vapor Cloud is
simple. In Terminal, type the following:

```
# 1
git add .
# 2
git commit -m "Add authentication to the website"
# 3
git push
```

Here's what these commands do:

1. Add the new files so Git tracks them.

2. Commit your changes with the message "Add authentication to the website".

3. Push your local commits up to the remote repository on GitHub.

Now, you've committed and pushed, you can deploy your updated application to Vapor Cloud. In Terminal, type the following:

```
vapor cloud deploy --env=production --build=incremental -y
```

This command is the same as previous **vapor cloud deploy** commands, with the following parameters:

• Deploy the application to the **production** environment.

• Use the **incremental** build type since you have included no new packages.

• Automatically deploy without waiting at the confirmation screen.

When the deployment has finished go to **https://<YOUR-URL>.vapor.cloud**. If you click **Create An Acronym**, you'll need to log in. Once logged in, the home page displays the **Log out** link:

Where to go from here?

In this chapter, you learned how to add authentication to the application's web site. You also learned how to make use of both sessions and cookies. You might want to look at adding CSRF tokens to the other POST routes, such as deleting and editing acronyms. In the next chapter, you'll learn how to use Vapor's validation library to automatically validate objects, request data and inputs.

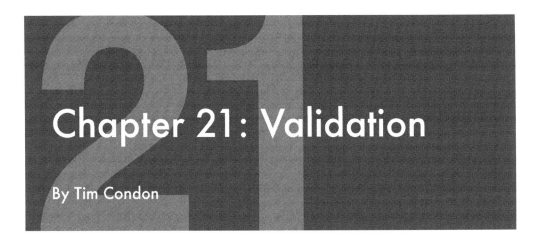

Chapter 21: Validation

By Tim Condon

In previous chapters, you built a fully-functional API and website. Users can send requests and fill in forms to create acronyms, categories and other users. In this chapter, you'll learn how to use Vapor's Validation library to verify some of the information users send the application. You'll create a registration page on the website for users to sign up. You'll validate the data from this form and display an error message if the data isn't correct. Finally, you'll deploy the code to Vapor Cloud.

The registration page

Create a new file in **Resources/Views** called **register.leaf**. This is the template for the registration page. Open **register.leaf** and add the following:

```
#set("content") {
<h1>#(title)</h1>

<form method="post">
  <div class="form-group">
    <label for="name">Name</label>
    <input type="text" name="name" class="form-control"
      id="name"/>
  </div>

  <div class="form-group">
    <label for="username">Username</label>
    <input type="text" name="username" class="form-control"
      id="username"/>
  </div>

  <div class="form-group">
```

```
      <label for="password">Password</label>
      <input type="password" name="password" class="form-control"
        id="password"/>
    </div>

    <div class="form-group">
      <label for="confirmPassword">Confirm Password</label>
      <input type="password" name="confirmPassword"
        class="form-control" id="confirmPassword"/>
    </div>

    <button type="submit" class="btn btn-primary">
      Register
    </button>
  </form>
}

#embed("base")
```

This is very similar to the templates for creating an acronym and logging in. The template contains four input fields for:

* name

* username

* password

* password confirmation

Next, open **WebsiteController.swift** and at the bottom of the file add the following context for the registration page:

```
struct RegisterContext: Encodable {
  let title = "Register"
}
```

Next, below `logoutHandler(_:)` add the following route handler for the registration page:

```
func registerHandler(_ req: Request) throws -> Future<View> {
  let context = RegisterContext()
  return try req.view().render("register", context)
}
```

Like the other routes handlers, this creates a context then calls `render(_:_:)` to render **register.leaf**.

Next, at the bottom of **WebsiteController.swift**, create the `Content` for the POST request for registration:

```
struct RegisterData: Content {
  let name: String
  let username: String
  let password: String
  let confirmPassword: String
}
```

This `Content` type matches the expected data received from the registration POST request. The variables match the names of the inputs in **register.leaf**. Next, add the following after `registerHandler(_:)` to create a route handler for this POST request:

```
// 1
func registerPostHandler(
  _ req: Request,
  data: RegisterData
) throws -> Future<Response> {
  // 2
  let password = try BCrypt.hash(data.password)
  // 3
  let user = User(
    name: data.name,
    username: data.username,
    password: password)
  // 4
  return user.save(on: req).map(to: Response.self) { user in
    // 5
    try req.authenticateSession(user)
    // 6
    return req.redirect(to: "/")
  }
}
```

Here's what's going on in the route handler:

1. Define a route handler that accepts a request and the decoded `RegisterData`.

2. Hash the password submitted to the form.

3. Create a new `User`, using the data from the form and the hashed password.

4. Save the new user and unwrap the returned future.

5. Authenticate the session for the new user. This automatically logs users in when they register, thereby providing a nice user experience when signing up with the site.

6. Return a redirect back to the home page.

Next, in `boot(router:)` add the following below
`authSessionRoutes.post("logout", use: logoutHandler)`:

```
// 1
authSessionRoutes.get("register", use: registerHandler)
// 2
authSessionRoutes.post(RegisterData.self, at: "register",
                        use: registerPostHandler)
```

Here's what this does:

1. Connect a GET request for **/register** to `registerHandler(_:)`.

2. Connect a POST request for **/register** to `registerPostHandler(_:data:)`.
   Decode the request's body to `RegisterData`.

Finally, open **base.leaf**. Before the closing `</ul>` in the navigation bar, add the
following:

```
#// 1
#if(!userLoggedIn) {
  #// 2
  <li class="nav-item #if(title == "Register"){active}">
    #// 3
    <a href="/register" class="nav-link">Register</a>
  </li>
}
```

Here's what the new Leaf code does:

1. Check to see if there's a logged in user. You only want to display the register link if
   there's no user logged in.

2. Add a new navigation link to the navigation bar. Set the `active` class if the current
   page is the **Register** page.

3. Add a link to the new **/register** route.

Build and run, then visit **http://localhost:8080** in your browser.

You'll see the new navigation link:

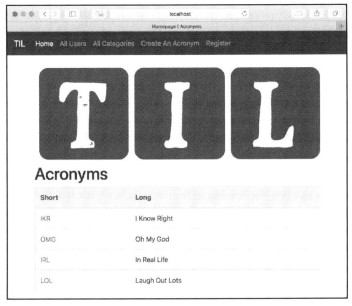

Click **Register** and you'll see the new register page:

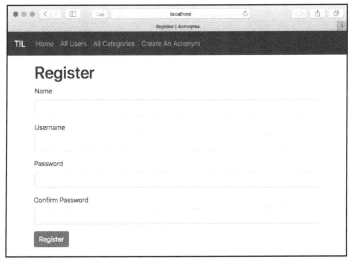

If you fill out the form and click **Register**, the app takes you to the home page. Notice the **Log out** button in the top right; this confirms that registration automatically logged you in.

Basic validation

Vapor provides a validation module to help you check data and models. Open **WebsiteController**, and add the following at the bottom:

```
// 1
extension RegisterData: Validatable, Reflectable {
  // 2
  static func validations() throws
    -> Validations<RegisterData> {
    // 3
    var validations = Validations(RegisterData.self)
    // 4
    try validations.add(\.name, .ascii)
    // 5
    try validations.add(\.username,
                        .alphanumeric && .count(3...))
    // 6
    try validations.add(\.password, .count(8...))
    // 7
    return validations
  }
}
```

Here's what this does:

1. Extend `RegisterData` to make it conform to `Validatable` and `Reflectable`. `Validatable` allows you to validate types with Vapor. `Reflectable` provides a way to discover the internal components of a type.

2. Implement `validations()` as required by `Validatable`.

3. Create a `Validations` type to contain the various validators.

4. Add a validator to ensure `RegisterData`'s name contains only ASCII characters. **Note**: Be careful when adding restrictions on names like this. Some countries, such as China, don't have names with ASCII characters.

5. Add a validator to ensure the username contains only alphanumeric characters and is at least 3 characters long. `.count(_:)` takes a Swift `Range`, allowing you to create both open-ended and closed ranges, if required.

6. Add a validator to ensure the password is at least 8 characters long.

7. Return the validations for Vapor to test.

As you can see, Vapor allows you to create powerful validations on models or incoming data. Because you use key paths, Vapor creates type-safe validations. Be aware the `.ascii` validator works only on `String` types. It won't work on `Int`, for example.

In `registerPostHandler(_:data:)`, add the following at the top of the method:

```
do {
  try data.validate()
} catch {
  return req.future(req.redirect(to: "/register"))
}
```

This calls `validate()` on the decoded `RegisterData`, checking each validator you added previously. `validate()` can throw `ValidationError`. In an API, you can let this error propagate back to the user but, on a website, that doesn't make for a good user experience. In this case, you redirect the user back to the "register" page.

Build and run, then visit the "register" page in your browser. If you enter information that doesn't match the validators, the app sends you back to try again.

Custom validation

If you've been following closely, you'll notice a flaw in the validation: Nothing ensures the passwords match! Vapor's validation library doesn't provide a built-in way to check that two strings match. However, it's easy to add custom validators. In the `validations()` for `RegisterData`, before `return validations`, add the following:

```
// 1
validations.add("passwords match") { model in
  // 2
  guard model.password == model.confirmPassword else {
    // 3
    throw BasicValidationError("passwords don't match")
  }
}
```

Here's what the new validator does:

1. Use `Validation`'s `add(_:_:)` to add a custom validator for `RegisterData`. This takes a readable description as the first parameter. The second parameter is a closure that should throw if validation fails.

2. Verify that `password` and `confirmPassword` match.

3. If they don't, throw `BasicValidationError`.

Build and run, then try registering a user with mismatched password. The application redirects you back to the "register" form.

Displaying an error

Currently, when a user fills out the form incorrectly, the application redirects back to the form with no indication anything went wrong. Open **register.leaf** and add the following under `<h1>#(title)</h1>`:

```
#if(message) {
  <div class="alert alert-danger" role="alert">
    Please fix the following errors:<br />
    #(message)
  </div>
}
```

If the page context includes `message`, this displays it in a new `<div>`. You style the new message appropriately by setting the `alert` and `alert-danger` classes. Open **WebsiteController.swift**, and add the following to the end of `RegisterContext`:

```
let message: String?

init(message: String? = nil) {
  self.message = message
}
```

This is the message to display on the registration page. Remember that Leaf handles `nil` gracefully, allowing you to use the default value in the normal case.

This is the flag the template uses. In `registerHandler(_:)`, replace:

```
let context = RegisterContext()
```

with the following:

```
let context: RegisterContext
if let message = req.query[String.self, at: "message"] {
  context = RegisterContext(message: message)
} else {
  context = RegisterContext()
}
```

This checks the request's query. If **message** exists — i.e., the URL is **/register?message=some-string** — the route handler includes it in the context Leaf uses to render the page.

Finally, in `registerPostHandler(_:data:)`, replace the `catch` block with:

```
catch (let error) {
  let redirect: String
```

```
    if let error = error as? ValidationError,
      let message = error.reason.addingPercentEncoding(
        withAllowedCharacters: .urlQueryAllowed) {
      redirect = "/register?message=\(message)"
    } else {
      redirect = "/register?message=Unknown+error"
    }
    return req.future(req.redirect(to: redirect))
}
```

When validation fails, the route handler extracts the `message` from the
`ValidationError`, escapes it properly for inclusion in a URL, and adds it to the
redirect URL. Then, it redirects the user back to the registration page. Build and run,
then visit **http://localhost:8080/register** in your browser.

Submit the empty form and you'll see the new message:

Deploy to Vapor Cloud

As in previous chapters, deploying the changes from this chapter to Vapor Cloud is
simple. In Terminal, type the following:

```
# 1
git add .
# 2
git commit -m "Add registration with validation"
# 3
git push
```

Here's what these commands do:

1. Add the new files so Git tracks them.

2. Commit your changes with the message "Add registration with validation".

3. Push your local commits up to the remote repository on GitHub.

Now you've committed and pushed, you can deploy your updated application to Vapor Cloud. In Terminal, type the following:

```
vapor cloud deploy --env=production --build=incremental -y
```

This command is the same as previous **vapor cloud deploy** commands, with the following parameters:

- Deploy the application to the **production** environment.

- Use the **incremental** build type since you haven't included any new packages.

- Automatically deploy without waiting at the confirmation screen.

When the deployment finishes, go to **https://<YOUR-URL>.vapor.cloud**. You'll see the new **Register** link where you can register as a user:

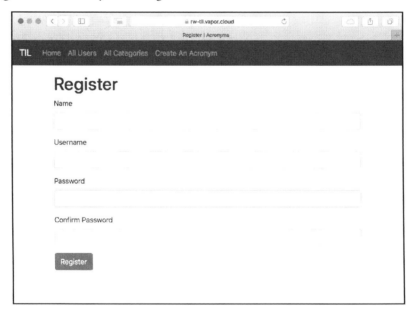

Where to go from here?

In this chapter, you learned how to use Vapor's validation library to check request's data. You can apply validation to models and other types as well.

In the next chapter, you'll learn how to integrate the TIL application with an OAuth provider. This lets you delegate login and registration to Facebook or Google, allowing users to sign in with an existing account.

Section IV: Advanced Server Side Swift

This section covers a number of different topics you may need to consider when developing server-side applications. These chapters will provide you the necessary building blocks to continue on your Vapor adventure and build even more complex and wonderful applications.

The chapters in this section deal with more advanced topics for Vapor and were written by the Vapor Core Team members.

Specifically, you'll learn:

- **Chapter 23: Database/API Versioning & Migration:** In this chapter, you'll make two modifications to the TILApp using migrations. First, you'll add a new field to `User` to contain a Twitter handle. Second, you'll ensure that categories are unique. Finally, you're going to modify the app so it creates the admin user only when your app runs in development or testing mode.

- **Chapter 24: Caching:** Whether you're creating a JSON API, building an iOS app, or even designing the circuitry of a CPU, you'll eventually need a cache. Caches are a method of speeding up slow processes and, without them, the Internet would be a terribly slow place. Some examples of slow processes you may encounter are, large database queries, requests to external services or complex computation such as parsing a large document.

- **Chapter 25: Middleware:** In the course of building your application, you'll often find it necessary to integrate your own steps into the request pipeline. The most common mechanism for accomplishing this is to use one or more pieces of middleware. They allow you to do things like log incoming requests, catch errors and display messages or rate-limit traffic to particular routes.

- **Chapter 26: Deploying with Heroku:** Heroku is a popular hosting solution that simplifies deployment of web and cloud applications. It supports a number of popular languages and database options. In this chapter, you'll learn how to deploy a Vapor web app with a Postgres database on Heroku.

- **Chapter 27: Websockets:** WebSockets, like HTTP, define a protocol used for communication between two devices. Unlike HTTP, the WebSocket protocol is designed for realtime communication. WebSockets can be a great option for things like chat, or other features that require realtime behavior. Vapor provides a succinct API to create a WebSocket server or client. This chapter focuses on building a basic server.

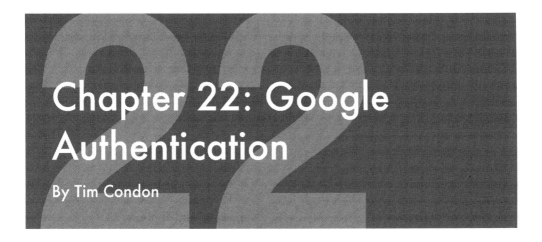

Chapter 22: Google Authentication

By Tim Condon

In the previous chapters, you learned how to add authentication to the TIL web site. However, sometimes users don't want to create extra accounts for an application and would prefer to use their existing accounts.

In this chapter, you'll learn how to use OAuth 2.0 to delegate authentication to Google, so users can log in with their Google accounts instead.

OAuth 2.0

OAuth 2.0 is an authorization framework that allows third-party applications to access resources on behalf of a user. Whenever you log in to a website with your Google account, you're using OAuth.

When you click **Login with Google**, Google is the site that authenticates you. You then authorize the application to have access to your Google data, such as your email. Once you've allowed the application access, Google gives the application a token. The app uses this token to authenticate requests to Google APIs. You'll implement this technique in this chapter.

> **Note**: You must have a Google account to complete this chapter. If you don't have one, visit https://accounts.google.com/SignUp to create one.

Imperial

Writing all the necessary scaffolding to interact with Google's OAuth system and get a token is a time-consuming job!

There's a community package called Imperial, https://github.com/vapor-community/Imperial, that does the heavy lifting for you. At the time of writing, it has integrations for Google and GitHub with more planned.

Adding to your project

Open **Package.swift** in Xcode to add the new dependency. Replace `.package(url: "https://github.com/vapor/auth.git", from: "2.0.0-rc")` with:

```
.package(url: "https://github.com/vapor/auth.git",
        from: "2.0.0-rc"),
.package(url: "https://github.com/vapor-community/Imperial.git",
        from: "0.7.1")
```

Next, add the dependency to your **App** target's dependency array, after `"Authentication"`:

```
dependencies: ["FluentPostgreSQL",
               "Vapor",
               "Leaf",
               "Authentication",
               "Imperial"]
```

In Terminal, create a file for a new controller to manage Imperial's routes:

```
touch Sources/App/Controllers/ImperialController.swift
```

Finally, in Terminal, regenerate the Xcode project to pull in the new dependency and include the new file:

```
vapor xcode -y
```

When the project opens in Xcode, open **ImperialController.swift** and create a new empty controller:

```
import Vapor
import Imperial
import Authentication

struct ImperialController: RouteCollection {
  func boot(router: Router) throws {
```

```
    }
  }
```

This creates a new type, `ImperialController`, that conforms to `RouteCollection`, implementing the required `boot(router:)`.

Open **routes.swift** and add the controller to your application at the bottom of `routes(_:)`:

```
let imperialController = ImperialController()
try router.register(collection: imperialController)
```

Setting up your application with Google

To be able to use Google OAuth in your application, you must first register the application with Google. In your browser, go to https://console.developers.google.com/apis/credentials.

If this is the first time you've used Google's credentials, the site prompts you to create a project:

Click **Create** to create a project for the TIL application. Fill in the form with an appropriate name, e.g. **Vapor TIL**:

When the project is created, the site takes you back to the Google credentials page. This time, click **Select** and select the created project. Click **Create Credentials** to create credentials for the TIL app and choose **OAuth client ID**:

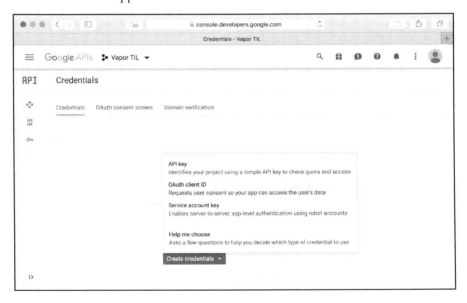

Next click **Configure consent screen** to set up the page Google presents to users, so they can allow your application access to their details.

Add a product name and click **Save**:

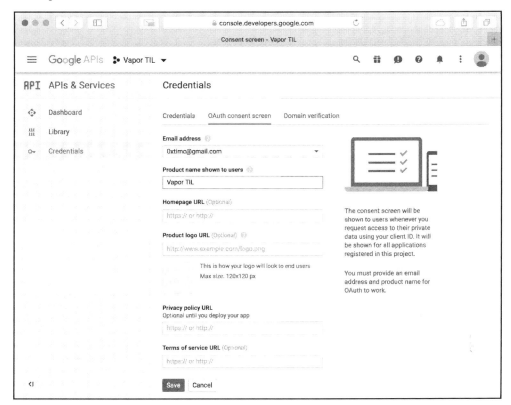

When creating a client ID, choose **Web application**. Add a redirect URI for your application for testing — **http://localhost:8080/oauth/google**.

This is the URL that Google redirects back to once the user has allowed your application access to their data.

If you are deploying to Vapor Cloud, add another redirect for your Vapor Cloud URL — e.g., **https://rw-til.vapor.cloud/oauth/google**:

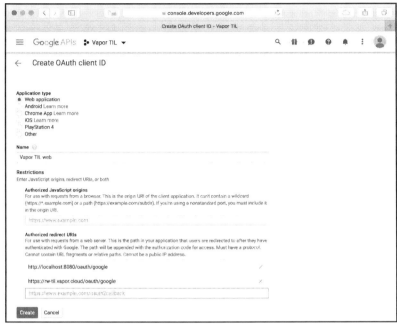

Click **Create** and the site gives you with your client ID and client secret:

> **Note**: You *must* keep these safe and secure. Your secret allows you access to Google's APIs and you should not share or checked the secret into source control. You should treat it like a password.

Setting up the integration

Now that you've registered your application with Google, you can start integrating Imperial. Open **ImperialController.swift** and add the following under boot(router:):

```
func processGoogleLogin(request: Request, token: String)
  throws -> Future<ResponseEncodable> {
    return request.future(request.redirect(to: "/"))
}
```

This defines a method to handle the Google login. The handler simply redirects the user to the home page — the same way that the regular login works. Imperial uses this method as the final callback once it has handled the Google redirect. Notice the use of request.future(_:) to create a future from request.redirect(to:), since the function that Imperial uses requires a future.

Next, set up the Imperial routes by adding the following in boot(router:):

```
guard let callbackURL = Environment.get("GOOGLE_CALLBACK_URL")
else {
  fatalError("Callback URL not set")
}
try router.oAuth(
  from: Google.self,
  authenticate: "login-google",
  callback: callbackURL,
  scope: ["profile", "email"],
  completion: processGoogleLogin)
```

Here's what this does:

- Get the callback URL from an environment variable — this is the URL you set up in the Google console.

- Register Imperial's Google OAuth router with your app's router.

- Tell Imperial to use the Google handlers.

- Set up the /login-google route as the route that triggers the OAuth flow. This is the route the application uses to allow users to log in via Google.

- Provide the callback URL to Imperial.

- Request the **profile** and **email** scopes from Google — the application needs these to create a user.

- Set the completion handler to `processGoogleLogin(request:token:)` - the method you created above.

In order for Imperial to work, you need to provide it the client ID and client secret that Google gave you. You provide these to Imperial using environment variables. To do this in Xcode, click the **Run** scheme, then click **Edit scheme**:

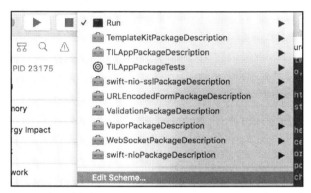

Under the **Arguments** tab, add three new **Environment Variables** as shown below:

- **GOOGLE_CALLBACK_URL**: **http://localhost:8080/oauth/google** — this is the URL you provided to Google.

- **GOOGLE_CLIENT_ID**: The client ID provided by Google.

- **GOOGLE_CLIENT_SECRET**: The client secret provided by Google.

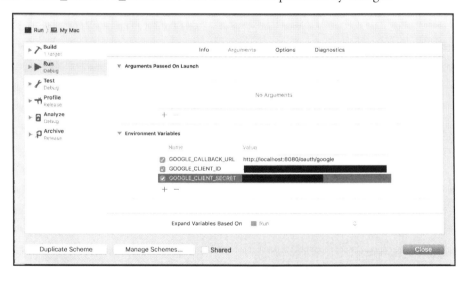

Integrating with web authentication

It's important to provide a seamless experience for users and match the experience for the regular login. To do this, you need to create a new user when a user logs in with Google for the first time. To create a user, you can use Google's API to get the necessary details using the OAuth token.

Sending requests to third-party APIs

At the bottom of **ImperialController.swift**, add a new type to decode the data from Google's API:

```
struct GoogleUserInfo: Content {
    let email: String
    let name: String
}
```

The request to Google's API returns many fields. However, you only care about the email, which becomes the username, and the name.

Next, under `GoogleUserInfo`, add the following:

```
extension Google {
  // 1
  static func getUser(on request: Request)
  throws -> Future<GoogleUserInfo> {
    // 2
    var headers = HTTPHeaders()
    headers.bearerAuthorization =
      try BearerAuthorization(token: request.accessToken())

    // 3
    let googleAPIURL =
      "https://www.googleapis.com/oauth2/v1/userinfo?alt=json"
    // 4
    return try request
      .client()
      .get(googleAPIURL, headers: headers)
      .map(to: GoogleUserInfo.self) { response in
      // 5
      guard response.http.status == .ok else {
        // 6
        if response.http.status == .unauthorized {
          throw Abort.redirect(to: "/login-google")
        } else {
          throw Abort(.internalServerError)
        }
      }
```

```
    // 7
    return try response.content
      .syncDecode(GoogleUserInfo.self)
  }
 }
}
```

Here's what this does:

1. Add a new function to Imperial's `Google` service that gets a user's details from the Google API.

2. Set the headers for the request by adding the OAuth token to the authorization header.

3. Set the URL for the request — this is Google's API to get the user's information.

4. Use `request.client()` to create a client to send a request. `get()` sends an HTTP GET request to the URL provided. Unwrap the returned future response.

5. Ensure the response status is `200 OK`.

6. Otherwise return to the login page if the response was `401 Unauthorized` or return an error.

7. Decode the data from the response to `GoogleUserInfo` and return the result.

Next, replace the contents of `processGoogleLogin(request:token:)` with the following:

```
// 1
return try Google
  .getUser(on: request)
  .flatMap(to: ResponseEncodable.self) { userInfo in
    // 2
    return User
      .query(on: request)
      .filter(\.username == userInfo.email)
      .first()
      .flatMap(to: ResponseEncodable.self) { foundUser in

      guard let existingUser = foundUser else {
        // 3
        let user = User(name: userInfo.name,
                        username: userInfo.email,
                        password: "")
        // 4
        return user
          .save(on: request)
          .map(to: ResponseEncodable.self) { user in
          // 5
```

```
        try request.authenticateSession(user)
        return request.redirect(to: "/")
      }
    }
  }
  // 6
  try request.authenticateSession(existingUser)
  return request.future(request.redirect(to: "/"))
  }
}
```

Here's what the new code does:

1. Get the user information from Google.

2. See if the user exists in the database by looking up the email as the username.

3. If the user doesn't exist, create a new `User` using the name and email from the user information from Google. Set the password to blank, since you don't need it.

4. Save the user and unwrap the returned future.

5. Call `request.authenticateSession(_:)` to save the created user in the session so the website allows access. Redirect back to the homepage.

6. If the user already exists, authenticate the user in the session and redirect to the homepage.

The final thing to do is to add a button on the website to allow users to make use of the new functionality! Open **login.leaf** and, under `</form>`, add the following:

```
<a href="/login-google">
  <img class="mt-3" src="/images/sign-in-with-google.png"
    alt="Sign In With Google">
</a>
```

The sample project for this chapter contains a new, Google-provided image, **sign-in-with-google.png**, to display a **Sign in with Google** button. This adds the image as a link to **/login-google** — the route provided to Imperial to start the login. Build and run the application and then visit **http://localhost:8080** in your browser.

Click **Create An Acronym** and the application takes you to the login page. You'll see the new **Sign in with Google** button:

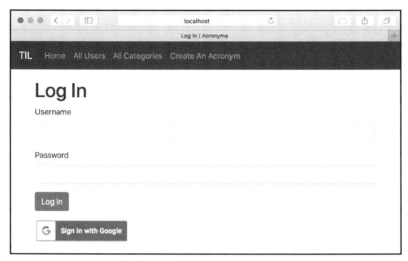

Click the new button and the application take you to a Google page to allow the TIL application access to your information:

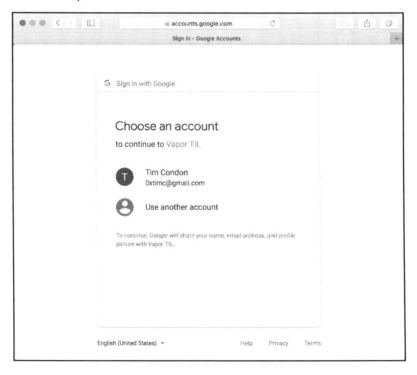

Select the account you want to use and the application redirects you back to the home page. Go to the **All Users** screen and you'll see your new user account. If you create an acronym, the application also uses that new user.

Deploying to Vapor Cloud

As in previous chapters, deploying the changes from this chapter to Vapor Cloud is simple. In Terminal, type the following:

```
# 1
git add .
# 2
git commit -m "Add Google login to the website"
# 3
git push
```

Here's what these commands do:

1. Add the new files so Git tracks them.

2. Commit your changes with the message "Add Google login to the website".

3. Push your local commits up to the remote repository on GitHub.

Now you've committed and pushed, you can deploy your updated application to Vapor Cloud. However, before you deploy, you need to provide your Vapor Cloud application the OAuth client ID, secret and callback URL. In Terminal, type the following:

```
vapor cloud config modify config set --env=production \
  GOOGLE_CALLBACK_URL=https://<YOUR_VAPOR_CLOUD_URL>/oauth/google

vapor cloud config modify config set --env=production \
  GOOGLE_CLIENT_ID=<YOUR_CLIENT_ID>

vapor cloud config modify config set --env=production \
  GOOGLE_CLIENT_SECRET=<YOUR_CLIENT_SECRET>
```

Answer with **y** when prompted. This sets the environment variables for **GOOGLE_CALLBACK_URL**, **GOOGLE_CLIENT_ID** and **GOOGLE_CLIENT_SECRET** in your application's container so they are available at runtime. This allows you to pass secret information to your Vapor Cloud instance without storing that information in source control.

> Eagle-eyed readers may notice these commands differ from what Vapor Toolbox shows in its help display. There is currently a bug in the Toolbox that requires you to enter two extra words after `config` to make the command work. You're free to enter `vapor cloud config modify x x ...` if you like.

Finally, deploy your application. In Terminal, type the following:

```
vapor cloud deploy --env=production --build=update -y
```

This command is the same as previous **vapor cloud deploy** commands, with the following parameters:

- Deploy the application to the **production** environment.

- Use the **update** build type to update the packages and pull in Imperial.

- Automatically deploy without waiting at the confirmation screen.

When the deployment has finished go to **https://<YOUR-URL>.vapor.cloud**. If you click **Create An Acronym**, you'll need to log in.

On the login page, you'll see the new **Log in with Google** button. Click the button and log in with Google:

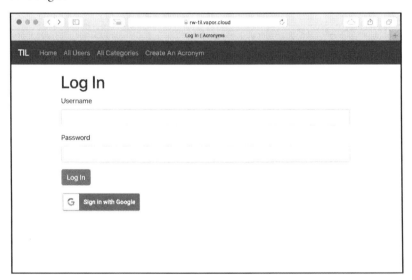

Where to go from here?

In this chapter, you've learned how to integrate Google login into your website using Imperial and OAuth. You've now built a fully-featured API that demonstrates many of the capabilities of Vapor. You've built an iOS application to consume the API, as well as a front-end website using Leaf. You've also learned how to test your application.

These sections have given you all the knowledge you need to build the back ends and web sites for your own applications! The next chapters cover more advanced topics that you may need, such as database migrations and caching.

Chapter 23: Database/API Versioning & Migration

By Jonas Schwartz

In the first three sections of the book, whenever you made a change to your model, you had to delete your database and start over. That's no problem when you don't have any data. Once you have data, or move your project to the production stage, you can no longer delete your database. What you want to do instead is modify your database, which in Vapor, is done using migrations.

In this chapter, you'll make two modifications to the TILApp using migrations. First, you'll add a new field to `User` to contain a Twitter handle. Second, you'll ensure that categories are unique. Finally, you're going to modify the app so it creates the admin user only when your app runs in development or testing mode.

> **Note**: This chapter requires that you have set up and configured PostgreSQL. Follow the steps in Chapter 6, "Configuring a Database", to set up PostgreSQL in Docker and configure the Vapor application.

Modifying tables

Modifying an existing database is always a risky business. You already have data you don't want to lose, so deleting the whole database is not a viable solution. At the same time, you can't simply add or remove a property in an existing table since all the data is entangled in one big web of connections and relations.

Instead, you introduce your modifications using Vapor's `Migration` protocol. This allows you to cautiously introduce your modifications while still having a revert option should it not work as expected.

> Modifying your production database is always a delicate procedure. You must make sure to test any modifications properly before rolling them out in production. If you have a lot of important data, it's a good idea to take a backup before modifying your database.

To keep your code clean and make it easy to view the changes in chronological order, you should create a directory containing all your migrations. Each migration should have its own file. For file names, use a consistent and helpful naming scheme, for example: **YY-MM-DD-FriendlyName.swift**. This allows you to see the versions of your database at a glance.

Writing migrations

A `Migration` is generally written as a `struct` when it's used to update an existing model. This `struct` must, of course, conform to `Migration`. `Migration` requires you to provide three things:

```
typealias Database: Fluent.Database
static func prepare(on connection: Database.Connection)
  -> Future<Void>
static func revert(on connection: Database.Connection)
  -> Future<Void>
```

Typealias Database

First, you must specify what type of database the migration can run on. Migrations require a database connection to work correctly as they must be able to query the `MigrationLog` model. If the `MigrationsLog` is not accessible, the migration will fail and, in the worst case, break your application.

Prepare method

`prepare(on:)` contains the migration's changes to the database. It's usually one of two options:

- Creating a new table

- Modifying an existing table by adding a new property.

Here's an example that adds a new model to the database:

```
static func prepare(on connection: PostgreSQLConnection)
  -> Future<Void> {
  // 1
```

```
    return Database.create(
      NewTestUser.self,
      on: connection
    ) { builder in
      // 2
      builder.field(for: \.id, isIdentifier: true)
    }
  }
```

1. You specify the action to perform and the model to use. If you're adding a new
   `Model` type to the database, you use `create(_:on:closure:)`. If you're adding a
   field to an existing `Model` type, you use `update(_:on:closure:)`. This example
   uses `create(_:on:closure:)` to create a new model with the field `id`.

2. Next, you specify a closure that accepts a `SchemaBuilder` for your model and
   performs the actual modifications. You call `field(for:)` on the builder to describe
   each field you're adding to your model. Normally, you don't need to include the type
   of the field as Fluent can infer the best one to use.

Revert method

`revert(on:)` is the opposite of `prepare(on:)`. Its job is to undo whatever
`prepare(on:)` did. If you use `create(_:on:closure:)` in `prepare(on:)`, you use
`delete(_:on:)` in `revert(on:)`. If you use `update(_:on:closure:)` to add a field,
you also use it in `revert(on:)` to remove the field with `deleteField(for:)`.

Here's an example that pairs with the `prepare(on:)` you saw earlier:

```
  static func revert(on connection: PostgreSQLConnection)
    -> Future<Void> {
    return Database.delete(NewTestUser.self, on: connection)
  }
```

Again, you specify the action to perform and the model to revert. Since you used
`create(_:on:closure:)` to add the field, you use `delete(_:on:)` here.

This method executes when you boot your app with the `--revert` option.

Adding users' Twitter handles

First, you need to create a new folder to hold all your migrations and a new file to hold
the `AddTwitterToUser` migration. In Terminal, enter:

```
# 1
cd ~/Vapor/TILApp/
```

```
# 2
mkdir Sources/App/Migrations
# 3
touch Sources/App/Migrations/18-06-05-AddTwitterToUser.swift
# 4
vapor xcode -y
```

Here's what this does:

1. Navigate to the directory where the TIL application lives.

2. Create a new directory, **Migrations**, in the **App** module.

3. Create a new file, **18-06-05-AddTwitterToUser.swift**, in the **Migrations** directory you just created.

4. Regenerate the Xcode project to add the new file to the **App** target.

In Xcode, open **User.swift** and add the following property to User below var password: String:

```
var twitterURL: String?
```

This adds the property of type String? to the models. You declare it as an optional string since your existing users don't have the property and future users don't necessarily have an account.

Next, replace the initializer with the following:

```
init(name: String,
     username: String,
     password: String,
     twitterURL: String? = nil) {
  self.name = name
  self.username = username
  self.password = password
  self.twitterURL = twitterURL
}
```

Next, add the new property to Public after var username: String:

```
var twitterURL: String?
```

Next, replace the initializer for Public with the following:

```
init(id: UUID?,
     name: String,
     username: String,
     twitterURL: String? = nil) {
  self.id = id
```

```
    self.name = name
    self.username = username
    self.twitterURL = twitterURL
  }
```

Finally, find the following extension:

```
extension User {
  func convertToPublic() -> User.Public {
    return User.Public(id: id, name: name, username: username)
  }
}
```

and replace it with the following to use the new initializer:

```
extension User {
  func convertToPublic() -> User.Public {
    return User.Public(
      id: id,
      name: name,
      username: username,
      twitterURL: twitterURL)
  }
}
```

When you use a migration to add a new property to an existing model, it's important you modify the initial migration so that it adds *only* the original fields. By default, `prepare(on:)` adds every property it finds in the model. If, for some reason — running your test suite, for example — you revert your entire database, allowing it to continue to add all fields in the initial migration will cause your new migration to fail.

Find the existing `prepare(on:)` in the `User: Migration` extension and replace `try addProperties(to: builder)` with the following:

```
builder.field(for: \.id, isIdentifier: true)
builder.field(for: \.name)
builder.field(for: \.username)
builder.field(for: \.password)
```

This manually adds the existing properties — excluding the new `twitterURL` — to the database.

Now, open **18-06-05-AddTwitterToUser.swift** and add the following to create a migration that adds the new `twitterURL` field to the model:

```
import FluentPostgreSQL
import Vapor
```

```
// 1
struct AddTwitterURLToUser: Migration {

  // 2
  typealias Database = PostgreSQLDatabase

  // 3
  static func prepare(
    on connection: PostgreSQLConnection
  ) -> Future<Void> {
    // 4
    return Database.update(
      User.self, on: connection
      ) { builder in
      // 5
      builder.field(for: \.twitterURL)
      }
  }

  // 6
  static func revert(
    on connection: PostgreSQLConnection
  ) -> Future<Void> {
    // 7
    return Database.update(
      User.self, on: connection
      ) { builder in
      // 8
      builder.deleteField(for: \.twitterURL)
      }
  }
}
```

Here's what this does:

1. Define a new type, AddTwitterURLToUser, that conforms to Migration.

2. As required by Migration, define your database type with a typealias.

3. Define the required prepare(on:).

4. Since User already exists in your database, use update(_:on:closure:) to modify the database.

5. Inside the closure, use field(for:) to add a new field corresponding to the key path \.twitterURL.

6. Define required revert(on:).

7. Since you're modifying an existing Model, you again use update(_:on:closure:) to remove the new field.

8. Inside the closure, use `deleteField(for:)` to remove the field corresponding to the key path `\.twitterURL`.

Now open **configure.swift** and register `AddTwitterURLToUser` as one of the migrations.

Since migrations are performed in order, it must be after the existing migrations in the list. Add the following immediately before `services.register(migrations)`:

```
migrations.add(
  migration: AddTwitterURLToUser.self,
  database: .psql)
```

The next time you launch the app, the new property is added to `User`. As with `AdminUser`, you should use the `add(migration:database:)` to register the migration since it isn't a full model. Build and run your application; you should be able to see the new property in your table.

> On your development machine, you can see the table's properties by entering the following in Terminal:

```
docker exec -it postgres psql -U vapor
\d "User"
\q
```

Updating the web site

Your app now has all it needs to store a user's Twitter handle and the API is complete. You need to update the web site to allow a new user to provide a Twitter address during the registration process.

Open **register.leaf** and add the following after the form group for **name**:

```
<div class="form-group">
  <label for="twitterURL">Twitter handle</label>
  <input type="text" name="twitterURL" class="form-control"
    id="twitterURL"/>
</div>
```

This adds a field for the Twitter handle on the registration form. Next, open **user.leaf** and replace `<h2>#(user.username)</h2>` with the following:

```
<h2>#(user.username)
#if(user.twitterURL) {
```

```
  - #(user.twitterURL)
}
</h2>
```

This shows the Twitter handle, if it exists, on the user information page. Finally, open **WebsiteController.swift** and add the following to the end of `RegisterData`:

```
let twitterURL: String?
```

This allows your form handler to access the Twitter information sent from the browser. In `registerPostHandler(_:data:)`, replace

```
let user = User(
  name: data.name,
  username: data.username,
  password: password)
```

with:

```
var twitterURL: String?
if let twitter = data.twitterURL,
  !twitter.isEmpty {
  twitterURL = twitter
}
let user = User(
  name: data.name,
  username: data.username,
  password: password,
  twitterURL: twitterURL)
```

If the user doesn't provide a Twitter handle, you want to store `nil` rather than an empty string in the database.

Build and run. Visit **http://localhost:8080/** in your browser and register a new user, providing a Twitter handle. Visit the user's information page to see the results of your handiwork!

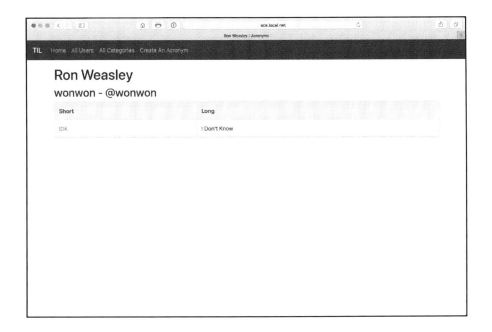

Making categories unique

Just as you've required usernames to be unique, you really want category names to be unique as well. Everything you've done so far to implement categories has made it impossible to create duplicates but you'd like that enforced in the database as well. It's time to create a `Migration` that guarantees duplicate category names can't be inserted in the database.

First, create a new file inside the **Migrations** directory. In Terminal, enter:

```
touch Sources/App/Migrations/18-06-05-MakeCategoriesUnique.swift
vapor xcode -y
```

This creates a new file to contain the new `Migration` and regenerates your Xcode project.

In Xcode, open **18-06-05-MakeCategoriesUnique.swift** and enter the following:

```
import FluentPostgreSQL
import Vapor
// 1
struct MakeCategoriesUnique: Migration {
  // 2
  typealias Database = PostgreSQLDatabase
```

```
// 3
static func prepare(
  on connection: PostgreSQLConnection
) -> Future<Void> {
  // 4
  return Database.update(
    Category.self,
    on: connection
  ) { builder in
    // 5
    builder.unique(on: \.name)
  }
}
// 6
static func revert(
  on connection: PostgreSQLConnection
) -> Future<Void> {
  // 7
  return Database.update(
    Category.self,
    on: connection
  ) { builder in
    // 8
    builder.deleteUnique(from: \.name)
  }
}
}
```

1. Define a new type, `MakeCategoriesUnique`, that conforms to `Migration`.

2. As required by `Migration`, define your database type with a `typealias`.

3. Define the required `prepare(on:)`.

4. Since `Category` already exists in your database, use `update(_:on:closure:)` to modify the database.

5. Inside the closure, use `unique(on:)` to add a new unique index corresponding to the key path `\.name`.

6. Define required `revert(on:)`.

7. Since you're modifying an existing `Model`, you again use `update(_:on:closure:)` to remove the new index.

8. Inside the closure, use `deleteUnique(from:)` to remove the index corresponding to the key path `\.name`.

Finally, open **configure.swift** and register `MakeCategoriesUnique` as one of the migrations. Add the following immediately before `services.register(migrations)`:

```
migrations.add(
  migration: MakeCategoriesUnique.self,
  database: .psql)
```

Build and run; observe the new migration in the console.

Seeding based on environment

In Chapter 18, "API Authentication, Part 1," you seeded an admin user in your database. As mentioned there, you should never use "password" as your admin password. But, it's easier when you're still developing and just need a dummy account for testing locally. One way to ensure you don't add this user in production is to detect your environment before adding the migration. In **configure.swift** replace:

```
migrations.add(migration: AdminUSer.self, database: .psql)
```

with the following:

```
switch env {
case .development, .testing:
  migrations.add(migration: AdminUser.self, database: .psql)
default:
  break
}
```

Now the **AdminUser** is only added to the migrations if the application is in either the development (the default) or testing environment. If the environment is production, the migration won't happen. Of course, you still want to have an admin in your production environment that has a random password. In that case you can switch on the environment inside **AdminUser** or you can create two versions, one for development and one for production.

Deploy to Vapor Cloud

In the previous chapters, you had to delete your whole database whenever you made any changes to your models. Now that the changes are made in migrations, that's no longer necessary. In Terminal, do the following:

```
# 1
git add .
# 2
```

```
git commit -m "Add twitterURL to User and make Categories
unique"
# 3
git push
# 4
vapor cloud deploy --env=production --build==incremental -y
```

Here's what this does:

1. Add all files so that Git picks up the new migration files.

2. Commit your changes with the message "Add twitterURL to User and make Categories unique."

3. Push your local commits to the remote repository on GitHub.

4. Deploy the application containing the modifications to the user and categories.

Where to go from here?

In this chapter, you learned how to modify your database after your app enters production using migrations. You saw how to add an extra property — twitterUrl — to User, how to revert this update, and how to enforce uniqueness of category names. Finally, you saw how to switch on your environment in **configure.swift**, allowing you to exclude migrations from the production environment.

You can learn more about migrations in the Vapor documentation at https:// docs.vapor.codes/3.0/fluent/migrations/.

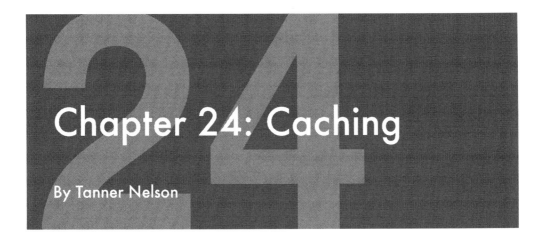

Chapter 24: Caching

By Tanner Nelson

Whether you're creating a JSON API, building an iOS app, or even designing the circuitry of a CPU, you'll eventually need a cache. Caches (pronounced *cashes*) are a method of speeding up slow processes and, without them, the Internet would be a terribly slow place. The philosophy behind caching is simple: store the result of a slow process so you only have to run it once. Some examples of slow processes you may encounter while building a web app are:

- Large database queries.

- Requests to external services, e.g., other APIs.

- Complex computation, e.g., parsing a large document.

By *caching* the results of these slow processes, you can make your app feel snappier and more responsive.

Cache storage

As part of `DatabaseKit`, Vapor defines the protocol `KeyedCache`. This protocol creates a common interface for different cache storage methods. The protocol itself is quite simple; take a look:

```
public protocol KeyedCache {
  // 1
  func get<D>(_ key: String, as decodable: D.Type)
    -> Future<D?> where D: Decodable

  // 2
  func set<E>(_ key: String, to encodable: E)
```

```
    -> Future<Void> where E: Encodable

  // 3
  func remove(_ key: String) -> Future<Void>
}
```

Here's what each method does:

1. `get(_:as:)` fetches stored data from the cache for a given key. If no data exists for that key, it returns `nil`.

2. `set(_:to:)` stores data in the cache at the supplied key. If a value existed previously, it's replaced.

3. `remove(_:)`: Removes data, if any, from the cache at the supplied key.

Each method returns a `Future` since interaction with the cache may happen asynchronously.

Now you understand the concept of caching and the `KeyedCache` protocol, it's time to take a look at some of the actual caching implementations available with Vapor.

In-memory caches

Vapor comes with two memory-based caches: `MemoryKeyedCache` and `DictionaryKeyedCache`. These caches store their data in your program's running memory. This makes both of these caches great for development and testing because they have no external dependencies. However, they may not be perfect for all uses as the storage is cleared when the application restarts and can't be shared between multiple instances of your application. Most likely though, this memory volatility won't affect a well thought out caching design.

The differences between `MemoryKeyedCache` and `DictionaryKeyedCache` are subtle but important. Here's a more in-depth look.

Memory cache

The contents of a `MemoryKeyedCache` are shared across all your application's event loops. This means once something is stored in the cache, all future requests will see that same item regardless of which event loop they are assigned to. This is great for testing and development because it simulates how an external cache would operate. However, the implementation of this cache is *not* thread safe and, thus, requires synchronized access. This makes `MemoryKeyedCache` unsuitable for use in production systems.

Dictionary cache

The contents of a `DictionaryKeyedCache` are local to each event loop. This means that subsequent requests assigned to different event loops may see different cached data. This behavior is fine for purely performance-based caching, such as caching the result of a slow query, but can cause problems if you're using a `DictionaryKeyedCache` for something like session storage. Because `DictionaryKeyedCache` does not share memory between event loops, it *is* suitable for use in production systems.

Database caches

All DatabaseKit-based caches support using a configured database as your cache storage. This includes all of Vapor's Fluent mappings (FluentPostgreSQL, FluentMySQL, etc.) and database drivers (PostgreSQL, MySQL, Redis, etc.).

If you want your cached data to persist between restarts and be shareable between multiple instances of your application, storing it in a database is a great choice. If you already have a database configured for your application, it's easy to set up.

You can use your application's main database for caching or you can use a separate, specialized database. For example, it's common to use a Redis database for caches.

Redis

Redis is an open-source, cache storage service. It's used commonly as a cache database for web applications and is supported by most deployment services like Vapor Cloud, Heroku, and more. Redis databases are usually very easy to configure and they allow you to persist your cached data between application restarts and share the cache between multiple instances of your application. Redis is a great, fast and feature-rich alternative to in-memory caches and it only takes a little bit more work to configure.

Now that you know about the available caching implementations in Vapor, it's time to add caching to an application.

Example: Pokédex

When building a web app, making requests to other APIs can introduce delays. If the API you're communicating with is slow, it can make your API feel slow. Additionally, external APIs may enforce rate limits on the number of requests you can make to them in a given time period. Fortunately, with caching, you can store the results of these external API queries locally and make your API feel much faster.

You're going to use a cache to improve the performance of "Pokédex", an API for storing and listing all Pokémon you've captured.

You've already learned how to create a basic CRUD API and how to make external HTTP requests. As a result, this chapter's starter project already has the basics implemented. In Terminal, change to the starter project's directory and use the following command to generate and open an Xcode project to work in:

```
vapor xcode -y
```

Overview

This simple Pokédex API has two routes:

• **GET /pokemon**: Returns a list of all captured Pokémon.

• **POST /pokemon**: Stores a captured Pokémon in the Pokédex.

When you store a new Pokémon, the Pokédex API makes a call to the external API pokeapi.co to verify that the Pokémon name you've entered is real. While this check works, the pokeapi.co API can be pretty slow to respond, thereby making your app feel slow.

Normal request

A typical Vapor requests takes only a couple of milliseconds to respond, when working locally. In the screenshot below, you can see the **GET /pokemon** route has a total response time of about 40ms.

PokeAPI dependent request

In the screenshot below, you can see that the **POST /pokemon** route is 25x slower at around 1,500ms. This is because the **pokeapi.co** API can be slow to respond to the query.

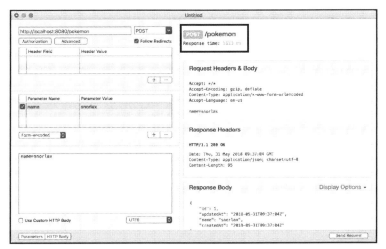

Now you're ready to take a look at the code to better understand what's making this route slow and how a cache can fix it.

Verifying the name

In Xcode, open **PokeAPI.swift** and look at verifyName(_:on:).

This class is a simple wrapper around an HTTP client and makes querying the PokeAPI more convenient. It verifies the legitimacy of a supplied Pokémon name. If the name is real, the method returns true, wrapped in a Future.

Now look at fetchPokemon(named:). This method sends the request to the external pokeapi.co and returns the Pokémon's data. If a Pokémon with the supplied name doesn't exist, the API — and, therefore, this method — returns a 404 Not Found response.

fetchPokemon(named:) is the cause of the slow response time on the **POST /pokemon** route. A KeyedCache is just what the doctor ordered!

Creating a KeyedCache

The first task is to create a `KeyedCache` for the `PokeAPI` wrapper. In **PokeAPI.swift**, add a new property to store the cache after `let client: Client`:

```
let cache: KeyedCache
```

Next, replace the implementation of `init` to account for the new property:

```
public init(client: Client, cache: KeyedCache) {
   self.client = client
   self.cache = cache
}
```

Finally, fix the remaining compiler error by replacing the `return` statement in `makeService(for:)` with:

```
return try PokeAPI(client: container.make(),
                   cache: container.make())
```

Build and run, then create a new request in RESTed. Configure the request as follows:

- **URL**: http://localhost:8080/pokemon

- **method**: POST

- **Parameter encoding**: JSON-encoded

Add one parameter with name and value:

- **name**: Test

You'll see the following error:

```
[ ERROR ] ServiceError.ambiguity: Please choose which KeyedCache
you prefer, multiple are available: MemoryKeyedCache,
DictionaryKeyedCache,
DatabaseKeyedCache<ConfiguredDatabase<SQLiteDatabase>>.
(Config.swift:72)
[ DEBUG ] Suggested fixes for ServiceError.ambiguity:
`config.prefer(MemoryKeyedCache.self, for: KeyedCache.self)`.
`config.prefer(DictionaryKeyedCache.self, for:
KeyedCache.self)`.
`config.prefer(DatabaseKeyedCache<ConfiguredDatabase<SQLiteDatab
ase>>.self, for: KeyedCache.self)`. (Logger+LogError.swift:20)
```

This may look intimidating at first, but don't worry, it's expected. Since this application is configured to use FluentSQLite as its database, there are multiple `KeyedCache` implementations available. Since Fluent is already configured, you'll use `SQLiteCache` (`DatabaseKeyedCache<ConfiguredDatabase<SQLiteDatabase>>`).

Open **configure.swift** and add following line before
`services.register(migrations)`:

```
migrations.prepareCache(for: .sqlite)
```

Just as you have to run a migration to set up your models in the database, you must
allow Fluent to configure the underlying database schema for storing cache data.

Next, add the following at then end of `configure(_:_:_:)`:

```
config.prefer(SQLiteCache.self, for: KeyedCache.self)
```

This tells Vapor to use SQLite as your application's `KeyedCache`. This resolves the
ambiguity error.

> **Note**: Fluent uses the table `fluentcaches` to store the cache data.

Build and run. Use RESTed to send the same request to **POST /pokemon**. You'll now
see the following in the **Response Body**:

```
{
    "error": true,
    "reason": "Invalid Pokemon Test."
}
```

Great! You've created your `KeyedCache`. Time to put it to work.

Fetch and Store

Now that the `PokeAPI` wrapper has access to a working `KeyedCache`, you can use the
cache to store responses from the pokeapi.co API and subsequently fetch them much
more quickly.

Open **PokeAPI.swift** and replace the implementation of `verifyName(_:on:)` with the
following:

```
public func verifyName(_ name: String, on worker: Worker)
    -> Future<Bool> {
    // 1
    let key = name.lowercased()
    // 2
    return cache.get(key, as: Bool.self).flatMap { result in
        if let exists = result {
            // 3
            return worker.eventLoop.newSucceededFuture(result: exists)
```

```
    }

    // 4
    return self.fetchPokemon(named: name).flatMap { res in
      switch res.http.status.code {
      case 200..<300:
        // 5
        return self.cache.set(key, to: true).transform(to: true)
      case 404:
        return self.cache.set(key, to: false)
          .transform(to: false)
      default:
        let reason =
          "Unexpected PokeAPI response: \(res.http.status)"
        throw Abort(.internalServerError, reason: reason)
      }
    }
  }
}
```

1. Create a consistent cache key by lowercasing the name. This ensures that both "Pikachu" and "pikachu" share the same cache result.

2. Query the cache to see if it contains the desired result.

3. If a cached result exists, return that result. This means that calls to verifyName(_:on:) will never invoke fetchPokemon(named:) a second time for a given name. This is the key step that will improve performance.

4. When fetchPokemon(named:) completes, store the result of the API query in the cache.

Build and run. Once again, use RESTed to send the same request to **POST /pokemon** . Take note of the response time for the first request. It'll likely be a couple of seconds. Now, make a second request and note the time; it should be much faster!

Where to go from here?

Caching is an important concept in Computer Science, and understanding how to use it will help make your web applications feel fast and responsive. There are several methods for storing your cache data for web applications: in-memory, Fluent database, Redis, and more. Each has distinct benefits over the other.

You can checkout the different types of algorithms available for caching such as Least Recently Used (LRU), Random Replacement (RR) or Last In First Out (LIFO). Each of these has pros and cons depending on the type of application you're writing and the type of data you're caching within it.

In this chapter, you learned how to configure a Fluent database cache. Using the cache to save the results of a request to an external API, you significantly increased the responsiveness of your app.

If you'd like a challenge, try configuring your app to use a Redis or in-memory cache instead of the `SQLiteCache`.

Chapter 25: Middleware

By Tanner Nelson

In the course of building your application, you'll often find it necessary to integrate your own steps into the request pipeline. The most common mechanism for accomplishing this is to use one or more pieces of middleware. They allow you to do things like:

- Log incoming requests.

- Catch errors and display messages.

- Rate-limit traffic to particular routes.

Middleware instances sit between your router and the client connected to your server. This allows them to view, and potentially mutate, incoming requests before they reach your controllers. A middleware instance may choose to return early by generating its own response, or it can forward the request to the next responder in the chain. The final responder is always your router. When the response from the next responder is generated, the middleware can make any modifications it deems necessary, or choose to forward it back to the client as is. This means each middleware instance has control over both incoming requests *and* outgoing responses.

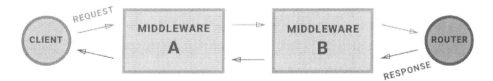

As you can see in the diagram above, the first middleware instance in your application — Middleware A — receives incoming requests from the client first. The first middleware may then choose to pass this request on to the next middleware — Middleware B — and so on. Eventually, some component generates a response, which then traverses back through the middleware in the opposite direction. Take note that this means the first middleware receives responses *last*.

The protocol for `Middleware` is fairly simple, and should help you better understand the previous diagram:

```
public protocol Middleware {
  func respond(
    to request: Request,
    chainingTo next: Responder) throws -> Future<Response>
}
```

In the case of Middleware A, `request` is the incoming data from the client, while `next` is Middleware B. The async response returned by Middleware A goes directly to the client.

For Middleware B, `request` is the request passed on from Middleware A. `next` is the router. The future response returned by Middleware B goes to Middleware A.

Vapor's middleware

Vapor includes some middleware out of the box. This section introduces you to the available options to give you an idea of what middleware is commonly used for.

Error middleware

The most commonly used middleware in Vapor is `ErrorMiddleware`. It's responsible for converting both synchronous and asynchronous Swift errors into HTTP responses. Uncaught errors cause the HTTP server to immediately close the connection and print an internal error log. Using the ErrorMiddleware ensures all errors you throw are rendered into appropriate HTTP responses.

In production mode, `ErrorMiddleware` converts all errors into opaque 500 Internal Server Error responses. This is important for keeping your application secure, as errors may contain sensitive information. You can opt into providing different error responses by conforming your error types to `AbortError`, allowing you to specify the HTTP status code and error message. You may also use `Abort`, a concrete error type that conforms to `AbortError`. For example:

```
throw Abort(.badRequest, "Something's not quite right.")
```

File middleware

Another common type of middleware is `FileMiddleware`. This middleware serves files from the Public folder in your application directory. This is useful when you're using Vapor to create a front-end website that may require static files like images or stylesheets.

Other Middleware

Vapor also provides a `SessionsMiddleware`, responsible for tracking sessions with connected clients. Other packages may provide middleware to help them integrate into your application. For example, Vapor's Authentication package contains middleware for protecting your routes using basic passwords, simple bearer tokens, and even JWTs (JSON Web Tokens).

Example: Todo API

Now that you have an understanding of how various types of middleware function, you're ready to learn how to configure them and how to create your own custom middleware types.

To do this, you'll implement a basic Todo list API. This API has three routes:

```
$ swift run Run routes
+----------+------------------+
| GET      | /todos           |
+----------+------------------+
| POST     | /todos           |
+----------+------------------+
| DELETE   | /todos/:todo     |
+----------+------------------+
```

You'll create and configure two different middleware types for this project:

1. `LogMiddleware`: Logs response times for incoming requests.

2. `SecretMiddleware`: Protects private routes from being accessed without permission by requiring a secret key.

Log middleware

The first middleware you'll create will log incoming requests. It will display the following information for each request:

• Request method

- Request path

- Response status

- How long it took to generate the response

Open the starter project directory in Terminal and generate an Xcode project for it by entering:

```
vapor xcode -y
```

Once Xcode opens, navigate to **Middleware/LogMiddleware.swift**. There you'll find an empty `LogMiddleware` class. Ignore the `TimeInterval` extension for now; you'll use that later.

Start by conforming `LogMiddleware` to the `Middleware` protocol. Only one method is required: `respond(to:chainingTo:)`. For now, the middleware will just log the incoming request's description. Replace `LogMiddleware` with the following:

```swift
final class LogMiddleware: Middleware {
  // 1
  let logger: Logger

  init(logger: Logger) {
    self.logger = logger
  }

  // 2
  func respond(
    to req: Request,
    chainingTo next: Responder) throws -> Future<Response> {
    // 3
    logger.info(req.description)
    // 4
    return try next.respond(to: req)
  }
}

// 5
extension LogMiddleware: ServiceType {
  static func makeService(
    for container: Container) throws -> LogMiddleware {
    // 6
    return try .init(logger: container.make())
  }
}
```

Here's a breakdown of the code you just added:

1. Create a stored property to hold a `Logger`.

2. Implement the `Middleware` protocol requirement.

3. Send the request's description to the Logger as an informational log.

4. Forward the incoming request to the next responder.

5. Allow `LogMiddleware` to be registered as a service in your application.

6. Initialize an instance of `LogMiddleware`, using the container to create the necessary `Logger`.

Now that you've created a custom middleware, you need to register it to your application. Open **configure.swift** and add the following line to under `// register custom service types here`:

```
services.register(LogMiddleware.self)
```

Once `LogMiddleware` is registered, you can use `MiddlewareConfig` to integrate it. Next, add the following line under `var middleware = MiddlewareConfig()`:

```
middleware.use(LogMiddleware.self)
```

This enables `LogMiddleware` globally. The ordering is important here as well: Since LogMiddleware is added before ErrorMiddleware, it receives requests first and responses last. This ensures that `LogMiddleware` logs the original request from the client unmodified by other middleware and the final response right before it goes out to the client.

Finally, build and run your application, then make a request to **GET /todos** using `curl`:

```
curl localhost:8080/todos
```

Take a look at the log output from your running application. You'll see something similar to:

```
[ INFO ] GET /todos HTTP/1.1
Host: localhost:8080
User-Agent: curl/7.54.0
Accept: */*
<no body> (LogMiddleware.swift:15)
```

This is a great start! But you can improve `LogMiddleware` to provide more useful, readable output. Open **LogMiddleware.swift** and replace the implementation of `respond(to:chainingTo:)` with the following methods:

```
func respond(
  to req: Request,
  chainingTo next: Responder) throws -> Future<Response> {
```

```
  // 1
  let start = Date()
  return try next.respond(to: req).map { res in
    // 2
    self.log(res, start: start, for: req)
    return res
  }
}

// 3
func log(_ res: Response, start: Date, for req: Request) {
  let reqInfo = "\(req.http.method.string) \(req.http.url.path)"
  let resInfo = "\(res.http.status.code) " +
    "\(res.http.status.reasonPhrase)"
  // 4
  let time = Date()
    .timeIntervalSince(start)
    .readableMilliseconds
  // 5
  logger.info("\(reqInfo) -> \(resInfo) [\(time)]")
}
```

Here's a breakdown of how the new methods work:

1. First, create a start time. Do this before any additional work is done to get the most accurate response time measurement.

2. Instead of returning the response directly, map the future result so that you can access the Response object. Pass this to log(_:start:for:).

3. This method logs the response for an incoming request using the response start date.

4. Generate a readable time using timeIntervalSince(_:) and the extension on TimeInterval at the bottom of the file.

5. Log the information string.

Now that you've updated LogMiddleware, build and run and curl **GET /todos** again.

```
curl localhost:8080/todos
```

If you check the output of your application, you'll see a new, more concise output format.

```
[ INFO ] GET /todos -> 200 OK [1.9ms] (LogMiddleware.swift:32)
```

Secret middleware

Now that you've learned how to create middleware and apply it globally, you'll learn how to apply middleware to specific routes.

Two of the Todo List APIs routes can make changes to the database:

- **POST /todos**

- **DELETE /todos/:id**

If this were a public API, you'd want to protect these routes with a secret key using middleware. That's exactly what `SecretMiddleware` will do.

Open **Middleware/SecretMiddleware.swift** and replace the class definition of `SecretMiddleware` with the following code:

```
final class SecretMiddleware: Middleware {
  // 1
  let secret: String

  init(secret: String) {
    self.secret = secret
  }

  // 2
  func respond(
    to request: Request,
    chainingTo next: Responder) throws -> Future<Response> {
    // 3
    guard
      request.http.headers.firstValue(name: .xSecret) == secret
    else {
      // 4
      throw Abort(
        .unauthorized,
        reason: "Incorrect X-Secret header.")
    }
    // 5
    return try next.respond(to: request)
  }
}
```

Here's a breakdown of how `SecretMiddleware` works:

1. Create a stored property to hold the secret key.

2. Implement `Middleware` protocol requirement.

3. Check the **X-Secret** header in the incoming request against the configured secret key.

4. If the header value does not match, throw an error with `unauthorized` HTTP status.

5. If the header matches, chain to the next middleware normally.

Now you just need to conform `SecretMiddleware` to `ServiceType` so that it can be used as a service in your application.

Add the following code after the `SecretMiddleware` implementation.

```
extension SecretMiddleware: ServiceType {
  static func makeService(
    for worker: Container) throws -> SecretMiddleware {
    // 1
    let secret: String
    switch worker.environment {
    // 2
    case .development: secret = "foo"
    default:
      // 3
      guard let envSecret = Environment.get("SECRET") else {
        let reason = """
          No $SECRET set on environment. \
          Use "export SECRET=<secret>"
          """
        throw Abort(
          .internalServerError,
          reason: reason)
      }
      secret = envSecret
    }
    // 4
    return SecretMiddleware(secret: secret)
  }
}
```

Here's a breakdown of how this code works:

1. Create a local variable to store the configured secret key.

2. If the current environment is development, just use **foo** as the key.

3. If the current environment is not development, attempt to fetch the key from the process environment at key **$SECRET**.

4. Initialize an instance of `SecretMiddleware` using the configured key.

Time to register the new middleware. Open **configure.swift** and add the following under the comment `// register custom service types`.

```
services.register(SecretMiddleware.self)
```

Now you've created and registered `SecretMiddleware`, you can use it to protect the desired routes. Open **routes.swift** and replace the **POST** and **DELETE** routes with the following code:

```
// 1
router.group(SecretMiddleware.self) { secretGroup in
  // 2
```

```
    secretGroup.post("todos", use: todoController.create)
    secretGroup.delete(
      "todos",
      Todo.parameter,
      use: todoController.delete)
  }
```

Here's what this does:

1. Create a new route group wrapped by `SecretMiddleware`.

2. Register the **POST** and **DELETE** routes in the newly created route group instead of the global router.

Build and run the application, then create a new request in RESTed. Configure the request as follows:

- **URL**: http://localhost:8080/todos

- **method**: POST

Add a parameter with name and value:

- **title**: This is a test TODO!

Click **Send Request** and notice the response:

```
  {
      "error": true,
      "reason": "Incorrect X-Secret header."
  }
```

The middleware is protecting the routes! If you try querying **GET /todos** you'll notice it still works.

Add **X-Secret: foo** to the headers section in RESTed and send the request again. Now you'll notice that the response has changed. The middleware is allowing this request through to the controller now it has the appropriate headers.

Where to go from here?

Middleware is extremely useful for creating large web applications. It allows you to apply restrictions and transformations globally or to just a few routes using discrete, re-usable components. In this chapter, you learned how to create a global `LogMiddleware` that displayed information about all incoming requests to your app. You then created `SecretMiddleware` which could protect select routes from public access.

For more information about using middleware, be sure to check out Vapor's API Docs:

- `Middleware`: https://api.vapor.codes/vapor/latest/Vapor/Protocols/Middleware.html

- `MiddlewareConfig`: https://api.vapor.codes/vapor/latest/Vapor/Structs/MiddlewareConfig.html

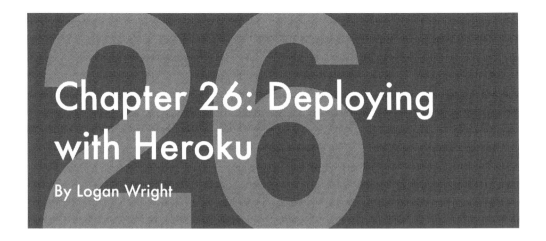

Chapter 26: Deploying with Heroku

By Logan Wright

Heroku is a popular hosting solution that simplifies deployment of web and cloud applications. It supports a number of popular languages and database options. In this chapter, you'll learn how to deploy a Vapor web app with a Postgres database on Heroku.

Setting up Heroku

If you don't already have a Heroku account, sign up for one now. Heroku offers free options and setting up an account is painless. Simply visit https://signup.heroku.com/ and follow the instructions to create an account.

Installing CLI

Now that you have a Heroku account, install the Heroku CLI tool. The easiest way to install on macOS is through Homebrew. In Terminal, enter:

```
brew install heroku/brew/heroku
```

If you don't wish to use Homebrew, or are running on Linux, there are other installation options available at https://devcenter.heroku.com/articles/heroku-cli#download-and-install

Logging in

With the Heroku CLI installed, you need to log in to your account. In Terminal, enter:

```
heroku login
```

Follow the prompts entering your email and password. Once you've logged in, you can verify success by checking `whoami` to ensure it outputs the correct email. Use the following command:

```
heroku auth:whoami
```

That's it; Heroku is all setup on your system. Now it's time to create your first project.

Create an application

Visit heroku.com in your browser to create a new application. Heroku.com should redirect you to dashboard.heroku.com. If it does not, make sure you've logged in and try again. Once at the dashboard, in the upper right hand corner, there's a button that says **New**. Click it and select **Create new app**.

Enter application name

At the next screen, choose the deployment region and a unique app name. If you don't want to choose your app's name, leave the field blank and Heroku automatically generates a unique slug to identify the application for you. Whether you create a name, or Heroku assigns you one, make note of it; you'll use it later when configuring your app.

Click **Create app**.

Add PostgreSQL database

After creating your application, Heroku redirects you to your application's page. Near the top, under your application's name, there is a row of tabs. Select **Resources**.

Under the section titled **Add-ons**, enter **postgres** and you'll see an option for **Heroku Postgres**. Select this option.

This takes you to one more screen that asks what type of database to provision. For now, provision a **Hobby Dev - Free** version to use.

Click the **Provision** button and Heroku does the rest.

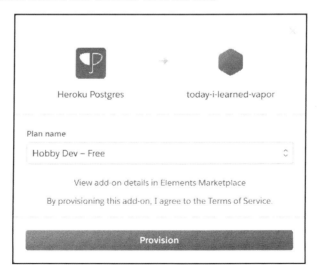

Once you've finished, you'll see the database has been added under the **Resources** tab.

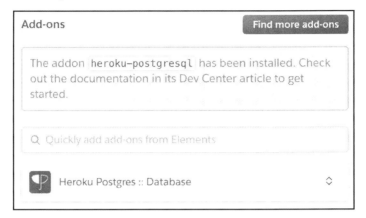

Setting up your Vapor app locally

Your application is now setup with Heroku; the next step is to configure the Vapor app locally. Download and open the project associated with this chapter. If you've been following along with the book, it should look like the TIL project you've been working on and you're free to use your own instead.

Git

Heroku uses Git to deploy your app, so you'll need to put your project into a Git repository, if it isn't already.

First, determine whether your application already has a Git repository. To do this, enter the following command in Terminal:

```
git rev-parse --is-inside-work-tree
```

It should output **true**. If it doesn't, then you must initialize a Git repository. Otherwise, skip the next section.

Initialize Git

If you need to add Git to your project, enter the following command in Terminal:

```
git init
```

Branch

Heroku deploys the **master** branch. Make sure you are on this branch and have merged any changes you wish to deploy.

To see your current branch, enter the following in Terminal:

```
git branch
```

The output will look something like the following. The branch with the asterisk next to it is the current branch:

```
* master
  commander
  other-branches
```

If you're not currently on **master**, navigate there by entering:

```
git checkout master
```

Commit changes

Make sure all changes are in your master branch and committed. You can verify by entering the following command. If you see any output, it means you have uncommitted changes.

```
git status --porcelain
```

If you have uncommitted changes, enter the following commands to commit them:

```
git add .
git commit -m "a description of the changes I made"
```

This ensures your project is in your local repository.

Connect with Heroku

Heroku needs to configure another remote on your Git repository. Enter the following command in Terminal, substituting your app's Heroku name:

```
$ heroku git:remote -a your-apps-name-here
```

You can confirm the format of this command by clicking the **Deploy** tab on the Heroku dashboard in your browser and looking at the command under **Existing Git repository**.

Set Buildpack

Heroku uses something called a Buildpack to provide the recipe for building your app when you deploy it. The Vapor Community currently provides a Buildpack designed for Vapor apps. To set the Buildpack for your application, enter the following in Terminal:

```
heroku buildpacks:set https://github.com/vapor-community/heroku-
  buildpack
```

Swift version file

Now that your Buildpack is set, Heroku needs a couple of configuration files. The first of these is **.swift-version**. This is used by the Buildpack to determine which version of Swift to install for the project. Enter the following command in Terminal:

```
echo "4.1" > .swift-version
```

This creates your **.swift-version** with 4.1 as its contents.

Procfile

Once the app is built on Heroku, Heroku needs to know what type of process to run and how to run it. To determine this, it utilizes a special file named **Procfile**. Enter the following command to create your Procfile:

```
echo "web: Run serve --env production" \
  "--hostname 0.0.0.0 --port \$PORT" > Procfile
```

This gives Heroku the needed command to run your app.

Commit changes

As mentioned earlier, Heroku uses Git and the master branch to deploy applications. Since you configured Git earlier, you've added two files: **Procfile** and **.swift-version**. These need to be committed before deploying or Heroku won't be able to properly build the application. Enter the following commands in Terminal:

```
git add .
git commit -m "adding heroku build files"
```

Configure the database

There's one more thing to do before you deploy your app: You must configure the database within your app. Start by listing the configuration variables for your app.

In Terminal, enter:

```
heroku config
```

You should see output similar to the following. It provides you with information about the database you provisioned for this project.

```
=== today-i-learned-vapor Config Vars
DATABASE_URL: postgres://cybntsgadydqzm:
2d9dc7f6d964f4750da1518ad71hag2ba729cd4527d4a18c70e024b11cfa8f4b
@ec2-54-221-192-231.compute-1.amazonaws.com:5432/dfr89mvoo550b4
```

There are two parts to this output; the first is **DATABASE_URL**. This represents the name of the environment variable. The second component will be similar to the following:

```
postgres://cybntsgadydqzm:
2d9dc7f6d964f4750da1518ad71hag2ba729cd4527d4a18c70e024b11cfa8f4b
@ec2-54-221-192-231.compute-1.amazonaws.com:5432/dfr89mvoo550b4
```

This component represents the actual value of the environment variable. In this case, it's the direct link to your Postgres database. You can use this direct url for purposes of manually connecting to the database should you need to for some reason. However, it's important that you **NEVER** hard code this value into your application. Not only is it bad practice and unsafe, Heroku specifies that the value of this environment variable could change at any time, rendering the absolute value useless.

The important part is the environment variable's name: **DATABASE_URL**.

Open your Vapor app in Xcode and navigate to **configure.swift**. Find the section that sets up the database configuration. It begins with:

```
let hostname =
  Environment.get("DATABASE_HOSTNAME") ?? "localhost"
```

and ends with:

```
let databaseConfig = PostgreSQLDatabaseConfig(
   hostname: hostname,
   username: username,
   database: databaseName,
   password: password)
```

This block of code must become an `else` block. Insert the following before it:

```
let databaseConfig: PostgreSQLDatabaseConfig
if let url = Environment.get("DATABASE_URL") {
```

```
    databaseConfig = PostgreSQLDatabaseConfig(url: url)!
} else {
```

Now insert a

```
}
```

following that block and **remove the** `let` **keyword** from the `databaseConfig` assignment at the end of your new `else` block. This allows the project to retrieve the database URL from the environment if it's running on Heroku. If **DATABASE_URL** isn't set in the environment, the app continues to use the previous method for determining its database.

Once again, you need to save your changes in Git. Enter the following in Terminal:

```
git add .
git commit -m "configured heroku database"
```

Configure Google environment variables

If you completed Chapter 22, "Google Authentication", and are using that as your project here, you must configure the same Google environment variables you used there.

Enter the following commands in Terminal:

```
heroku config:set \
  GOOGLE_CALLBACK_URL=https://<YOUR_HEROKU_URL>/oauth/google

heroku config:set GOOGLE_CLIENT_ID=<YOUR_CLIENT_ID>

heroku config:set GOOGLE_CLIENT_SECRET=<YOUR_CLIENT_SECRET>
```

You can find your Heroku URL on the **Settings** tab of the Heroku dashboard. This sets the environment variables for **GOOGLE_CALLBACK_URL**, **GOOGLE_CLIENT_ID** and **GOOGLE_CLIENT_SECRET** so they're available at runtime. Remember to visit https://console.developers.google.com to add the Heroku callback URL as an authorized redirect. See Chapter 22, "Google Authentication," if you need a refresher.

Deploy to Heroku

You're now ready to deploy your app to Heroku. Push your master branch to your Heroku remote and wait for everything to build. This can take a while, particularly on a large application.

To kick things off, enter the following in Terminal:

```
git push heroku master
```

Once everything deploys, Heroku notifies you of your app's status. Heroku normally starts your app automatically when it finishes building. In the unlikely event it doesn't, enter the following in Terminal to start your app:

```
heroku ps:scale web=1
```

Going forward, pushing the **master** branch to Heroku will redeploy your app. Open your app by visiting the app URL as seen in the **Settings** tab of the Heroku dashboard in your browser. You can also open the site in a browser by entering the following in Terminal:

```
heroku open
```

Reverting your database

If you followed the chapters in the first three sections, you encountered the need to revert the database on Vapor Cloud. It's a simple matter to run a database revert or migration on Heroku, as well.

To revert the last batch of migrations, enter the following in Terminal:

```
heroku run Run -- revert --yes --env production
```

This tells your Heroku instance to run the program **Run** — your Vapor app's main entry point — and pass it the **revert** command. To revert your entire database, enter the following in Terminal:

```
heroku run Run -- revert --all --yes --env production
```

Finally, to run your migrations again:

```
heroku run Run -- migrate --env production
```

Where to go from here?

In this chapter, you learned how to set up the app in the Heroku dashboard, configure your Git repository, add the necessary configuration files to your project, and deploy your app. Explore your dashboard and the Heroku Help to learn even more options!

Chapter 27: WebSockets

By Logan Wright

WebSockets, like HTTP, define a protocol used for communication between two devices. Unlike HTTP, the WebSocket protocol is designed for realtime communication. WebSockets can be a great option for things like chat, or other features that require realtime behavior. Vapor provides a succinct API to create a WebSocket server or client. This chapter focuses on building a basic server.

In this chapter, you'll build a simple server/client application that allows users to share their current location with others, who can then view this on a map in realtime.

Tools

Testing WebSockets can be a bit tricky since you can't visit a URL in the browser or use a simple CURL request. To work around this, you're going to utilize an aptly named Google Chrome extension called Simple WebSocket Client. It can be installed, for free, from https://chrome.google.com/webstore/detail/simple-websocket-client/pfdhoblngboilpfeibdedpjgfnlcodoo.

After you've installed the tool, open it in Chrome.

A basic server

Now your tools are ready, it's time to set up a very basic WebSocket server. Copy this chapter's starter project to your favorite location and open a Terminal window in that directory.

Enter the following to build and open an Xcode project:

```
cd location-track-server
vapor xcode -y
```

Echo server

Open **websockets.swift** and add the following to the end of `sockets(_:)` to create an echo endpoint:

```
// 1
websockets.get("echo-test") { ws, req in
  print("ws connnected")

  // 2
  ws.onText { ws, text in
    print("ws received: \(text)")
    ws.send("echo - \(text)")
  }
}
```

Here's what this does:

1. Create a route handler for the **echo-test** endpoint. It logs a message to the console each time it connects.

2. Create a listener that fires each time the endpoint receives text. It logs the received text to the console, and then echoes it back to the sender after prepending **echo -**.

In Xcode's scheme selector, choose the **Run** scheme and **My Mac** as the destination. Build and run. In Chrome, open Simple WebSocket Client and enter **ws://localhost: 8080/echo-test** in the URL field. Click **Open** and **Status** will change to **OPENED**.

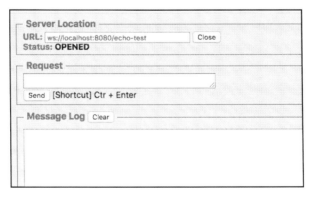

Check the Xcode console and you'll see **ws connected**.

```
Server starting on http://localhost:8080
ws connnected
```

Enter a message in Simple WebSocket Client and you'll see your server respond with an appropriate echo.

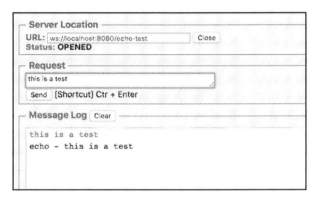

iOS project

The materials for this chapter include a nearly complete iOS app. You'll add the ability to follow a user later. The app includes a WebSocket client implementation written by Josh Baker. You can find more information and his original source code at https://github.com/tidwall/SwiftWebSocket.

> **Note**: You'll get several deprecation warnings in **WebSocket.swift** when you build the iOS project. These can safely be ignored.

Build and run your server project; leave it running. Now build and run the iOS project in the simulator. Tap the **Echo** button on the home screen several times. You should see output similar to the following in the Xcode console.

```
sending sending echo 1521066998.62272
got message: echo — sending echo 1521066998.62272
sending sending echo 1521066999.33329
got message: echo — sending echo 1521066999.33329
sending sending echo 1521066999.90972
got message: echo — sending echo 1521066999.90972
```

Awesome! Your server is communicating with the iOS app via a WebSocket!

> **Note**: If you try to run the iOS app on a device, you'll need to change the definition of host in **WebServices.swift**.

Server word API

Now you've verified your client and server can communicate, it's time to add more capabilities to the server. The server starter project includes a random word generator you'll use to create tracking session IDs.

To demonstrate this generator, open **routes.swift** and add the following to the end of routes(_:):

```
router.get("word-test") { request in
  return wordKey(with: request)
}
```

This defines a GET handler for the endpoint **word-test** that simply returns the result of a call to wordKey(with:).

Build and run. Visit **http://localhost:8080/word-test** in your browser. You'll see a result similar to the following:

```
exercise.green.power
```

Now you've built the basic structure of the server, it's time to add the location sharing endpoints.

Session Manager

Your server app supports two types of client users:

- **Poster**: a client sharing location for others to see.

- **Observer**: a client watching and charting a **Poster**'s location.

Posters and **Observers** are connected via a **TrackingSession**, identified with a random word generated as you saw earlier.

For the purposes of this tutorial, you're going to create a TrackingSessionManager to coordinate all of this. It will create tracking sessions, receive updates from Posters and notify Observers of those updates.

> **Note**: The solution you'll create is not scalable and only works with a single server instance. To extend this functionality in a more scalable way, you'd need to connect `TrackingSessionManager` to a large-scale, realtime database such as Redis.

Create a session

When a Poster creates a new tracking session, you must assign a new ID and return that to the user. The starter project includes a thread-safe `LockedDictionary` implementation to make storing session information simple.

Open **SessionManager.swift** and add the following inside `TrackingSessionManager`:

```
private(set) var sessions:
   LockedDictionary<TrackingSession, [WebSocket]> = [:]
```

Each `TrackingSession` is associated with an array of `WebSocket`s, each corresponding to an Observer.

A Poster needs a way to create a tracking session. Enter the following to the end of `TrackingSessionManager`:

```
func createTrackingSession(for request: Request)
  -> Future<TrackingSession> {
  // 1
  return wordKey(with: request)
    .flatMap(to: TrackingSession.self) { [unowned self] key in
      // 2
      let session = TrackingSession(id: key)

      // 3
      guard self.sessions[session] == nil else {
        return self.createTrackingSession(for: request)
      }

      // 4
      self.sessions[session] = []

      // 5
      return Future.map(on: request) { session }
    }
}
```

Here's what this does:

1. Generate a new session ID. `wordKey(with:)` returns a `Future<String>` so it must be unwrapped to use in subsequent steps.

2. Create a `TrackingSession` for this new session, using the created ID.

3. Ensure the session ID is unique. If not, call yourself recursively to try again.

4. Record the new `TrackingSession` and give it an empty list of Observers.

5. Wrap the session in a future and return it.

Update location

The starter project includes a `Location` model that conforms to `Content`. Take advantage of this and add a bit of magic to make it easy to send locations as JSON. Close your Xcode project. In Terminal, enter the following:

```
touch Sources/App/WebSocket+Extensions.swift
vapor xcode -y
```

This adds the file in the correct place in your project structure and generates an updated Xcode project. Add the following implementation in **WebSocket+Extensions.swift**:

```
import Vapor
import WebSocket
import Foundation

extension WebSocket {
  func send(_ location: Location) {
    let encoder = JSONEncoder()
    guard let data = try? encoder.encode(location) else {
      return
    }

    send(data)
  }
}
```

This method simply converts the `Location` model into JSON for transmission over the wire.

Open **SessionManager.swift** and add the following to the end of the class:

```
func update(_ location: Location,
            for session: TrackingSession) {
  guard let listeners = sessions[session] else {
    return
  }

  listeners.forEach { ws in
    ws.send(location)
  }
}
```

When a Poster sends an updated location to the server, this sends that new location to each registered Observer.

Close session

You've built logic that allows a Poster to create and update a tracking session. The final capability a Poster needs is that of closing a session.

Add the following to the end of the `TrackingSessionManager` class:

```
func close(_ session: TrackingSession) {
  guard let listeners = sessions[session] else {
    return
  }

  listeners.forEach { ws in
    ws.close()
  }

  sessions[session] = nil
}
```

This closes each Observer's WebSocket and removes the `TrackingSession` from the list of active sessions.

With all of the Poster's required behaviors complete, it's time to implement the Observer interactions.

Observer behaviors

The Tracking Session Manager must provide two interactions for Observers:

• Register for updates.

• Disconnect from the server.

Open **SessionManager.swift**, and add the following to the end of `TrackingSessionManager`:

```
func add(listener: WebSocket, to session: TrackingSession) {
  // 1
  guard var listeners = sessions[session] else {
    return
  }

  listeners.append(listener)
  sessions[session] = listeners

  // 2
```

```
    listener.onClose.always { [weak self, weak listener] in
      guard let listener = listener else {
        return
      }

      self?.remove(listener: listener, from: session)
    }
  }

  func remove(listener: WebSocket,
              from session: TrackingSession) {
    // 3
    guard var listeners = sessions[session] else {
      return
    }

    listeners = listeners.filter { $0 !== listener }
    sessions[session] = listeners
  }
```

Here's what this does:

1. Verify that the session exists and add the Observer's WebSocket to the list of listeners.

2. Register an `onClose` handler that triggers when the Observer's client closes the WebSocket. This handler removes the WebSocket from the list of listeners.

3. Verify the session exists and remove the Observer's WebSocket from the list of listeners.

Endpoints

Now that `TrackingSessionManager` is complete, you must create some endpoints to make its behaviors accessible to clients. The endpoints that support the Poster can all be implemented as regular HTTP routes. It doesn't need to use WebSockets because it doesn't require realtime updates.

Create

Open **routes.swift** and add the following to the end of `routes(_:)`:

```
router.post("create", use: sessionManager.createTrackingSession)
```

An empty POST request to **/create** will create and return a new tracking session to the client.

Build and run. Test session creation by entering the following in Terminal:

```
curl -X POST http://localhost:8080/create
```

The server will return a JSON object that looks something like this:

```
{"id":"pumped.arch.dime"}
```

Close

Next up, it's time to implement "close" support. To do this, you'll create an endpoint at **/close/:tracking-session-id**. Add the following to the end of `routes(_:)`:

```
router.post("close", TrackingSession.parameter) {
  req -> HTTPStatus in
  let session = try req.parameters.next(TrackingSession.self)
  sessionManager.close(session)
  return .ok
}
```

This code receives the `TrackingSession` as a parameter, closes the session with the session manager, and subsequently returns an empty `HTTPResponse` to indicate success.

Build and run. Create a session as you did previously. Use the returned tracking session ID to send a close request as follows:

```
curl -w "%{response_code}\n" -X POST \
  http://localhost:8080/close/<tracking.session.id.goes.here>
```

You'll see **200** printed on the next line, showing the server sent a `200 OK` HTTP status.

Update

Finally, the Poster needs an endpoint to receive location updates. You'll create an endpoint at **/update/:tracking-session-id** to implement this. Add the following to the end of `routes(_:)`:

```
// 1
router.post("update", TrackingSession.parameter) {
  req -> Future<HTTPStatus> in
  // 2
  let session = try req.parameters.next(TrackingSession.self)
  // 3
  return try Location.decode(from: req)
                    .map(to: HTTPStatus.self) { location in
    // 4
    sessionManager.update(location, for: session)
```

```
        return .ok
    }
}
```

Here's what this does:

1. Create a POST handler for the endpoint.

2. Extract the tracking session ID from the URL.

3. Create a `Location` from the POST request's body.

4. Call the session manager to broadcast the updated location and then return a `200 OK` HTTP status.

Build and run. Create a session as you did earlier. Use the returned tracking session ID to send an update request as follows:

```
curl -w "%{response_code}\n" \
  -d '{"latitude": 37.331, "longitude": -122.031}' \
  -H "Content-Type: application/json" -X POST \
  http://localhost:8080/update/<tracking.session.id.goes.here>
```

That's it! You have implemented everything your Posters need!

Observer endpoint

An Observer only needs one endpoint, used to connect a WebSocket. To do this, you must define a new WebSocket route. Open **websockets.swift** and add the following to the end of `sockets(_:)`:

```
// 1
websockets.get("listen", TrackingSession.parameter) { ws, req in
  // 2
  let session = try req.parameters.next(TrackingSession.self)
  // 3
  guard sessionManager.sessions[session] != nil else {
    ws.close()
    return
  }
  // 4
  sessionManager.add(listener: ws, to: session)
}
```

Here's what this does:

1. Create a WebSocket handler for the endpoint **/listen/:tracking-session-id**.

2. Extract the tracking session ID from the URL.

3. Ensure the session is still valid. Close the WebSocket if it isn't.

4. Add the WebSocket to the session as an Observer.

That's it! Your server is complete and ready to run your new location sharing application. Build and run. Leave the server running in one window and open the iOS app's project in another.

iOS follow location

As you saw earlier, the starter project iOS app is nearly complete. All that remains is for you to implement its WebSocket abilities. When a user wishes to observe a Poster, the app prompts for a tracking session ID. It then calls `startSocket()` to register as an Observer and process the location updates.

Open **FollowViewController.swift** and replace the existing `startSocket()` with the following:

```
func startSocket() {
  // 1
  let ws = WebSocket("ws://\(host)/listen/\(session.id)")

  // 2
  ws.event.close = { [weak self] code, reason, clean in
    self?.navigationController?
      .popToRootViewController(animated: true)
  }

  // 3
  ws.event.message = { [weak self] message in
    guard let bytes = message as? [UInt8] else {
      fatalError("invalid data")
    }
    let data = Data(bytes: bytes)
    let decoder = JSONDecoder()
    do {
      // 4
      let location = try decoder.decode(
        Location.self,
        from: data
      )
      // 5
      self?.focusMapView(location: location)
    } catch {
      print("decoding error: \(error)")
    }
```

```
    }
  }
```

Here's the play-by-play:

1. Open a WebSocket to the server using the tracking session ID the user entered.

2. Set up an event handler that's called when the WebSocket is closed.

3. Set up an event handler that's called when the WebSocket receives data.

4. Decode the received message into a `Location`.

5. Plot the received location on the map.

Build and run. Tap the **Echo** button to verify that the app and your server are communicating. You'll use `curl` commands in Terminal to simulate a Poster. Enter the following in Terminal to create a new session:

```
curl -X POST http://localhost:8080/create
```

As you've come to expect, you'll receive a JSON response containing your tracking session ID. It will look something like this:

```
{"id":"rabbit.callsign.skirt"}
```

In the iOS Simulator, tap **FOLLOW** and enter the tracking session ID and tap **Track**.

You now need to send a location update.

In Terminal, enter the following, inserting your tracking session ID as appropriate:

```
curl -w "%{response_code}\n" \
  -d '{"latitude": 37.331, "longitude": -122.031}' \
  -H "Content-Type: application/json" -X POST \
  http://localhost:8080/update/<tracking.session.id.goes.here>
```

The app on the Simulator will immediately jump to the newly received location, which happens to be Apple's Headquarters.

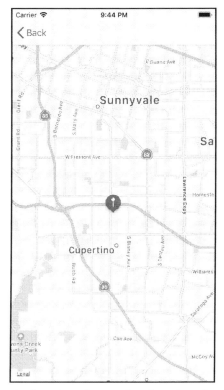

Verify the map updates as the location changes by changing the numbers slightly.

Enter the following in Terminal and watch the map update:

```
curl -w "%{response_code}\n" \
  -d '{"latitude": 37.332, "longitude": -122.030}' \
  -H "Content-Type: application/json" -X POST \
  http://localhost:8080/update/<tracking.session.id.goes.here>
```

Make one final test. Enter the following in Terminal:

```
curl -w "%{response_code}\n" \
   -d '{"latitude": 51.510, "longitude": -0.134}' \
   -H "Content-Type: application/json" -X POST \
   http://localhost:8080/update/<tracking.session.id.goes.here>
```

The map will jump to Piccadilly Circus in London!

Where to go from here?

You've done it. Your iOS Application communicates in realtime via WebSockets with your Swift server. Many different kinds of apps can benefit from the instantaneous communications made possible by WebSockets, including things such as chat applications, games, live stock tickers, and so much more. If the app you imagine needs to respond in real time, WebSockets may be your answer!

Challenges

For more practice with WebSockets, try these challenges:

• Add some more data to the application to personalize it a bit. Maybe an Observer includes a name or some other identifying information so the Poster knows who's watching.

• Provide the Poster with a live list of the Observers.

• Try hosting your basic application on a remote server. Make sure to update the `host` variable in your iOS application and see if you can make it run with a couple of iPhones. You and a friend can move around and test your location updates.

Conclusion

Throughout this book, you've learned how to build complex server applications using the Vapor framework. The book covers everything you need to know to build the applications to support your apps and front-end websites. All the basic building blocks for any application are in the book as well, as more complex use cases. You've learned everything from the basics of routing in Vapor to creating large templates for generating HTML. There should be nothing stopping you from taking Vapor and your new found knowledge and using it wherever you need.

We hope this book provides an awesome reference as you use Vapor throughout your projects and as server-side Swift becomes ever more popular.

If you have any questions or comments as you work through this book, please stop by our forums at http://forums.raywenderlich.com and look for the particular forum category for this book.

Thank you again for purchasing this book. Your continued support is what makes the tutorials, books, videos, conferences and other things we do at raywenderlich.com possible, and we truly appreciate it!

Wishing you all the best in your continued adventures with server-side Swift,

– Tim, Logan, Jonas, Tanner, Richard and Darren

The *Server Side Swift with Vapor* team

More Books You Might Enjoy

We hope you enjoyed this book! If you're looking for more, we have a whole library of books waiting for you at https://store.raywenderlich.com.

New to iOS or Swift?

Learn how to develop iOS apps in Swift with our classic, beginner editions.

iOS Apprentice

https://store.raywenderlich.com/products/ios-apprentice

The iOS Apprentice is a series of epic-length tutorials for beginners where you'll learn how to build four complete apps from scratch.

Each new app will be a little more advanced than the one before, and together they cover everything you need to know to make your own apps. By the end of the series you'll be experienced enough to turn your ideas into real apps that you can sell on the App Store.

These tutorials have easy to follow step-by-step instructions, and consist of more than 900 pages and 500 illustrations! You also get full source code, image files, and other resources you can re-use for your own projects.

Swift Apprentice

https://store.raywenderlich.com/products/swift-apprentice

This is a book for complete beginners to Apple's brand new programming language — Swift 4.

Everything can be done in a playground, so you can stay focused on the core Swift 4 language concepts like classes, protocols, and generics.

This is a sister book to the iOS Apprentice; the iOS Apprentice focuses on making apps, while Swift Apprentice focuses on the Swift 4 language itself.

Experienced iOS developer?

Level up your development skills with a deep dive into our many intermediate to advanced editions.

Data Structures and Algorithms in Swift

https://store.raywenderlich.com/products/data-structures-and-algorithms-in-swift

Understanding how data structures and algorithms work in code is crucial for creating efficient and scalable apps. Swift's Standard Library has a small set of general purpose collection types, yet they definitely don't cover every case!

In Data Structures and Algorithms in Swift, you'll learn how to implement the most popular and useful data structures, and when and why you should use one particular datastructure or algorithm over another. This set of basic data structures and algorithms will serve as an excellent foundation for building more complex and special-purpose constructs. As well, the high-level expressiveness of Swift makes it an ideal choice for learning these core concepts without sacrificing performance.

Realm: Building Modern Swift Apps with Realm Database

https://store.raywenderlich.com/products/realm-building-modern-swift-apps-with-realm-database

Realm Platform is a relatively new commercial product which allows developers to automatically synchronize data not only across Apple devices but also between any combination of Android, iPhone, Windows, or macOS apps. Realm Platform allows you to run the server software on your own infrastructure and keep your data in-house which more often suits large enterprises. Alternatively you can use Realm Cloud which runs a Platform for you and you start syncing data very quickly and only pay for what you use.

In this book, you'll take a deep dive into the Realm Database, learn how to set up your first Realm database, see how to persist and read data, find out how to perform migrations and more. In the last chapter of this book, you'll take a look at the synchronization features of Realm Cloud to perform real-time sync of your data across all devices.

Design Patterns by Tutorials

https://store.raywenderlich.com/products/design-patterns-by-tutorials

Design patterns are incredibly useful, no matter what language or platform you develop for. Using the right pattern for the right job can save you time, create less maintenance work for your team and ultimately let you create more great things with less effort. Every developer should absolutely know about design patterns, and how and when to apply them. That's what you're going to learn in this book!

Move from the basic building blocks of patterns such as MVC, Delegate and Strategy, into more advanced patterns such as the Factory, Prototype and Multicast Delegate pattern, and finish off with some less-common but still incredibly useful patterns including Flyweight, Command and Chain of Responsibility.

Server Side Swift with Vapor

https://store.raywenderlich.com/products/server-side-swift-with-vapor

If you're a beginner to web development, but have worked with Swift for some time, you'll find it's easy to create robust, fully featured web apps and web APIs with Vapor 3.

Whether you're looking to create a backend for your iOS app, or want to create fully featured web apps, Vapor is the perfect platform for you.

This book starts with the basics of web development and introduces the basics of Vapor; it then walks you through creating APIs and web backends; creating and configuring databases; deploying to Heroku, AWS, or Docker; testing your creations and more1

iOS 11 by Tutorials

https://store.raywenderlich.com/products/ios-11-by-tutorials

This book is for intermediate iOS developers who already know the basics of iOS and Swift development but want to learn the new APIs introduced in iOS 11.

Discover the new features for developers in iOS 11, such as ARKit, Core ML, Vision, drag & drop, document browsing, the new changes in Xcode 9 and Swift 4 — and much, much more.

Advanced Debugging and Reverse Engineering

https://store.raywenderlich.com/products/advanced-apple-debugging-and-reverse-engineering

In Advanced Apple Debugging and Reverse Engineering, you'll come to realize debugging is an enjoyable process to help you better understand software. Not only will you learn to find bugs faster, but you'll also learn how other developers have solved problems similar to yours.

You'll also learn how to create custom, powerful debugging scripts that will help you quickly find the secrets behind any bit of code that piques your interest.

After reading this book, you'll have the tools and knowledge to answer even the most obscure question about your code — or someone else's.

RxSwift: Reactive Programming with Swift

https://store.raywenderlich.com/products/rxswift

This book is for iOS developers who already feel comfortable with iOS and Swift, and want to dive deep into development with RxSwift.

Start with an introduction to the reactive programming paradigm; learn about observers and observables, filtering and transforming operators, and how to work with the UI, and finish off by building a fully featured app in RxSwift.

454   *Server Side Swift with Vapor*

Core Data by Tutorials

https://store.raywenderlich.com/products/core-data-by-tutorials

This book is for intermediate iOS developers who already know the basics of iOS and Swift 4 development but want to learn how to use Core Data to save data in their apps.

Start with with the basics like setting up your own Core Data Stack all the way to advanced topics like migration, performance, multithreading, and more!

iOS Animations by Tutorials

https://store.raywenderlich.com/products/ios-animations-by-tutorials

This book is for iOS developers who already know the basics of iOS and Swift 4, and want to dive deep into animations.

Start with basic view animations and move all the way to layer animations, animating constraints, view controller transitions, and more!

watchOS by Tutorials

https://store.raywenderlich.com/products/watchos-by-tutorials

This book is for intermediate iOS developers who already know the basics of iOS and Swift development but want to learn how to make Apple Watch apps for watchOS 4.

tvOS Apprentice

https://store.raywenderlich.com/products/tvos-apprentice

This book is for complete beginners to tvOS development. No prior iOS or web development knowledge is necessary, however the book does assume at least a rudimentary knowledge of Swift.

This book teaches you how to make tvOS apps in two different ways: via the traditional method using UIKit, and via the new Client-Server method using TVML.

Want to make games?

Learn how to make great-looking games that are deeply engaging and fun to play!

2D Apple Games by Tutorials

https://store.raywenderlich.com/products/2d-apple-games-by-tutorials

In this book, you will make 6 complete and polished mini-games, from an action game to a puzzle game to a classic platformer!

This book is for beginner to advanced iOS developers. Whether you are a complete beginner to making iOS games, or an advanced iOS developer looking to learn about SpriteKit, you will learn a lot from this book!

3D Apple Games by Tutorials

https://store.raywenderlich.com/products/3d-apple-games-by-tutorials

Through a series of mini-games and challenges, you will go from beginner to advanced and learn everything you need to make your own 3D game!

This book is for beginner to advanced iOS developers. Whether you are a complete beginner to making iOS games, or an advanced iOS developer looking to learn about SceneKit, you will learn a lot from this book!

Unity Games by Tutorials

https://store.raywenderlich.com/products/unity-games-by-tutorials

Through a series of mini-games and challenges, you will go from beginner to advanced and learn everything you need to make your own 3D game!

This book is for beginner to advanced iOS developers. Whether you are a complete beginner to making iOS games, or an advanced iOS developer looking to learn about SceneKit, you will learn a lot from this book!

Want to learn Android or Kotlin?

Get a head start on learning to develop great Android apps in Kotlin, the newest first-class language for building Android apps.

Android Apprentice

https://store.raywenderlich.com/products/android-apprentice

If you're completely new to Android or developing in Kotlin, this is the book for you!

The Android Apprentice takes you all the way from building your first app, to submitting your app for sale. By the end of this book, you'll be experienced enough to turn your vague ideas into real apps that you can release on the Google Play Store.

You'll build four complete apps from scratch — each app is a little more complicated than the previous one. Together, these apps will teach you how to work with the most common controls and APIs used by Android developers around the world.

Kotlin Apprentice

https://store.raywenderlich.com/products/kotlin-apprentice

This is a book for complete beginners to the new, modern Kotlin language.

Everything in the book takes place in a clean, modern development environment, which means you can focus on the core features of programming in the Kotlin language, without getting bogged down in the many details of building apps.

This is a sister book to the Android Apprentice the Android Apprentice focuses on making apps for Android, while the Kotlin Apprentice focuses on the Kotlin language fundamentals.

53421272R00252

Made in the USA
Columbia, SC
15 March 2019